Ethics and Profits
A Convergence
of Corporate America's
Economic and Social
Responsibilities

R. Eric Reidenbach
Professor of Marketing
Director of the Center
for Business Development and Research
University of Southern Mississippi

Donald P. Robin
Professor of Marketing
Department of Marketing
Louisiana Tech University

Prentice Hall
Englewood Cliffs, New Jersey 07632

Library of Congress Cataloging-in-Publication Data

Reidenbach, R. Eric.
  Ethics and profits.

  Includes index.
  1. Industry--Social aspects--United States.
  2. Corporate culture--United States. 3. Business
  ethics. I. Robin, Donald P. II. Title.
  HD60.5.U5R45 1989   302.3'5   88-30664
  ISBN 0-13-290214-1

Editorial/production supervision
    and interior design: Jacqueline A. Jeglinski
Cover design: Ben Santora
Manufacturing buyer: Mary Ann Gloriande

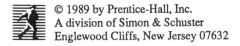

© 1989 by Prentice-Hall, Inc.
A division of Simon & Schuster
Englewood Cliffs, New Jersey 07632

The publisher offers discounts in this book when ordered
in bulk quantities. For more information, write:
    Special Sales/College Marketing
    Prentice-Hall, Inc.
    College Technical and Reference Division
    Englewood Cliffs, NJ 07632

Printed in the United States of America
10 9 8 7 6 5 4 3 2 1

ISBN 0-13-290214-1

Prentice-Hall International (UK) Limited, *London*
Prentice-Hall of Australia Pty. Limited, *Sydney*
Prentice-Hall Canada Inc., *Toronto*
Prentice-Hall Hispanoamericana, S.A., *Mexico*
Prentice-Hall of India Private Limited, *New Delhi*
Prentice-Hall of Japan, Inc., *Tokyo*
Simon & Schuster Asia Pte. Ltd., *Singapore*
Editora Prentice-Hall do Brasil, Ltda., *Rio de Janeiro*

Contents

Contents

Contents

Preface

The underlying proposition of this book is that the "ethics crisis" facing corporate America is first and foremost a management problem. Business has learned to manage effectively many aspects of its operations from materials acquisition to distribution of finished product. The expanded knowledge base with its constituent technologies responsible for making corporate America productive and efficient has ignored one singularly important area of management concern, namely how to manage the business in an ethical manner.

Managers have relegated the importance of ethics to concerns for productivity and profits and failed to judge accurately the response of the many and varied constituencies that business serves. Academic response, in our opinion, has been somewhat misdirected. There has been a thunder of emotional breast-beating and a chorus of normative advice. Many philosophers have found in the business ethics problem a rejuvenation as they espouse moral philosophies with little regard or perhaps awareness for the complex dynamics that drive American business.

The solution is not simply memorizing philosophical dialectic, but rather, it is incorporating those transcendent rules of moral philosophy into a creative and constructive management system which will reduce the probability of ethical misconduct. This is what this book is all about. The core of what we offer is a parallel planning system which accommodates concerns for ethics, social responsibility, and the demands for corporate profitability. Through the management of the corporation's culture, plans can be translated into ethical actions with a heightened probability that the right thing will be done.

We do not offer a simple solution. In fact, the size of the book belies the magnitude of the content. We offer a solution to those managers who truly want to be part of an ethical organization. Like most successful endeavors, this system of management requires constant vigilance and effort.

Chapter 1 examines what has been called corporate America's ethics crisis. Chapter 2 looks at several reasons why our corporations are losing the respect of the American public and what we can and cannot do to win back this respect. Chapter 3 discusses the differences between the concepts of social responsibility and ethics and examines them as tools for responding to the ethics problem. Chapter 4 examines corporate culture which is central to our parallel planning system. The actual parallel planning system is discussed in Chapter 5 with a focus on how ethical concerns can be placed on an equal footing with concerns for profitability and productivity. Chapter 6 examines several tools that make the parallel planning system work, while Chapter 7 looks at the implementation and control functions associated with the management of the system. Chapter 8 concludes the book with a brief discussion and evaluation of the system relevant to a number of criteria put forth by leading exponents of business ethics.

There are several people that we are indebted to in this effort. First is our families who have tolerated the selfishness that a book like this requires. Second, we would like to thank all of the people who helped us fine tune our ideas. They are too many to mention but their contribution was significant.

R. Eric Reidenbach
Donald P. Robin

Chapter 1

Corporate America's Ethics Crisis

ITEM: Anheuser-Busch, America's undisputed King of Beer, has been the object of allegations that key Anheuser-Busch marketing executives have received kickbacks from one of its suppliers. The allegations state that Hanley Worldwide Inc., a St. Louis promotional firm, paid $13,500 toward a Porsche sports car which was bought by Anheuser-Busch's director of promotions. In addition, depositions claim that two other executives had received in excess of $150,000 in kickbacks from Hanley.

ITEM: In June 1987, Chrysler was presented with a 16-count indictment alleging that executives of the Chrysler Corporation had driven Chrysler automobiles with their odometers disconnected and then sold the cars as new. Chrysler officials countered that there was no attempt to mislead the public and that Chrysler officials had done nothing illegal or improper.

ITEM: General Dynamics, one of the country's biggest defense contractors, was twice suspended from doing business with the U.S. government because Pentagon investigations revealed that executives at General Dynamics had been fraudulently billing the government.

ITEM: General Electric and Rockwell International, two highly regarded members of corporate America, were found guilty of defrauding the U.S. government and overcharging on defense contracts.

ITEM: E. F. Hutton & Company pleaded guilty to 2,000 counts of mail and wire fraud in a scheme to overdraw checking accounts, a practice in the trade that is called kiting checks.

ITEM: The SEC and other regulatory bodies are attempting to unravel all the connections in the Ivan Boesky case. Mr. Boesky admitted to charges of insider trading on Wall Street. He was fined $100,000,000 and given immunity to provide leads to other insider trading suspects.

These are just a few of the incidents that are forcing virtually all segments of American society to question the morality of American business and American business people. With increasing frequency we are being bombarded with new revelations of wrongdoing and unethical behavior on the part of many of our highly regarded business institutions. And, as is the case with many of these types of situations, there is a strong likelihood that the American public has been exposed to only the tip of the iceberg and that many of the wrongdoers and their actions go unnoticed. One study by Amitai Etzioni of George Washington University indicates that two thirds of the nation's 500 largest industrial corporations have been involved in at least one significant illegal incident in the past decade.[1]

Consider also that arrests for fraud have increased 75 percent in the ten-year period between 1976 and 1986. In that same time period, arrests for embezzlement have increased 26 percent.[2]

This mounting evidence and disaffection with the ethical practices of corporate America has lead many critics and supporters of business alike to suggest that corporate America is facing an "ethics crisis."

THE NATURE OF THE CONCERN

The concern about corporate America's behavior is not isolated. An institution as large and pervasive as business cannot help but touch numerous groups and segments of our society. How do Americans feel about business and those that are charged with its management?

1. Steven P. Rosenfeld, "Business Crime: Just a Few Bad Apples, or the Barrel?" *The Commercial Appeal*, December 15, 1985, p. C2.

2. Michael H. Gallagher, Jo Ann Tooley, Marianna I. Knight, Andrew Torach and Edwina Anderson, "Ethics 101" *U.S. News & World Report*, March 14, 1988, p. 76.

3

Americans Distrust Business and Business People

If polls about business provide any indication about people's attitudes toward business and business people, then there is significant cause for alarm. For example, a *New York Times* poll found that 55 percent of the American public feel that American corporate executives are not honest.[3] A study by Brenner and Molander found that even business executives themselves are more cynical about their peers than they were 15 years ago.[4] Another poll conducted by *U.S. News & World Report* indicated that 69 percent of the public thinks most or many employees take office supplies and small tools home from work with them; 60 percent think that most or many business people with expense accounts pad them; 47 percent think most or many labor leaders use union funds for their personal expenses.[5] A poll conducted for *Time* magazine found that 76 percent of the American public saw lack of ethics in business people as contributing to a decline in moral standards.[6] A poll by Yankelovich, Skelly, and White reported that in 1968, 70 percent of the American public believed that business tried to strike a balance between profits and the public interest. Ten years later, the percentage dropped to 15 percent.[7] In 1966, a Harris poll reported that 55 percent of the American public had respect for and confidence in our business leaders, where more recently, only 20 percent say that they now do.[8] Michael Hoffman, founding director of the Center for Business Ethics at Bentley College, notes that a poll done for the Center by Gallup found that "big business was rapidly becoming,

3. W. Williams, "White Collar Crime: Booming Again," *New York Times,* June 9, 1985, p. 4:1.

4. S. Brenner and E. Molander, "Is the Ethics of Business Changing?" *Harvard Business Review,* 55(1), 1977, pp. 57–71.

5. Merrill McLoughlin, Jerry Sheled, and Gordon Witkin, "A Nation of Liars," *U.S. News & World Report,* February 23, 1987, pp. 55–60.

6. Ezra Bowen, "Ethics: Looking to its Roots," *Time Magazine,* May 25, 1987, pp. 26–29.

7. W. Michael Hoffman, "Developing the Ethical Corporation," *Business Insights,* 2, no. 2 (Fall 1986), p. 10.

8. Ibid.

in the public's view, the biggest threat to the country's future."[9] Study after study, poll after poll reveal the cynicism that most Americans have in regard to the moral and ethical integrity of business and business people.

Business is no less harsh a critic of its own behavior. A Touche Ross survey of over 1,000 directors, top executives of U.S. companies, and business school deans expressed the feeling that the business community, as a whole, has an ethics problem. When asked if they thought the issue of business ethics has been overblown by the media, more than two thirds of the directors and top executives said the issue had not been overblown.[10]

Business Schools are Becoming More Involved

A sure sign that the behavior of American business is causing concern is evidenced by a growing involvement of America's business schools. This involvement pervades the entire spectrum of business schools. Most notably, Harvard has recently announced the receipt of a gift of $30 million to fund a teaching program in ethics for MBAs. The money was given by outgoing Security and Exchange Commission Chairman John S. R. Shad.

In addition, a debate over whether business schools should be teaching ethics and whether such a program would do any good has been waged in newspapers and business magazines across the country. Critics question whether ethics can be taught with any effect on students, while supporters of the idea argue that students will be better equipped to deal with decisions that involve ethical consequences.

The American Assembly of Collegiate Schools of Business (AACSB) has long required coverage of ethics in business school curricula. That coverage need not be concentrated in a single course but documentation during accreditation times must be provided indicating that it is covered sufficiently in other courses.

9. Ibid.
10. "Ethics in American Business," Touche Ross, January 1988.

Reactions from the Legal System

Unethical business behavior has spawned numerous laws designed to provide a minimum level of permissible behavior. Recent laws enacted by Congress include Truth in Lending, Truth in Advertising, the Corrupt Foreign Practices Act, the Automobile Information Disclosure Act, and Consumer Credit Protection Act. Some of the more famous and historical pieces of legislation are the Sherman Antitrust Act, Clayton Act, and the Robinson-Patman Act. All of these legal constraints on business activity have evolved because of the unwillingness of business to regulate the ethics of its own behavior.

David Vogel comments on the causal nexus between ethical impropriety and ensuing legislation. "In the 20th century, corporate misdeeds have been commonly ascribed to the lack of adequate government controls over business. As a result, new scandals often lead to the establishment of a new statute, regulation or regulatory agency."[11] This linkage between unethical behavior and subsequent rule making is underscored by Congress's recent decision to investigate insider trading and to seek a definition of the practice so that legislation defining insider trading and identifying the types of information that can be used can be legislated.

The concern over the ethical behavior or lack of ethical behavior of business touches many segments of our society. We have become so aware of the numerous ethical trespasses of business that some business commentators are suggesting that corporate America is in the midst of an ethics crisis. A crisis typically describes a situation or period in time where a turning point is reached. That behavior or series of events which produced the turning point, if continued, will lead to less than desirable outcomes. Is corporate America in the midst of an ethics crisis? What are the less than desirable outcomes of continued unethical behavior?

11. David Vogel, "Could an Ethics Course Have Kept Iran From Going Bad?" *Wall Street Journal*, April 27, 1987, p. 18.

DOES ETHICS PAY?

Another way of examining the dysfunctional outcomes of continued unethical behavior is to ask "Does it pay to be unethical?" Most managers and executives are "bottom-line" people and this question is a bottom-line question. There are a number of ways of assessing the payoff of ethical or unethical behavior.

Profits

Unfortunately, there exists no concrete evidence that conclusively indicates that ethical companies are more profitable companies. It is the belief of the authors that in general, and in the long run, ethical performance has a positive effect on profitability. However, we also recognize that in certain situations, and especially in the short run, unethical behavior can produce greater profits than ethical behavior. Following an unethical path to greater profits, by its very nature, increases risks to the organization since outcomes are never totally predictable. Even so, if executives choose to follow an unethical path to greater profits, there may be occasions where they can do so successfully.

Attempts to measure the success of "ethical" companies and compare that success to other companies has produced questionable results. We cite as weak and admittedly limited evidence those so-called socially responsible mutual funds that invest in only those companies which they consider to be good corporate citizens. Typically, these funds have not done as well as other funds.

Comparing so-called ethical corporations with corporations that make no statement about their ethics poses a significant problem. As consultants to several national and many regional firms, we have never encountered an entire corporation which was unethical by design. Rather, corporations often receive the tag of being unethical because of the actions of one individual or a small group of individuals. Many times these actions are not necessarily intended but result from insufficient knowledge of a situation or faulty reasoning about the consequences of an action.

Studies which purport to compare the profitability of ethical companies with unethical companies are suspect on yet another ground. Consider the company that has broken South African law by desegregating worker environments. This is illegal by South African law and accordingly, by some definitions, unethical. This company has not withdrawn from South Africa because to do so, according to its management, is to forfeit its ethical duty to bring about needed social change. This company would not therefore be included in a CSR mutual fund on the basis of it not being an ethical company. Is this company properly excluded from inclusion in a CSR mutual fund? The issues are not that clear cut; consequently, statements concerning the profitability of ethics are not to be relied upon.

One measure of the cost of unethical and illegal behavior in corporate America estimates that between $40 billion to $300 billion a year is lost.[12] While estimates may vary, it is clear that the cost is great, impacting government receipts from taxes and increasing the price paid for products and services by consumers. Interestingly, 65 percent of the directors in the Touche Ross survey felt that higher ethical standards made a company a stronger competitor.[13]

Legal Ramifications of Unethical Behavior

There is perhaps a better measure of the consequences of ethical behavior and the ultimate profitability of such behavior. As mentioned before, increased legislation and concern by the government over the conduct of business is evident. Much of this legal intervention has carried with it fines and jail sentences.

Chrysler faced fines of up to $120 million for its practice of disconnecting odometers and then reconnecting them to sell the cars, which may have up to 400 actual miles on them, as brand new automobiles.

E. F. Hutton, found guilty of a kiting scheme, was fined $12 million dollars. Ivan Boesky, who admitted to charges of insider

12. Steven B. Rosenfeld, "Business Crime: Just a Few Bad Apples, or the Barrel?" *The Commercial Appeal*, December 15, 1985, p. C2.

13. "Ethics in American Business," Touche Ross, January 1988.

trading was fined $100 million. General Dynamics, the Bank of Boston, Chemical New York and General Electric have all faced fines for corporate behavior found to be unethical.

Perhaps more important is the growing propensity of the legal system to pierce the corporate veil and hold individuals responsible for corporate behavior. The most significant case to date concerns a firm called Film Recovery Systems located in Elk Grove Village, Illinois, a suburb of Chicago. This company extracted silver from old X-ray film with a chemical process that involved the use of cyanide. Stefan Golab, a worker at FRS, became weak and nauseated while working near a large, foaming vat. He collapsed, lost consciousness and was rushed to a hospital where he was pronounced dead on arrival. The district attorney, under Illinois law, was empowered to bring murder charges whenever an individual "knowingly creates a strong probability of death or great bodily harm." Three executives of FRS, Steven O'Niel, the president, Charles Kirschbaum, the plant director, and Daniel Rodriguez, the foreman, were indicted and convicted of murder. The three were sentenced to 25 years in prison. Legal consultants concur that the FRS case has set a precedent providing legal access to corporate executives that heretofore was not available. [14] This exposure of corporate executives to legal prosecution was indelibly etched in the minds of a number of employees at Kidder Peabody and Goldman Sachs when federal marshals arrested Richard Wigton, the head of arbitrage and over-the-counter trading at Kidder Peabody and Robert Freeman, the head of the arbitrage department at Goldman Sachs.

The Image of a Crooked Company

Does ethical behavior pay? Ask executives at E. F. Hutton who, in the wake of the check kiting scandal, had to hire Bill Cosby in an attempt to restore credibility to a company name that had been tarnished by unethical behavior. Ask the Bank of Boston whose survival depends on ethics and a pristine image damaged by refusing to report massive cash transactions of alleged mob leaders. Ask Lee

14. Robert Melury, "Murder on the Shop Floor," *Across the Board*, June 15, 1982, pp. 24–31.

Iacocca who had fought so hard to restore the image of the Chrysler Corporation only to have it damaged by the odometer problem. Ask executives at Nestlé who fought worldwide boycotts concerning their marketing of infant formula in less developed countries (LDCs), a practice that resulted in the infant deaths.

Traders at investment houses in New York City are suffering from the disclosures of insider trading that have plagued that industry. One *Wall Street Journal* headline reads: "I AM NOT A CROOK," IMAGE PROBLEM DOGS INVESTMENT BANKERS".[15] As if this were not enough for the industry to deal with, a rash of jokes about the integrity of investment bankers has surfaced. For example, "What do you get if you cross a pig with a Wall Streeter?" The response: "Nothing. There are some things even a pig won't do!" Or, "Two drunks were stumbling through the graveyard of Trinity Church, in the heart of New York's financial district, when one trips on a tombstone. He peers down and reads the inscription: 'Here lies an investment banker and an honest man,' it says. "Hey Charlie," the drunk yells to his friend, "it's getting so crowded in here they're burying them two to a grave!"[16]

The point is unethical behavior carries with it a stigma that can alienate markets and create massive employee morale problems. These consequences are often unmeasured side effects of unethical behavior that can linger long after the last dollar of a fine has been paid. They are consequences that require additional dollar expenditures to correct and in some cases cannot be totally corrected.

The Hidden Costs of Increased Legislation

Another cost of unethical behavior that often goes uncited is the cost of conforming to increased legislation. We alluded to the increasing amount of legislation that has been promulgated because of businesses failing to act ethically. This increased legislation has a number of insidious impacts, other than fines, on corporate America.

15. Michael M. Miller and Laurie P. Cohen, "I am Not a Crook: Image Problem Dogs Investment Bankers," *Wall Street Journal*, March 9, 1987, pp. 1, 12.
16. Ibid.

One of the more notable impacts is the increase in the size of the legal departments of American business. The increased legislation means that executives must now consult more lawyers more frequently to determine whether proposed actions and programs are legal or have the potential for leading the company into a legal problem. Corporate legal staffs have increased significantly in an effort to navigate the murky waters of corporate liability.

A second impact of increased legislation is a narrowing of acceptable business practices making it more and more difficult for businesses to compete. Legislation aimed at limiting permissible business behavior has the effect of circumscribing the playing field making it more expensive and more difficult to compete. Corporate disregard for the environment, for example, has resulted in numerous regulations and agencies designed to monitor and control pollution. If this problem had been addressed by business and treated as an ethical challenge to doing business, there is a strong likelihood that subsequent solutions to the problem would have resulted in fewer inspections, less paperwork, lower costs, and fewer laws.

While the short-term returns of unethical behavior may appear attractive to both individuals and organizations, a mounting body of evidence suggests that individuals and corporations alike are at risk if they pursue an unethical business tack. Increased legislation, individual prosecution, and image problems can easily offset what appeared to be readily obtainable profits. When all of these potential consequences are considered, we would argue that in the long run unethical behavior does not pay.

Business Needs a Level Playing Field

One of the more compelling reasons for ethical behavior is the need for a competitive environment that allows all businesses equal opportunity to survive and grow. Imagine a system in which lying, cheating, bribing, giving kickbacks and other types of unethical behavior were the norm rather than the exception. Doing business as we know it would be unrecognizable and more like gang warfare. All businesses and business people need to expect ethical behavior from fellow workers, their bosses, and competitors. Without this expectation, a relatively uncontrolled free market system cannot operate.

WHO IS TO BLAME?

In the previous sections we have seen the depth and the breadth of the declining moral record of corporate America. In addition, we have looked at what we think are the key consequences of unethical behavior and how they will affect individuals, businesses, and society. We have arrived at the point in the discussion where it is logical to ask who or what is to blame for the ethical problems we are experiencing in corporate America. To answer this question it is necessary to look at the two major factors related to the problem: our society and our corporations.

A Changing Societal Ethics System

Business does not operate in a vacuum. It is a subsystem of our social order and as such is not immune to the changing social ethic that impacts other institutions. We have been concentrating on business to the exclusion of two other major social institutions; the church and government. We would be remiss not to point out that the apparent moral decline associated with business is also seen in matters related to the government and church.

Government, at all levels, is plagued with questions of ethics and moral wrongdoing. At the federal level more than 100 Reagan administration officials have faced allegations of questionable ethical practices. This list includes the Attorney General, several former advisors and cabinet officials, as well as a host of minor officials. State and local governments are not faring much better. In Mississippi, Operation Pretense, a program to identify corrupt county supervisors, has resulted in a large number of arrests and convictions for such crimes as bribery, extortion, and fraud. This type of program has been extended to other states and is currently in effect in New York.

Of all our institutions, one would think that the church would be least susceptible to moral backsliding. Recent revelations, however, suggest this is not so. Perhaps most noteworthy are the ethical and possibly illegal problems uncovered in the TV evangelical ministry of the PTL. Questions concerning the raising and use of millions of dollars of contributions remain unanswered as well as questions of the impropriety of the money-raising schemes. The ethics of Oral Robert's ploy of claiming that if he did not raise certain sums of money the Lord would "call him home" have been questioned.

Many have argued that our entire social ethic has changed. Jody Powell, former press secretary to President Carter, suggests that "There is a growing degree of cynicism and sophistication in our society—a sense that all things are relative and that nothing is absolutely right or wrong."[17] This sense of relativism suggests that absolute notions of good and bad, right and wrong no longer apply. Rather, there exist certain factors that make ideas of morality contingent upon factors embedded within a particular situation. This type of thinking says that stealing or lying may be permissible depending upon the situation. Winston Churchill had this sense of relativism in mind when he stated, "In wartime, truth is so precious that she should be attended by a bodyguard of lies."

Contributing to this sense of relativism is what many see as a breakdown in the important institutions of family and religion—two of the more important sources of moral teaching. Young people are not being taught key values about truth telling, cheating, and stealing.

Still others maintain that the problem is caused by greed unleashed by the relative laissez-faire economic program of the Reagan administration. Says Myron Magnet, writing in *Fortune* about the current ethos embraced by many young Wall Streeters:

> The ethic they have, half articulate but deeply felt, takes the
> idea of the free market and turns economic theory into a per-

17. Ezra Bowen, "Ethics: Looking to its Roots," *Time Magazine*, May 25, 1987, pp. 26–29.

sonal moral code, making nonsense of reasonable propositions by exaggeration and distortion. "Okay" the rising generation says, "the mechanism of the market insures that each individual, pursuing his own interest in his own way, will augment the wealth of the nation, thereby advancing the public interest by self-interest. This means that whatever I do in my own race for wealth—spill the company's secrets, or put that one into play or lie to a third—is fine. It is only mistaken sentimentality to say these things are wrong."[18]

Observes Getty Foundation chief and ex-Norton Simon C.E.O. Harold Williams: "The concept of 'let the market govern' relieves one of one's sense of responsibility."[19]

Many proponents of the free market regulating the behavior of individuals point to their mentor, Milton Friedman, a longstanding advocate of capitalism and profit making. However, even Friedman recognizes the importance of law and ethics. He contends that corporate executives have a responsibility to "make as much money as possible *while conforming to the basic rules of society, both those embodied in law and those embodied in ethical custom*"[20] (emphasis added).

Mismanagement of Corporate Ethics

It is convenient to speak of corporations being unethical. This, we believe, is erroneous. Corporations are comprised of individuals and it is the individual who acts, not the corporation. In the past, wrongdoing has been ascribed to the corporation which, in essence, locates the responsibility and blame for an action to a piece of paper or a building. That is where a corporation actually exists, both legally and physically. By focusing on the corporation and ascribing to it moral agency, ethical problems are depersonalized and obscured. This focus on the legal entity of corporations rather than the individuals who run them is critical because it diffuses the responsibility from those who acted to all who belong to the corporation.

18. Myron Magnet, "The Decline and Fall of Business Ethics," *Fortune*, December 8, 1986, pp. 65, 66, 68, 72.

19. Ibid.

20. Milton Friedman, "The Social Responsibility of Business is to Increase its Profits," *New York Times Magazine*, September 13, 1970.

It confounds any real attempts to deal with the situation by failing to hold the true perpetrators responsible.

We are recognizing that corporations do exert a vital force that impacts the lives of those who work for that organization. We refer to this environmental force as a corporate culture that is comprised, over time, of individual values and beliefs of the employees, top management, industry, and the founders of the corporation. Each individual in the corporation contributes to and partakes of this culture. That means that each individual brings to the corporation his or her notions of, among other things, right and wrong, good and bad. These notions are combined with rules, policies, and regulations to become part and parcel of the corporation's culture.

W. Michael Hoffman, director of the Center for Business Ethics at Bentley College, effectively expresses this reciprocal dynamic between individual and corporation:

> E. F. Hutton and General Dynamics and the rest are blamed only because certain individuals committed wrongful actions; hence we should focus our attention on developing individual integrity which will lead to institutional integrity. Although there is some truth to this claim, it nevertheless overlooks the essential dynamics and reciprocity between individuals and organizations. Just as organizations are made up of individuals, individuals are dependent on organizations. Individuals gain meaning, direction, and purpose by belonging to and acting out of organizations, out of social cultures that are formed around common goals, shared beliefs, and collective duties. . . . Corporations, like other social organizations, can and do influence individual decisions and actions. Corporations are social cultures with character—character that can exercise good or bad influences depending on goals, policies, structures, strategies and other characteristics that formalize relations among the individuals who make up corporations.[21]

The Real Problem

The real problem facing corporations today with respect to ethical behavior is a management problem. How is it possible to ef-

21. W. Michael Hoffman, "Developing the Ethical Corporation," *Business Insights,* vol. 2, no. 2 (Fall 1986), p. 10.

fectively manage the reciprocal relationship between individual and institution so that the probability of ethical action is increased?

In developing our response to this question we begin by asking what factors are under the corporation's control. For example, corporate managers and executives cannot control directly what is being taught in the school systems, what is being preached in the churches, what mothers and fathers are or are not teaching their children, what business schools are teaching their graduates, and so forth. Yet studies indicate that business people overwhelmingly feel that the decay in our cultural and social institutions are eroding business ethics. While this may be an accurate sociological explanation, these factors are out of the control of the typical business organization and are therefore not part of the solution to the problem.

What is under the control of the organization is its management system, both the formal and informal aspects of it. The corporate culture, the organization's planning processes, the way it implements the plans and controls its actions are all critical factors that will have a significant impact on the probability that its subsequent actions will be judged as ethical or unethical. The rest of this book is dedicated to examining these critical management factors and suggesting ways in which they can be incorporated into a management system to increase the probability of ethical corporate behavior.

Exercises for Chapter 1

Bribery of Retail Buyers Is Called Pervasive: Cash, Gifts from Vendors Spur Many Firms to Attack Practice*

Donald G. Parker was making a pretty good living buying shoes for T. G. & Y. Stores Co., an Oklahoma City-based retailer. Just how good became apparent when the company's security officials opened his bank safe-deposit box.

*Hank Gilman, *Wall Street Journal*, April 1, 1985, p. 6. Used with permission.

Inside were more than $70,000 in cash, stock certificates valued at $1,000, a Rolex watch, two diamonds, an 18-karat gold bracelet, 13 gold Krugerrands and a 6.2-ounce gold bar. Mr. Parker also owned three homes and, the company has alleged, stock in a Dallas company that was a T. G. & Y. supplier.

Mr. Parker, who allowed the chain to open the safe-deposit box after he was confronted with the company's allegations, built his nest egg by taking at least $525,000 in kickbacks from T. G. & Y.'s suppliers, the concern charges in a lawsuit.

Until recently, many retailers thought such chicanery was a thing of the past, from a time when vendors curried favor by dazzling buyers with cash and lavish gifts. But industry officials say bribery is back with a vengeance, triggered by overseas buying trips, more competition among vendors and just plain greed. "It's pervasive, it's all over the place," says Herbert Robinson, a New York lawyer specializing in white-collar crime. "It's in the largest chains and in the smallest chains. Even the most pious ones."

The ultimate losers in this type of bribery are retailers, whose profit can suffer, and customers, who often must pay higher prices.

Polygraph Tests

As a result, more retailers are closely scrutinizing their buyers with extensive background checks and polygraph (lie-detector) tests. Some "have personnel dedicated solely to white-collar crime investigations—that's how serious it has become," says Peter Schmidt, vice president for security with T. G. & Y.

In fact, retailers are so concerned that a few are taking buyers to court, a practice normally considered too costly and time consuming. For example:

- In late 1983, T. G. & Y filed seven separate civil complaints in state court in Oklahoma City, accusing Mr. Parker and six other buyers of taking about $735,000 in cash and gifts from the company's vendors. The suit seeks that amount and other damages. Two cases have been settled and negotiations continue in the others, including Mr. Parker's. Mr. Parker declines to comment pending resolution of the case. The company, a unit of Household International Inc., also filed suits in federal district court in Oklahoma City against 12 vendors who allegedly bribed T. G. & Y.'s buyers. Those cases were settled late last year; terms weren't disclosed.

• Recently, a health and beauty products buyer with Boston-based Stop & Shop Cos. agreed to return $389,000 in what the company said were kickbacks and interest. According to a civil complaint filed by Stop & Shop in federal district court in Boston, the buyer accepted payments equal to 1.5% of Stop & Shop's orders from Interstate Cigar Co., a Westbury, N.Y. supplier. Interstate allegedly mailed the kickbacks to the buyer's dummy corporation. The FBI said it is investigating further.

• Natco Industries Inc., which operates 211 men's apparel shops, filed a civil complaint in New York State Supreme Court accusing three former employees of taking "millions of dollars" in kickbacks from the company's overseas vendors. The company's suit seeks actual and punitive damages of $40 million. Natco says the U.S. attorney's office in New York is investigating the case based on evidence generated by the company. The U.S. attorney's office would neither confirm nor deny that an investigation is under way.

And, as Robert Nesbit, a New York-based recruiter of retail personnel notes, "For every court case, there are hundreds of situations where retailers just say 'goodbye, Al, goodbye, Pete,' " to crooked buyers.

Many industry experts trace the kickback surge to the rise of imports, which accounts for about 30 percent of the clothes sold in the U.S., compared with 12 percent in 1973. Foreign vendors pay kickbacks as high as 15 percent of an order, compared with the usual 1 percent to 3 percent in the U.S., industry officials say. "Graft is a way of life in some of those countries," says Mr. Nesbit, a vice president with Korn/Ferry International. "Now we have a whole new generation of bag men."

David Richenthal, general counsel and director of Natco, says Natco's former buyers may have solicited "as much as $10 million" in kickbacks from overseas vendors during a five-year period. According to Natco's suit, manufacturers paid some kickbacks to dummy corporations overseas, which were owned by Natco's merchandise executives.

The suit also alleges that Danny Markowitz, a former Natco vice president and director, collected $294,703 in kickbacks from one of Natco's 20 foreign vendors. Mr. Markowitz couldn't be reached for comment.

Buyers can be easy pickings for overseas vendors, retailers say. Roy Fisher, Natco's president and chief executive officer, offers this typical example: A buyer who paid $9.75 for a pair of blue jeans the year before negotiates a $9.00 price based on a larger order. However, another clothes maker says he'll deliver the same pants for $8.75 each. In order to retain the big order, the first vendor matches the $8.75 price and also "gives the buyer 25 cents a pair," Mr. Fisher explains. The bribe is undetectable because the buyer sets up a phony company that serves as a middleman in the transaction. The vendor bills the retailer for $9.00 a pair and funnels the 25 cents back to the buyer through the dummy corporation, calling it "an agency commission."

On the surface, everyone's happy. The vendor keeps the order and the retailer pays less for the pants than a year ago. The buyer figures, "I'm a hero; I deserve the money." Mr. Fisher says, however, that the retailer's price is never that good again because the buyer is obligated to the vendor.

Foreign vendors aren't the only culprits. Competition among U.S. manufacturers is fierce and gift-giving widespread. "And as long as the dollar is real strong, their overseas sales are going to decrease. They've got to sell locally," explains Howard Stone, a Chicago lawyer and former Internal Revenue Service agent. Some vendors even circumvent buyers and try to bribe a company's top executives, says Jack Shewmaker, vice chairman of Wal-Mart Stores Inc., the big discount chain. "I could have had percentages or cash payments," Mr. Shewmaker says.

Buyers take bribes for many reasons, officials say. Many who do are relatively low-paid, often disgruntled employees who have been passed over for promotions. "They're 40 years old to 50 years old, make about $30,000 a year and can't go anywhere else," explains Eugene Sampieri, an East Setauket, New York investigator who does security investigations for retailers. "So they make it up in other ways." Adds Arthur D'Antonio, an investigator with Kerin, Duffy & Heberer Inc., New York private detectives: "Some reasons are drugs, adultery and gambling. But in white-collar crime you have a fourth area—greed. The almighty dollar."

Losses Cited

While the vendors and buyers profit from kickback arrangements, retailers and consumers pay for it. Natco, for example, had losses four of the past six years, including a $3.2 million loss in 1982. "I'm convinced this (alleged buyers') scheme made a difference in the profitability of the company," says Mr. Richenthal, adding that the company often paid more for merchandise than its competitors.

Many retailers are forced into costly price cuts on unsalable merchandise purchased by a corrupt buyer. "When a manufacturer has an overrun, they'll call a buyer in their pocket to take the merchandise off their hands," says a buyer for a big apparel chain. Also, many dishonest buyers often don't demand discounts such as advertising allowances that are provided to honest merchandise executives. "On the very face of things, the buyer isn't using as sharp a pencil as she or he otherwise might," says Mr. Robinson, the New York attorney. "If you take goods in at 50 cents more, you will price them to your customer at least $1 more. You render yourself noncompetitive with retailers whose buyers aren't on the take."

Honest manufacturers are hurt by these schemes. One New York apparel vendor says he lost a $4 million account with one of the nation's largest retailers because he, unlike one competitor, didn't bribe the buyer with $20,000 cars and pricey stereo systems. The same vendor also says he was excluded from doing business with a corrupt buyer from a big East Coast discount chain.

Uncovering corruption is difficult. "It's more sophisticated now," says Mr. Sampieri, the private investigator. T. G. & Y.'s Mr. Schmidt says he has seen bribes ranging from stock-market tips to rare art prints. "One buyer bought from a (vendor) a house that was valued at $205,000," Mr. Schmidt recalls. "He paid $50,000 for it."

In fact, most chains discover kickbacks by accident. For example, after one unfruitful investigation, Natco's Mr. Fisher received a 7 A.M. telephone call on a Saturday from John F. Kennedy

Airport in New York. It "was one of our long-term suppliers from the Orient," Mr. Fisher recalls. He flew here to complain about paying excessive bribes and eventually provided documents linking the chain's overseas buyers with various kickback schemes, Mr. Fisher says.

Industry officials say the best way to ferret out corruption is to watch closely buyers' purchases for their stores. Mr. Stone, the Chicago lawyer, says retailers also must hire professional investigators to check corruption rumors and "pay attention" to how buyers live.

Many states have commercial-bribery laws that prohibit suppliers from giving anything of value to a buyer or any other purchasing agent—without the knowledge and consent of the employer. Also, there are various federal laws prohibiting employees from taking bribes from people with whom they do business. If kickbacks are paid by mail, for example, the buyer could be in violation of the federal Mail Fraud Act.

Bentonville, Arkansas-based Wal-Mart doesn't even allow its buyers to accept a free lunch. "It then turns out to be a dinner and theater tickets and subsequent to that a vacation in Las Vegas. And down the road, cash kickbacks," explains Mr. Shewmaker. Adds a security director for a West Coast department store: "People who shoplift don't start out with $5,000 furs."

Wall Street and the Age-old Tragic Flaw*

Second-guessing Wall Street's insider-trading scandal has become a growth industry. Politicians claim the whole thing could have been prevented by tougher regulations. Economists blame the system. "What do you expect," they ask, "when arbitragers' returns routinely reach 35 percent to 50 percent? Pussycats?"

Psychologists, too, are having a field day. They contend that the insatiable thirst for profit, the lavish life styles and the manipula-

*John K. Clemons, *Wall Street Journal*, March 18, 1987, p. 24. Used with permission.

tion of the market are all products of (you guessed it) lousy childhoods.

Come on.

Things are simpler than that. It's plain arrogance that has given Wall Street its biggest jolt in decades. The symptoms are easy to detect precisely because they are so inherently a part of human nature—the "we-are-so-powerful-we-can-do-anything" syndrome combined with the naive belief that once on a roll, always on a roll. It's an old story.

And it was told well by Sophocles, the fifth-century B.C. Greek playwright whose tragic characters illustrate the damage done by usurping authority, abusing power and lacking respect for others. Most important, they demonstrate that arrogance is downright bad business. Just change the names and places, and today's Levines, Boeskys and Siegels become the tragic protagonists in his stories.

Ajax, for example, is "top gun" among the Greeks in the Trojan War. In battle, he is likened to a lion, and enemy soldiers are understandably awed. Sophocles reveals Ajax's tragic flaw when Ajax is denied a promotion. The affront so rankles him that he seeks revenge by murdering the Greek leaders. But the gods intervene and turn him on the Greeks' livestock. After coming to his senses the next day, he is so overcome with shame that he kills himself.

Ajax's crime is not that he slaughtered a few goats and sheep or attempted revenge on his unappreciative bosses. His real offense is arrogance. Early in the play the youthful Ajax, leaving home to join the Greek army, is offered some parting advice by his father: "My son, seek victory in arms, but seek it always with the help of heaven." Ajax blusters, "Father, with the help of gods even a weak man might win, but I, even without their aid, trust to bring glory within my grasp." Youthful boasting? Perhaps. But when, as an adult, Ajax brags even to the gods that he is omnipotent, it is unpardonable.

To the ancient Greeks, there was nothing unusual about this. The idea that the gods would slap down any mortal who became too powerful, rich or ambitious was part of their culture. "The gods are accustomed to throw down whatever rises too high," said the Greek historian Herodotus. Words to Wall Street's wise.

Shakespeare's *Macbeth* is another story of arrogance, ambition and evil. As Thane of Glamis, Macbeth is the model young nobleman: brave and courageous, his king's most glorious general. But arrogance is to get the better of him:

> I have no spur
> To prick the sides of my intent, but only
> Vaulting ambition, which o'erleaps itself
> And falls on th' other—

When the king visits Macbeth's castle, Macbeth sneaks into his bedchamber and stabs him. Macbeth is crowned king, but he is consumed by guilt. Experiencing gradual disintegration, he utters the lines that signal the futility of his existence:

> Life's but a walking shadow, a poor player,
> That struts and frets his hour upon the stage,
> And then is heard no more. It is a tale
> Told by an idiot, full of sound and fury
> Signifying nothing.

Macbeth is finally beheaded by an avenging general.

Ajax and Macbeth dramatize clearly what's happening on Wall Street: unbridled arrogance and ambition leading to inevitable falls. Like Ivan Boesky's. His career began to self-destruct, not when the Securities and Exchange Commission accused him of insider trading, but when, in 1985, he arrogantly told a crowd of adoring business students: "Greed is all right, by the way. I want you to know that. I think greed is healthy. You can be greedy and still feel good about yourself." His is the all-too-common tale of a supersuccessful individual so contemptuous of others that he loses all sense of propriety. By the time he notices, it is too late.

Mr. Boesky—whose prep-school education presumably included an introduction to Greek and Shakespearean tragedies—may have been less surprised than others by his own downfall. Perhaps he remembered the line from Shakespeare's *Henry VIII:* "Cromwell, I charge thee, fling away ambition, by that sin fell the angels." And he knew that arrogance had infected him. Asked about

23

his obsessive money making, he once said: "It's a sickness I have, in the face of which I am helpless." He had a premonition of the end. "I can't predict my demise," he told an interviewer, "but I suspect it will occur abruptly."

That's a tragic story. But the oldest in the world.

Companies as Citizens: Should They Have a Conscience?*

The American corporation comes under attack in two new books, both of which accuse it of lacking "responsibility." But what the authors have in mind by that term reflect very different images of what social and economic role the corporation ought to play.

From the left, or thereabouts, comes *Rating America's Corporate Conscience: A Provocative Guide to the Companies Behind the Products You Buy Every Day*, a team effort by the Council on Economic Priorities (Addison-Wesley, $14.95 paper). Anyone who wishes to lug this fat tome to the supermarket can look up which brand of "non-dairy dessert whip" is made by the firm least involved in defense contracting, what firms have the best employee daycare arrangements, and so on.

From the right, or thereabouts, comes *Boone*, the memoir of Texas takeover artist T. Boone Pickens, Jr. (Houghton-Mifflin, $18.95). Mr. Pickens styles himself the avatar of the interests of the small shareholder, and ends his book with a plug for United Shareholders of America (USA—geddit?), a would-be mass shareholders lobby Mr. Pickens founded last year, which you can join for a mere $50.

The CEP's standards for "corporate responsibility" are: share of profits donated to charity; number of women and minorities among top officers and on boards of directors; willingness to disclose "social information" to nosy groups like the CEP; involvement in South Africa; conventional- and nuclear-weapons contracting, and PAC contributions.

*Michael Kinsley, *Wall Street Journal*, February 19, 1987, p. 25. Used with permission.

24

Many *Wall Street Journal* readers, of course, will disagree with these criteria. They might wish to buy their non-dairy dessert whip from the company that is doing more, not less, to strengthen America's defenses in a dangerous world. The authors, I think, would say: Fine, if those are your priorities. Their overarching concept is one of "corporate citizenship": the corporation as a political institution that should be dealt with as such. Others, who share the council's general political slant, will find some of its criteria laughably beside the point. Will the world really be a better place if Juanita Kreps and William Coleman snare a few more fat director's fees while Henry Kissinger snares a few less? Who cares?

But differing criteria aside, is it really a good idea to turn the economy into one huge secondary boycott? If consumers decide which brand of peanut butter to buy based on social and political criteria, it stands to reason that they will have to sacrifice economic criteria to some extent. They will either pay more or get worse peanut butter. Or, if there is no real price or quality competition among peanut butters anyway, shouldn't that be of even greater concern to the Council on Economic Priorities?

In short, isn't the CEP misunderstanding the nature of capitalism, a system whose basic structure it does not challenge? The proper social role of the corporation is to produce the best peanut butter at the lowest price, leaving to individuals and to the political system such matters as support for the arts and how much we spend on defense. There's a lot to be said, even from a left-wing viewpoint, for the idea that corporations should keep to their own sphere and not attempt to become all-embracing social-service agencies.

In particular, I am not impressed by corporate charity and cultural benefaction, which amount to executives playing Medici with other people's money. You wouldn't know, from the lavish parties corporate officers throw for themselves whenever they fund an art exhibit or a PBS series, that it's not costing them a penny. The shareholders, who aren't invited, pick up the tab for the parties, too. There's a Catch-22 logic behind corporate charity, which the CEP seems to endorse: It's good for the corporate image to be thought charitable; a good image is good for profits (the CEP will urge people to buy your peanut butter); therefore corporate charity is a justifiable expenditure of shareholders' money. But if it's actually a hard-nosed business decision, why give the corporation credit for generosity? In which case the syllogism unravels.

Mr. Picken's vision of the corporation is not as a free-floating social and political entity, but as a simple mechanism through which shareholders collectively maximize their profits. When he talks about corporate abuses, he means inept or greedy management, not dumping toxic wastes or closing factories. In fact, the ruthless rationalization he and his fellow raiders have forced on company after company has turned them away from exactly the sort of "soft" considerations for which the Council on Economic Priorities awards points.

Mr. Pickens is a phony in many ways. His "barefoot boy from Texas vs. the Wall Street slicksters" routine is a joke. His suits are as expensive as any; he has a vast public-relations apparatus; and he travels with a praetorian guard of special assistants. Despite his denials, he has taken greenmail, which is hardly a service to the 47 million American stockholders with average incomes of $37,000 whom he claims to represent. But he does represent a theory of the corporation that is more right than wrong. If you believe in capitalism, then you have to believe that the main social function of the corporation is to maximize its own profits in the production of goods and services, which the companies the raiders target have sometimes failed to do.

It's not quite as simple as the raiders and their defenders would have you believe, though. Shareholders are not just shareholders. We are all bundles of interests: We want a profit on our shares, we want clean air and water, we want a just society. Yet the Pickens theory slices off and maximizes just one interest. There is something a little crazy—not rational at all—about some bow-tied young investment banker in New York taking steps that will force a company to shut down a plant in the name of "maximizing value for the shareholders," when the shareholders might include the pension fund for the workers in that very plant, or other workers getting the same treatment from another investment banker down the street. Political action committees and lobbyists protect our interests as corporate shareholders far better than we can protect our political interests in less-organized aspects of our lives. The net result may or may not reflect the true political interests of people who happen to own shares, let alone people in general.

Apart from pure self-interest, the corporate system leads us to act as shareholders in ways we never would act as individuals. Most of us don't try to squeeze every penny out of life. A sole proprietor of a family firm in a small town can sacrifice profits out of sentimental pride in product or community concern in ways that could land a big corporate executive with a shareholder derivative suit, or at least have him looking over his shoulder to see if Boone Pickens or Carl Icahn was coming along to rationalize his hide.

I wouldn't want either Boone Pickens or the Council on Economic Priorities running my corporation.

Cigarette Ads Reveal a History of Deceit*

Cigarette ads are in the news:

Surgeon General C. Everett Koop told a House subcommittee last Friday that he personally supported legislation that would totally ban the advertising and promotion of tobacco products. Mr. Koop, a presidential appointee, put himself at odds with the Reagan administration, which opposes any such ban.

The Federal Trade Commission recently charged R. J. Reynolds Tobacco Co. with using advertising to misrepresent the findings of a scientific study in order to make it appear that smoking has not been proven to be a cause of heart disease.

Across the nation, more than 100 product-liability lawsuits have been filed against cigarette makers; plaintiffs allege, among other things, that cigarette advertising deceptively—even fraudulently—misrepresented the dangers of smoking.

Egregious Abuse

Cigarette makers like to frame the issue as one of freedom of speech. Any attempt to restrict their efforts to promote smoking is

*Joe B. Tye, *Wall Street Journal*, August 15, 1986, p. 26. Used with permission.

portrayed as a violation of First Amendment rights and the first step toward mass censorship of commercial speech. In fact, no other industry has abused freedom of speech so egregiously. For 60 years, cigarette firms have used unfounded health claims to encourage people to smoke despite the risk of harm.

In the early part of this century, advertising was used to offset the common-sense perception that smoking "coffin nails" was unhealthy. American Tobacco Co. led the campaign with its promise that Lucky Strike cigarettes caused "No throat irritation—no cough." One Luckies ad from 1929 showed a fist labeled "American intelligence" breaking the chain of "ignorance." The ad stated, "We removed the prejudice against cigarettes when we removed from the tobacco harmful corrosive acrids (pungent irritants) present in cigarettes manufactured the old-fashioned way."

In subsequent years, smokers were implored to "protect the delicate tissues in your throat" by smoking Luckies; were asked "Do you inhale? What's there to be afraid of?" and were told to "Smoke a Lucky to feel your level best." Famous singers were claimed to smoke Luckies because of a professional need to protect their throats.

R. J. Reynolds used affirmative health claims to promote Camel cigarettes. They were claimed to steady the nerves, to provide "a harmless restoration of the flow of natural body energy," to aid digestion and to increase manual dexterity. Famous athletes were used to convey the message that smoking would not impair physical conditioning. One read, "Olympic champions say: Camels don't get your wind. So mild! You can smoke all you want!"

As evidence mounted linking smoking with disease, cigarette makers used medical themes to promote smoking: "20,679 physicians say Luckies are less irritating to your throat," claimed American Brands. "More doctors smoke Camels than any other cigarette!" responded R. J. Reynolds. L & M cigarettes were "just what the doctor ordered," while Philip Morris were "recognized by eminent medical authorities." Lorillard claimed that the American Medical Association had proved its Kent brand to have the most effective filter, drawing a stinging rebuke from the AMA's medical journal.

During the early 1950s, public alarm grew as lung-cancer deaths increased at an epidemic rate. In response, cigarette health claims reached the apex of deception. Brown & Williamson claimed that the "new Health-Guard filter makes Viceroy better for your health." Philip Morris ads stated, "An ounce of prevention is worth a pound of cure. Philip Morris are scientifically proved far less irritating to the nose and throat." R. J. Reynolds claimed that Camel smokers had been examined by "noted throat specialists" who found "not one single case of throat irritation due to smoking Camels."

Liggett & Myers ran a series of ads claiming to "give you the scientific facts in support of smoking." Long-term Chesterfield smokers purportedly were given "a thorough examination including X-rays, and covering the sinuses, nose, ears, and throat." The subjects were followed (at least in the advertising) for about two years; in each ad their respiratory organs were claimed to have been "not adversely affected" by smoking Chesterfields.

One of the most duplicitous cigarette-advertising campaigns was that introducing Kent cigarettes in 1952. In an advertising blitz that saturated both television and the print media, readers were told that one out of three smokers were "unduly sensitive to the nicotine and tars in tobacco. They really need real health protection." Kent's new Micronite filter was claimed to provide "the greatest health protection in cigarette history."

When Kents were introduced, they did deliver less tar and nicotine than most competing brands. In fact, the levels were so low that addicted smokers complained that it was like "smoking through a mattress." By 1955, Kent's formula was changed to quadruple the nicotine content and increase tar delivery sixfold. Unfortunately, the millions of smokers who had switched to avail themselves of "the greatest health protection in cigarette history" were never informed of the change.

In the late 1960s, Liggett & Myers injected a new element into cigarette health claims by discussing "gas" (presumably carbon monoxide) in cigarette smoke. One ad, with a picture of a woman kissing a man's balding head, read, "Tell someone you like about Lark's Gas-Trap filter.... Maybe your husband already knows that almost 90% of cigarette smoke is gas." The ad claimed that Lark's filter removed "certain of those harsh gases by nearly twice as much as any other filter on any other popular brand."

More Subtle Deception

Today, the deception in cigarette advertising is more subtle than in past years, but still effective in communicating the message that it is reasonably safe to smoke. The ads seem to be having a diminishing effect on men, but now are being strongly and effectively targeted at young women. The imagery of ski-racers, windsurfers, aerobic dancers and other athletic role models belies the reality of addiction, disease and death.

Even a society committed to freedom of speech must establish limits. Every freedom, including freedom of speech, has a corresponding responsibility. For 60 years tobacco firms have used advertising to deceive smokers and potential smokers into thinking it is safe to smoke. The FTC action against RJR Nabisco comes late in the game. If it is no more successful in discouraging deceit in ads pitched at concern for public health than previous such forays have been, it may be time to consider whether cigarette makers haven't forfeited the freedom they have enjoyed to use deceptive commercial speech to promote use of their lethal product.

Ethics on the Job: Companies Alert Employees to Potential Dilemmas*

Eighteen men and a woman sit around a table discussing Kate Simpson's dilemma. Kate is a new employee at a small firm that specializes in helping nonprofit hospitals get financing. One of its clients wants to hire a consultant to advise it on acquiring a new facility, and Kate has been asked to analyze competing proposals from four firms. Of the three received so far, Roberts & Co.'s is clearly the best.

*Alan L. Otten, *Wall Street Journal*, July 14, 1986, p. 17. Used with permission.

Then Kate sees her boss's deputy, a brash go-getter, slip a copy of the Roberts proposal into an envelope. He tells her to take it to a friend of his who works at the firm whose bid isn't yet in. "I told him we'd let him glance at Roberts's version," he says. Kate's boss won't be back for hours. What should she do?

Kate should damn well do as she's told, several people around the table declare. "She's not on a level where she's supposed to think," says one. "She doesn't know all the facts," adds another. "It may not be what she thinks."

Others say Kate should refuse; the situation has a bad smell, and she should keep her own hands clean. The debate continues for almost an hour.

Until recently, these people—senior administrators at the Fort Worth, Texas division of General Dynamics Corp.—probably wouldn't have addressed such a problem unless it happened to them. But now General Dynamics and other American companies are setting up training seminars where managers and workers are presented with fictional ethical dilemmas they might someday have to confront. These ethics workshops, which tend to be more consciousness-raising sessions than formal instruction, are designed to alert employees to the ethical dimensions of their decisions and actions, provide them with some broad guidelines for attacking ethical dilemmas and give them practice in applying these models.

"It's not whether you will do right or wrong, but to find out what the pressures are on you," says Barbara Ley Toffler, a Harvard Business School professor who serves as ethics consultant to major companies.

Many corporations adopted codes of ethics or business standards in the 1970s, when illegal corporate campaign contributions and overseas bribes were making headlines. "A lot of them thought the job was done," says Gary Edwards, executive director of the Washington, D.C.-based, nonprofit Ethics Resource Center, which tries to spread ethics programs in the business community. "Now they come, codes in hand, and say, 'These don't seem to be doing the job.' They want to transform them into management tools— training, communication, education."

So in the past 18 months, companies like General Dynamics, McDonnell Douglas Corp., Chemical Bank and American Can Co.

have initiated ethics programs. "They raise the ethical awareness of everyone involved," says Sanford McDonnell, chairman of McDonnell Douglas. "When you talk things out, you get a better feel for the company's value system."

Much of the raised consciousness about ethics is an obvious reaction to scandals that, polls show, have exacerbated the public's suspicions that business and honesty aren't always synonymous. General Dynamics, General Electric Co. and other companies have been charged with defrauding the Pentagon; E. F. Hutton & Co. was caught in an illegal check-kiting scam; major banks have failed to report large cash deposits by suspected criminals; and top company officials have traded on inside information.

But rescuing their public images is only one reason some companies have adopted ambitious ethics programs. Others, including McDonnell Douglas, believe that ethical corporate conduct is not only morally right but also smart business in the long run. Changing business conditions—deregulation, mergers and acquisitions, foreign competition—create new problems that executives fear could, without precautions, lead to ethical lapses.

Bad ethical practices can also have expensive consequences—including fines and lawsuits, loss of reputation and perhaps, down the line, government regulation. "Many business leaders are coming to believe that Japanese companies, and many of the best U.S. companies, succeed due to management values rather than management procedures," says Kirk Hanson, a Stanford Business School professor and ethics consultant for General Dynamics, McDonnell Douglas and other companies.

Of the 279 top U.S. corporations that responded last year to a 1,000-company survey about ethics by the Center for Business Ethics at Bentley College in Waltham, Mass., 208 had written codes of conduct and 99 had formal training programs. Forty companies had created high-level ethics committees, and 17 had ombudsmen or hotlines to provide "escape routes" for people reluctant to raise ethical problems through normal channels.

Because everyone has a different definition of what is ethical, people who conduct training sessions frequently encounter distrust and suspicion, if not downright hostility. Managers and workers may feel their honesty is being questioned, or they may worry that ethical concerns will paralyze decision making.

"People think you're going to tell them how to be good, but that isn't what we do," says William May, director of the University of Southern California's Program in Business Ethics. "We try to give them tools, useful ways of thinking about it."

In discussing ethics, Mr. Hanson and several other consultants like to use the concept of "constituencies," groups that each person deals with in his or her job. They may be suppliers, customers, employees, colleagues, stockholders, the local community or the federal government. Instructors focus on the responsibilities that workers owe to each constituency and the ethical problems that might arise in their relationships. Finally, they try to come up with a checklist of procedures likely to produce a fair solution.

Another training technique suggests specific questions that workers confronted with an ethical dilemma might ask themselves. For example: How would I feel if my family found out about my decision? Or how would I feel if I saw it printed in the newspaper?

"We aren't teaching people right from wrong—we assume they know that," says Robert Rosenbloom of Chembank's Social Policy Group. "We aren't giving people moral courage to do what is right—they should be able to do that anyhow. We focus on dilemmas: What you owe the longtime employee who can't learn to use new machinery, what you owe a community no longer producing business."

Last spring, after charging General Dynamics with widespread overbilling on defense contracts, the Pentagon ordered it to set up a comprehensive ethics program. The company drew up and issued to all 100,000 employees a 20-page "Standards of Business Ethics and Conduct." Like codes at many other companies, much of the booklet is glittering generality, but many sections are also quite specific: "Shifting of costs to inappropriate contracts is strictly prohibited."

General Dynamics also created a committee of board members to review ethics policy and a corporate steering group to supervise

33

policy execution; and it installed Kent Druyvesteyn, former director of MBA programs at the University of Chicago, as corporate ethics director. He in turn named ethics directors in several company divisions and established 26 ethical complaint hotlines. Ethics workshops began at the top corporate rungs late last year; Mr. Druyvesteyn hopes that by December every employee will have been exposed to some form of ethics training. "A company like ours is showering in a glass-walled shower," he says.

Like all of General Dynamics's workshops, the Fort Worth one opened with a videotape in which Stanley Pace, chairman of the company, warns that "people are expecting more every day" in the way of ethical behavior. The film shows workers discussing what ethics means to them. To one woman, honesty on expense accounts means, "Do I order prime ribs or what I usually eat?"

Then training specialist Flora Brewer leads the group through some questions: What does ethics mean to you? Is there a difference between good business decisions and good ethical decisions? How do you know you have a dilemma?

"You have been making ethics decisions every day of your life," says Jerry Sills, the Fort Worth division's director of product planning and now also ethics program director. "We are going to help you by providing you with some rules of the road, thumbnail guides that will help you make those decisions better."

After the group discusses the Kate Simpson case, Ms. Brewer gradually points them to the decision-making checklist the company wants everyone to use: Recognize and define the dilemma. Get the facts. List your options. Test your options—are they legal, are they right, are they beneficial? Make your decision.

The McDonnell Douglas workshops are more formal—a training film coordinated with a program workbook. On the film, Mr. Hanson, the Stanford professor, may talk for a few minutes, then say, "Now turn to page 19 of your workbook." The group—in this case, a dozen middle-level technicians—settles down to the exercise on that page: List the most important constituencies you deal with and five decisions you're likely to have to make with respect to each constituency.

After a half hour of concentrated writing, the group discusses all the lists, which include such questions as, Do you say a request for engineering data is more urgent than it really is to make sure you get it on time? Should we give preference to local suppliers? Do you follow design procedures to a "T" even if you think you have a better way?

Does any of this really work? Certainly some heightened consciousness results. "When I check in at a motel, I get a coupon for a free drink—can I use it?" a salesman asks Mr. Druyvesteyn. (Answer: That's OK. What would be wrong is taking $50 to stay there in the first place.)

"Most difficult business decisions are made under time pressure," says Mr. Hanson, and ethics training "increases the chances an employee will reach the right answer when confronted with time pressure business decisions."

Some officials and consultants think businesses are still underestimating the difficulties in achieving change. "Corporations don't pay enough attention to the role of the organization in making it possible for managers and workers to behave ethically," says Ms. Toffler of Harvard. "Organizations may not realize how difficult even benign policies can be. Two statements in a company code may say, 'Do not discriminate in hiring and promotion' and 'Act affirmatively to hire and promote women and minorities.' What does the manager do?"

The great majority of companies "still just pass out another piece of paper," observes W. Michael Hoffman, director of Bentley College's Center for Business Ethics. "They don't communicate at all." He notes how few corporations yet have ethics committees or ombudsmen, and asks, "Who is supposed to put teeth in the ethics code?"

Mr. May of USC says it's "premature to say we are undergoing a great ethical renaissance. A lot of companies are simply responding to egg on their faces."

Most ethics training workshops ask participants to consider a hypothetical situation that poses several ethical dilemmas. Here, somewhat streamlined, are several case studies from recent seminars.

Budget Maneuver

For three years Dan Calvin, director of community relations for a New England utility, has worked with a downtown redevelopment association in the city where he works. Shortly after being chosen chairman of the association, Dan is told by his boss that a companywide economy wave means a 20 percent cut in his entertainment budget. At the same time, however, the boss's boss, a former community affairs officer, tells Dan to go all out on community relations work.

The development association holds a dinner to acquaint neighborhood leaders with its plans, and Dan thinks it would be good public relations for him to pick up the $625 tab. But caught between the directives from his two superiors, he decides to put the bill down as advertising costs, which are charged to another division's budget.

Eventually, Dan's action is discovered. You are the company personnel director and must decide how to deal with him. What's your decision?

Secret Envelope

Jack Smith, division vice president of a major defense contractor, opens a bulky envelope marked "Confidential and Personal." In it he finds a set of figures that appear to be cost data worked up by his company's major competitor for a Navy fighter-plane contract. An accompanying note from one of Jack's best marketing managers attests that the document is the real thing. Clearly, this could be a major advantage in preparing Jack's company's own bid.

He calls in two trusted aides to discuss the pros and cons of using the figures. His marketing vice president sees no problem; everyone in the industry tries to get reliable intelligence on competitors' plans, and Jack himself had recently reminded his top managers how vital this was. But Jack's executive assistant warns of possible risks. The figures might have been bought or obtained with a promise of some quid pro quo; if so, it could blow up in the company's face if discovered.

What should Jack do?

Smutty Pictures

You head the commercial-loan department of a large bank. You have been approached by a "finder," a person who secures loans for clients, with the request for a substantial loan for one of his customers. The customer is financially qualified, but his business is legal pornography—no kidporn or other truly rough stuff, but the usual brand of X-rated material found in "adult" theaters or on cable at home.

This finder brings a lot of business to you and your bank, but you're not sure if the bank should be involved in this type of loan. What do you do?

Rising Son

Yours is a small service unit of only six people in a large firm, and you all work at top speed to keep up. One of your best employees has indicated that she is eager to move up to a first-level supervisory position, but your boss tells you that because of escalating costs, you will not be able to replace anyone on your staff, no matter how much extra work this puts on the rest of your group.

A week later you hear on the grapevine that a first-line supervisory job is opening in the materials division, and you decide to check with the director of materials. As you enter the reception area outside his office, you hear the voice of a company vice president saying that "not only is my son a good prospect technically, but it has always been this company's practice to encourage the hiring of employees' relatives." This nepotism might affect your ability to get your employee the job; but complaining about it might hurt you. What do you do?

Questions

1. Do we have an ethics crisis or has this been a condition that has existed for some time?

2. What in your opinion are the principal reasons for ethics problems in American business?
3. "The proper social role of the corporation is to produce the best peanut butter at the lowest price. . . ." Evaluate this statement in light of what you have understood from Chapter 1. Use the article on cigarettes to defend your position.

Chapter 2

The Ethical Paralysis of Corporate America

The existence of an ethics crisis in corporate America was established in Chapter 1. Business has not managed this crisis well as evidenced by the headlines in the popular and business press. Since the objective of this book is to help business people do a better job, it is important that we establish an understanding of existing efforts at ethics and social responsibility. We begin by trying to understand the reasons for this crisis, followed by an exploration of what business has done in the past to solve these problems. The next step is to analyze why these approaches have not been more successful. Finally, we look ahead to future chapters that provide the information needed to break out of the ethical paralysis in which business finds itself.

UNDERSTANDING THE ETHICS CRISIS IN BUSINESS

After presenting several stories of ethical wrongdoing in American business, Saul Gellerman in his *Harvard Business Review* article states: ". . . we have to ask how usually honest, intelligent, compassionate human beings could act in ways that are callous, dishonest, and wrongheaded."[1] The question seems to imply that the values of the individuals involved are different when they are on the job than when they are off the job. If that is true, and it seems to be at least part of the problem, the question still remains as to why this is so. That people use different values in the different roles they play is hardly surprising. Findings supporting this thesis are part of the literature on role theory and have been around for many years. Even Shakespeare recognized that people play many roles when, in *As You Like It* (Act II, Scene VII) he says:

1. Saul Gellerman, "Why 'Good' Managers Make Bad Ethical Choices," *Harvard Business Review* (July–August 1986), pp. 85–90.

All the world's a stage,
And all the men and women merely players.
They have their exits and their entrances;
And one man in his time plays many parts . . .

Unfortunately, many of the individual roles played for organizations are directed by values which produce unacceptable behavior. As suggested, these values are often a phenomenon of an "on-the-job" role. Work role values can be overtly developed and established by the organization, or they can evolve due to a vacuum of specific organizational values. The latter situation usually produces unpredictable results that occur because of the personal values involved, pressures on that individual, and the existing organizational culture that has evolved. Cultures do evolve whether or not top management plays a role in developing their structure. Performance, as the key and perhaps only organizational value supported by top management, often distorts the ethical character of the individuals on the job and covertly creates an "anything goes" organizational value. Add to that situation the currently declining character of personal values and the organization can expect the worst. Obviously, the values that apply to the on-the-job role must be ethically and socially acceptable if the ethics crisis is to abate.

That we have seen important changes in American personal values is well documented. Since Americans do bring these values to the workplace, and since without proper guidance on the job we are likely to use them in that role as well, it seems appropriate to take a brief look at that part of the American character. One outstanding feature that can be noted about the values in the culture of the United States is that they are pluralistic. Individualism is present in the view of the cowboy, an American symbol that is part of myriad advertising themes, in songs ("I did it my way!"), in the wide variety and still growing number of religions actively practiced in this country, and in the "melting pot" backgrounds of the citizenry. Behind this individualism in personal values is a background of freedom and tolerance that have been an inherent part of the United States from its beginning.

Another factor important in fostering individual independence is simply the living space historically available in the United States. If you don't like one community or group, it has been possible to move on to another place. Many countries haven't had that quantity of living space (e.g., Japan and the Netherlands), and their people have tended to learn values of cooperation rather than independence. Further, cooperation of this type tends to produce similar, or at least compatible, values within these countries. Thus, instead of the pluralism of personal values, these countries produce more common or unified personal values. This situation is one of the reasons why Japanese management can be and is different from that in the United States. It is also why the managers of American organizations must be overt and direct in establishing organizational values for acceptable and unacceptable behavior.

The independent character of the American people is only one of the reasons for the differing values that have become a concern during the ethics crisis. The self-centeredness and greed apparent in most of the unethical activities say something about the nature of certain individual values. Further, business, political and even religious examples of self-indulgence in monetary and material things, and in sexual activities, followed by the hypocrisy and use of public relations damage control to deflect blame, strongly suggest that current personal values cannot be left to dominate organizational activities. The problem of weak personal values is aggrevated by the separation of ownership and management. In most large corporations owners are not managers and in many cases have little identity with that corporation. This separation produces a lack of involvement and often a lack of concern for how the public views the company. Henry Ford's name was on all of the products his company produced and a sense of pride usually exists when that occurs.

The effect of personal values can never be completely overcome by the organization, but with the careful selection of human resources, and substantial support from top management, the organization's values can dominate job performance. For those who doubt the truth of that statement, let us remind you of the surprising *misbehavior* exhibited by people doing their job, who would never think of doing similar things at home. Many students of the current ethical morass believe that the pressure of job objectives, and the culture in which the people work, are primary determinants of the problem. If these objectives and the culture are modified, it seems reasonable that many of the ethical problems will disappear.

Organizations must establish their own rules of ethical behavior, and these rules must be broad enough to cover most decisions that can move the organization into problem situations. Rules of that type can correctly be called organizational values. Suppose that the people involved found themselves in a work culture that rewarded ethically positive behavior and punished ethically negative behavior? Is it unreasonable to expect ethically positive results? Just as people can and have been steered in negative directions by job pressures and culture, we believe that people can be steered in positive directions with the same tools. It does, however, take a clear, organized effort by top management.

A BRIEF HISTORY OF BUSINESS ETHICS PLANNING AND CONCERN

Unfortunately, the literature and the practice of the strategic planning process are primarily, if not exclusively, aimed at identifying strategies and tactics for achieving specific economic objectives of the organization. Books, articles, and consulting efforts focus on identifying appropriate objectives through the analysis of external opportunities and threats and the internal strengths and weaknesses. The focus, predominantly economic in nature, is from external to internal—how existing situations in the environment can be used to satisfy the mission of the organization. First, objectives are set, then strategies and tactics developed based on an environmental analysis. Seldom are ethical or social responsibility concerns fully integrated into the analysis.

To the extent that ethics and social responsibility are considered in the strategic decision-making literature, the material appears as a separate consideration, apart from the strategic plan. If a decision is made to adopt a particular strategic plan, the implication seems to be that deliberations on questions of moral appropriateness, if made at all, are a secondary consideration. To perform an ex post facto review of the decision for its moral appropriateness invites inefficient planning at best, or negative public exposure and moral rationalizing of alternatives at worst. Although authors of the strategic business literature probably do not intend that their social responsibility and ethics materials be interpreted in that way, the separate treatment, rather than full integration of the issue, promotes just such an ex post facto analysis. It is not surprising that business people follow the lead of these writers in attempting to be ethical and socially responsible.

The following two cases illustrate the nature and problems of such one-way thinking. The first case is that of the classic Ford Pinto fuel system and focuses on the customer as the significant part of the impacted environment. The second case, Manville Corporation, focuses on the employee as the injured party.

The Ford Pinto

The Ford Pinto was an attempt to meet foreign competition. The design and its implementation were rushed to completion under the industry average by Lee Iacocca, as President of the Ford Motor Company. In order to meet the competition, both the weight and the cost of the vehicle were limited to 2,000 pounds and $2,000. The first car was presented to the public in 1970. Although other designs for the gas tank placement were apparently considered, the strap-on tank behind the rear axle was selected. It should be noted that virtually every American-made car of that time used this type of design, but it should also be noted that virtually all American-made cars were bigger and heavier.

Safety testing of the fuel tank was considered by Ford, and the company supported initial limited standards by the federal government of low fuel leakage when a 4,000-pound barrier struck a stationary vehicle at 20 mph. More stringent requirements, one of which was a 30 mph moving barrier test, were fought by the company. Ford did consider adaptations to the fuel system of the Pinto if it were forced to meet the 30 mph criterion, but none of these changes were used.

Public criticism of the Pinto fuel system began in earnest in late 1973 when an independent consultant on auto safety warned the

Department of Transportation that the fuel system design was "very vulnerable."[2] Other damaging charges seemed to be based on quotes from company engineers and confidential company memoranda. During this time, Ford continued to defend the Pinto against all attacks.

In September 1977, the National Highway Traffic Safety Administration (NHTSA) began an investigation of the Pinto's fuel tank system. It ran an engineering analysis of pre-1977 Pintos and found that "the fuel tank's location and the structural parts around it permitted easy crushing or puncturing of the tank in a crash."[3]

Ford management was angry because it felt that the reasons *for beginning* the NHTSA investigation were unsatisfactory. The agency began the investigation because of the considerable quantity of mail it received demanding that something be done about the Pinto.

In February 1978, a California jury assessed Ford $125 million in punitive damages in a case involving the crash and burning of a 1972 Pinto. Other suits followed. On May 9, 1978, the NHTSA reached an "initial determination" that a safety defect existed in the fuel systems of Ford Pintos for the 1971 through 1976 model years.

On June 9, 1978, Ford announced the recall of 1.5 million of its subcompacts, but the company insisted that it did not agree with the NHTSA's findings. Rather, it said that it was offering the modifications to "end public concern that had resulted from criticism of the fuel system."[4] Ford estimated that the recall could cost the company $20 million after taxes, about 1.3 percent of the previous year's earnings.

This brief review of the Ford Pinto case is classic from the one-way view of environmental effects on the plan and organizational objectives. The company's initial approach can be criticized for not adequately considering the effect of the new product's safety on the customers. Ford's effort was not totally lacking in environmental (customer) concern, but it did not go far enough. Further, it seemed

2. Lee Patrick Strobel, *Reckless Homicide?* (South Bend, Indiana: Books, 1980), p. 145.

3. "Car Trouble: Government Pressure Propels Auto Recalls Toward a New High," *Wall Street Journal*, August 16, 1978, p. 1.

4. "Ford Orders Recall of 1.5 Million Pintos for Safety Changes," *New York Times*, June 10, 1978, p. 1.

to lack appropriate organizational values for analyzing the product's impact. We might even arguably grant that Ford's initial problems were due to carelessness and competitive pressures. However, the continued failure to willingly correct the problem when evidence indicated a need to do so indicates irresponsible and unethical thinking.

The monetary and nonmonetary costs to the crash victims and to the company were substantial. They were certainly more than the cost of voluntarily fixing the problem before the first car rolled off the production line, or at least, as soon as the figures indicated that a problem existed. In this case the Ford Motor Company failed to make a "committed" analysis of the impact of the Pinto on their customers. That failure produced (1) a substantial short- and long-term monetary cost to the company, (2) increased the degree of government involvement in their production and marketing, (3) substantially reduced customer trust in the company, and (4) made it easier for foreign competition to increase its market in the United States. More important than all of these points is the fact of the increased pain and suffering incurred by the burn victims of rear-end crashes.

Manville Corporation

Asbestos fibers can remain permanently in the lungs once they are inhaled. Once in the lungs they cause a slow, irreversible tissue reaction. It can take 10 to 15 years from the time of the exposure before the injury to the lungs can be diagnosed, and of course, each exposure to the asbestos fibers can be injurious. Thus, someone who comes in contact with asbestos could incur considerable lung damage before a physician could identify that a problem exists.

One of the problems that tends to occur from inhaling asbestos fibers is asbestosis, a debilitating lung disease. Asbestosis is bad enough, but in addition, roughly 10 percent of the people with asbestosis die as a result of mesothelioma, a very painful cancer of the chest linings. This cancer is almost always fatal, and those with it usually live for about one year after diagnosis.

Johns-Manville was the largest producer of asbestos in the United States. For example, in 1979 it sold $168 million of asbestos fibers plus an additional several million dollars worth of asbestos-based products. In that year the company's pretax profits were $217 million and they were listed among the giants of American business. By 1986, Manville was in the process of turning over *80 percent* of its equity to a trust created to pay the claims of people who have sued the company because of asbestos-related injuries. The company's mismanagement of ethical problems with asbestos has all but destroyed them.

Apparently, the company's management had known the effects of breathing asbestos fibers in the mid-1930s or even before then. However, these effects were suppressed and the company continued to operate as usual. The company's approach to the problem of informing an employee when X-ray evidence indicated that he had contracted asbestosis was described by a Johns-Manville company physician as follows:

> . . . as long as the man is not disabled it is felt that he should not be told of his condition so that he can live and work in peace and the Company can benefit by his many years of experience.[5]

In a particularly damaging piece of testimony, a New Jersey attorney recounted an incident in which around the years 1942 to 1943 his cousin found that workers in a local asbestos plant had developed signs of asbestos disease. This attorney informed the plant manager who, in turn, arranged an appointment with the president and another officer of Johns-Manville. The attorney and the plant manager met with them and asked whether the Johns-Manville physical-examination program had found evidence that workers exposed to asbestos had developed lung disease. The answer was that X-ray evidence indicated that the relation did seem to exist but that workers were not told. The reason given was that if the workers were told, they would stop working and file claims against the company. The lawyer said that he was told "that it was Johns-Manville's policy to let them work until they quit work because of asbestosis or died as a result of asbestos-related diseases."

5. Paul Brodeur, *Outrageous Misconduct: The Asbestos Industry on Trial* (New York: Pantheon Books, 1985), p. 102.

He then asked, "...do you mean to tell me you would let them work until they dropped dead?" The response was "Yes, we save a lot of money that way."[6]

There may never have been a more classic one-way view of the organization and its environment than that of Johns-Manville. People were seen as mere factors of production, much the same as a piece of machinery. The approach was straightforward and simple, "How can we use the factors in the environment to help the organization meet its objective (profit)?" Obviously, the approach failed in reaching even that objective, if *long-run* profitability is the goal. Any kind of two-way analysis, involving a look at the cost of its policies on others in the environment, would have recognized that these practices were unethical.

Other Factors Influencing Ethical Planning Effectiveness

Articles by Friedman,[7] Carr,[8] and Gaski[9] further compound the problem. When someone as well known as Milton Friedman says that the only social responsibility of business is to increase its profits, business people are likely to listen. The problem is that all of these articles state, either explicitly or implicitly, that business is amoral. Societies have made a different judgment. The social realities in the United States and other developed capitalistic democracies seem to suggest that business and its leaders are to be held accountable for their behavior in a moral and ethical sense. The literature in business ethics strongly suggests that business must go beyond the belief that it is amoral. For example, DeGeorge states:

> The breakdown of the Myth of Amoral Business has been sig-
> naled in three fairly obvious ways: by the reporting of scandals

6. Ibid., p. 276.

7. Milton Friedman, "The Social Responsibility of Business Is to Increase Its Profits," *New York Times Magazine*, September 13, 1970, p. 33.

8. Albert Z. Carr, "Is Business Bluffing Ethical?" *Harvard Business Review*, 46 (January–February 1968), 145ff.

9. John F. Gaski, "Dangerous Territory: The Societal Marketing Concept Revisited," *Business Horizons*, 28 (July–August 1985), 42–47.

and the concomitant public reaction to these reports; by the formation of popular groups, such as the environmentalists and the consumerists; and by the concern of business, expressed in conferences, magazine and newspaper articles, the burgeoning of codes of ethical conduct, and so on.[10]

One hundred years ago in the United States, the environment of business was given substantial freedom of action with a corresponding power "to act." Since then, concerns about the irresponsible and unethical practices of business like those previously described have produced a negative reaction by society and reduced some of this freedom and power. The Iron Law of Responsibility suggests what business can expect if social responsibilities are not satisfied.[11] It states, "In the long run, those who do not use power in a way that society considers responsible will tend to lose it." In the case of social responsibility and ethics, the lost power is likely to be the freedom to act and the freedom to choose.

Like most human activities, business has been, and is likely to continue to be, evaluated from a moral point of view. Moreover, business is a subset of a greater social activity and depends on the prevailing social morality in order to exist. For example, if stealing and lying were the social rule rather than the exception to it, business as we know it would be impossible. Both customers and employees would practice these behaviors to a much greater degree and the potential for successfully running a business would be greatly reduced. Arguments that do not hold business to the same social requirements as the rest of society are unrealistic. There is nothing extraordinary in the concept of business that excuses it from what society believes to be ethical and responsible behavior.

Further, as the case against Film Recovery Systems cited earlier suggests, business cannot escape its moral role by appealing to its basic nonhuman nature, a frequently used rationalization. Though the corporation is essentially a legal entity, *people* are its

10. Richard R. DeGeorge, *Business Ethics,* 2nd ed. (New York: Macmillan Publishing Company, 1986).

11. Keith Davis and Robert L. Blomstrom, *Business and Its Environment* (New York: McGraw-Hill Book Company, 1966); ———— and William C. Frederick, *Business and Society: Management, Public Policy, Ethics,* 5th ed. (New York: McGraw-Hill Book Company, 1984).

legal agents and its owners, and both the organization and the individuals in it have been judged by society to be liable for the behavior of its agents. Society created the concept of the corporation and has the capacity, and apparently the will, to change it in any way it deems suitable. If moral considerations do not become a greater part of business practice, society, through its legislators, is likely to continue to impose corrective measures.

WHAT CAN (CAN'T) BUSINESS DO?

Let's start this discussion by recognizing an important limitation of business ethics. Business should not try to *directly* influence social values of individuals. The impact that it has should be indirect, developing naturally out of living with organizational values. Unfortunately, many critics of business feel that it should take an active, overt role in changing personal values. One reason often given is that since (they feel) business has a negative impact on human values, such as materialism, it is reasonable that it should overtly attempt to "correct these wrongs." However, to the extent that business influences personal values it usually does so without setting that outcome as its objective. Instead, just the fact of business doing the things that business normally does such as developing, producing, and marketing new products and services, creates a desire for those products. Taken together, the efforts of all businesses may well be to make people more materialistic. However, it is a gross misunderstanding of their capabilities to assume that business, either singularly or collectively, can overtly direct individual values away from values like materialism.

While organizations have more control over their employees than their customers, it would be just as wrong to assume that personal values within the organization can be radically changed. Once established during our youth, personal values tend to change slowly in reaction to many different forces. Certainly, the work environment is one of those forces, but other factors will often dominate. The family, the church, friends, and other environmental pressures can play a more significant role. Thus, while a business may wish to focus on one or two value-related character traits of an individual, the long-run success rate of attempting to change the social values of employees can be expected to be very low.

A much better approach is to focus on values of the organization, and then hire with consideration of existing personal values, train carefully, and enforce employees' compliance to these values. With this approach, it becomes clear that the organization's values dominate while the employee is on the job. If employees cannot operate in such a culture, they will typically leave the organization or be fired. However, if these values are positive and societally oriented in nature, the long-run impact from living and working with them can even have a positive effect on the employees' social values—albeit, a covert influence similar to the materialism example.

Bowen H. McCoy published a parable called "The Sadhu" in the *Harvard Business Review* in which several relevant ethical and social responsibility questions were presented.[12] The following quotation from that article focuses on those questions that are particularly relevant to business.

> Real moral dilemmas are ambiguous, and many of us hike right through them, unaware that they exist. When, usually after the fact, someone makes an issue of them, we tend to resent his or her bringing it up. Often, when the full impact of what we have done (or not done) falls on us, we dig into a defensive position from which it is very difficult to emerge.
>
> Had we . . . been free of physical and mental stress . . . we might have treated the (situation) differently. Yet, isn't stress the real test of personal and corporate values? The instant decisions executives make under pressure reveal the most about personal and corporate character.
>
> Among the many questions that occur to me when pondering my experience are: What are the practical limits of moral imagination and vision? Is there a collective or institutional ethic beyond the ethics of the individual? At what level of effort or commitment can one discharge one's ethical responsibilities? Not every ethical dilemma has a right solution . . . . In a busi-

12. Bowen H. McCoy, "The Parable of the Sadhu," *Harvard Business Review* (September–October 1983), pp. 103–8.

ness context, however, it is essential that managers agree on a *process* for dealing with dilemmas.

> One of our problems was that as a group we had no process for developing a consensus. We had no sense of purpose or plan. . . . Because it did not have a set of preconditions that could guide its action to an acceptable resolution, the group reacted instinctively as individuals. . . . We had no leader with whom we could all identify and in whose purpose we believed. [13]

It is the purpose of this book to help managers deal with all of the questions and problems addressed in the preceding quote. In fact, we agree with Bowen McCoy when he goes on to add: "Some organizations do have a value system that transcends the personal values of the managers. Such values, which go beyond profitability, are usually revealed when the organization is under stress."[14] About this system of corporate values, he states: ". . . for the corporation to be strong, the members need to share a preconceived notion of what is correct behavior, a 'business ethic,' and think of it as a positive force, not a constraint."[15] When such corporate values exist, the organization is ready to recognize ethical problems when they occur, and knows how to deal with them even under stressful situations. Without them, we are just as liable to fall into the same trap described in the quotation.

This book will also address the questions of "the practical limits of moral imagination and vision" as well as the "level of effort or commitment" appropriate to "discharge one's ethical responsibilities." It will provide guidelines for developing organizational values, and the rationale for those guidelines. With the organizational values and direction established, management can successfully analyze and control ethical situations. This approach will have enough flexibility to meet the needs of most organizations whether profit or nonprofit.

13. Ibid., pp. 106–7.
14. Ibid., p. 107.
15. Ibid., p. 107.

WHAT HAS BUSINESS DONE TO DEAL WITH THE ETHICS CRISIS?

The answer to the question in the section heading varies greatly, just as the personality of business organizations varies greatly. However, of those who have done anything, the most popular response has been to create or expand codes of ethics (codes of conduct, behavior codes, and so on). As currently constructed, these codes of ethics are not designed to meet organizational needs. They lack breadth, depth, and vision in dealing with the broad social and ethical problems of business, and they lack implementation and enforcement. The current codes of ethics tend to be legalistic documents that forbid very specific actions, rather than providing the more needed value-oriented guides to behavior. The only exceptions seem to be filled with platitudes that do little to give direction to behavior.

We believe that current codes of ethics are, for the most part, not ethical statements. Further, if as is suggested, codes are not currently very effective, then another question arises: "Should codes be used at all, and if they should, how can these efforts be designed to make them more effective?" The purpose of this section is to explore these questions and offer tentative answers to them.

There has been a considerable amount of effort spent in analyzing codes of ethics. However, two relatively recent articles summarize what seems to be a general feeling by many, but not all, researchers that codes lack much impact. Cressey and Moore, for example, in an elaborate analysis of corporate codes of ethics, state they are convinced "that any improvements in business ethics taking place in the last decade are not a consequence of business leaders' calls for ethics or of the codes themselves. We believe that, instead, any changes have stemmed from conditions imposed by outsiders."[16] Further, an empirical study by Chonko and Hunt involving marketing managers found that "The existence of corporate

16. Donald R. Cressey and Charles A. Moore, "Managerial Values and Corporate Codes of Ethics," *California Management Review* (Summer 1983), pp. 53–77.

or industry codes of ethics seems to be unrelated to the extent of ethical problems in marketing management."[17]

Both results seem to suggest that codes of ethics lack a major impact on important decisions involving ethical questions. It is entirely possible that codes accomplish other things such as communication of specific rules, but they seem to lack impact for what might be considered the "really important ethical problems." Unfortunately, corporate management seems to expect more from them. The Center for Business Ethics at Bentley College published the results of a study in which they inquired whether the respondent's company had been "taking steps to incorporate ethical values and concerns into the daily operations of your organization"[18] and if they had, what they hoped to achieve by doing so. About 80 percent of the 279 respondents said that they had taken such steps, and five objectives seemed to be most important to them. In order of perceived importance they were (1) to be a socially responsible corporation, (2) to provide guidelines for employees' behavior, (3) to improve management, (4) to comply with local, state, or federal guidelines, and (5) to establish better corporate culture. The first two were substantially more important, while the last three were seen as about equal in importance. Fully 93 percent of the respondents indicated that their company used codes of conduct to achieve these objectives. The next most popular approach of employee training in ethics was used by only 44 percent of the respondents.

There seems to be a very important gap between what managers hope to accomplish with corporate codes and what is accomplished. Compliance with local, state, or federal guidelines might be achieved based on the legalistic language of the codes. Also, *very specific* guidelines for employees' behavior might be achieved based on their specific character, but broad guidelines and the other objectives seem to be beyond what is currently attainable.

17. Lawrence B. Chonko and Shelby D. Hunt, "Ethics and Marketing Management: An Empirical Examination," *Journal of Business Research*, 13 (August 1985), pp. 339–59.

18. Center for Business Ethics, "Are Corporations Institutionalizing Ethics?" *Journal of Business Ethics* (April 1986), pp. 85–92.

The content and apparent intent of codes lack the direction and compliance in order to achieve these objectives.

Cressey and Moore, in their analysis of corporate codes of ethics, believe that these documents "tend to imitate the criminal law and thus contain few innovative ideas about how the ethical standards of a firm, let alone of business in general, can be improved."[19] In personally reviewing codes, we found that lawlike statements dominate, while broad, shared values are almost absent. Innovative ethical standards for a firm would seem to work best in the shared values of a corporate culture. These values could be adapted to the needs of the firm and its impacted publics, and thereby achieve much of what existing codes attempt to achieve plus a great deal more. Thus, this core value approach is suggested as an alternative to the current codes. More on this approach is developed later in the book.

As a hypothetical example of the code development process, suppose that E. F. Hutton were evaluating, as one of several opportunities and threats, the use of float that caused their recent problems. It is interesting to note that a rule against this behavior apparently existed at Hutton when their problems occurred. However, suppose again that management recognized (1) an opportunity for financial gain, (2) a threat of exposure with the concomitant fines, negative publicity and alienation of customers and other financial institutions, (3) that Hutton's financial strength and desirability as a customer could be used to keep the banks quiet, assuming that the actions were not extreme, and (4) one weakness was due to the number of people involved in the process because of the increased threat of detection. There are many other opportunities, threats, strengths, and weaknesses with this scheme, but for this example, the four mentioned should suffice.

Given this analysis, E. F. Hutton's top management might choose to overtly condemn such behavior but covertly condone it. Such an approach would tend to remove blame from them, and if they were risk takers, might produce greater profits. To undertake this approach all that is required is to establish a rule, as in a code of ethics, and then simply not enforce it. Obviously, there is little to

19. Cressey and Moore, "Managerial Values," p. 73.

suggest that E. F. Hutton's top management went through any such analysis. This situation is only an example of the kind of analysis that could occur by a firm in their situation. Even so it illustrates another reason why an item in a code of ethics might not only be ineffective but misleading.

A major problem with this fairly typical analysis is that it focuses on *the impact of the environment on the organization without considering the impact of the organization on its environment.* In this instance, the impacted environment includes current and future employees, directly affected financial institutions, the investing public, and other investment companies. The actual impacts are probably not worth belaboring in this example. However, it is important to note that both long- and short-run impacts should be considered.

When the results of the E. F. Hutton example are analyzed in light of any ethical reasoning, the company's use of float in this manner seems undesirable. For example, would Hutton's top management want their organization to operate in a world where everyone carried out the practice? Since we can presume that the Hutton organization would not like to have their best and most powerful customers doing the same thing to them, this action would fail one important ethical test. Other ethical tests, discussed in the next chapter, would produce the same results.

Obviously, another approach is needed to help management maintain sound business practices while operating in a manner that is ethically and socially acceptable. Platitudes and acrimony won't work. It was just such a frustrating environment that produced a call, albeit ineffective, for specific codes of ethics. As with most important matters in business, the solution is not straightforward or easy, but a sound reasoned approach does exist. As suggested in this chapter, it requires that we understand the impacted environment, that we understand how to make ethical and socially responsible judgments (and know the difference between the two), and that we have a framework or methodology for identifying and analyzing any action we may choose to undertake. The remainder of this book is designed to fulfill each of these needs.

A LOOK AHEAD

The first two chapters of this book have been used to establish that ethical and social responsibility problems exist for business and that a new, organized approach is needed if consistent improvement is to occur. The remainder of the book is a presentation of an approach that the authors believe can achieve the goals of social responsibility and ethical performance while still maintaining focus on the organization's other objectives.

In order to develop the type of approach that is desired, a certain amount of background is needed. First, decision rules for solving ethical or social responsibility problems are necessary. Second, since our approach suggests that a set of specific core values be created for the organization, and that these values become integrated into the corporate culture, a discussion of corporate culture is also necessary. Chapter 3 is a presentation of social responsibility and ethical tools that can be used in decision making. It discusses the differences between the two concepts and suggests methods for thinking about both of them. Chapter 4 presents a practical look at corporate culture. The culture is the primary bond that makes the organization an entity rather than a collection of individuals going in roughly the same direction. The values of that culture both direct and prohibit behavior to a degree that goes far beyond the normal written policies, procedures, and rules of the organization. Only through the values of the corporate culture can the huge variety of employee behaviors be consistently moved in an ethical and responsible direction.

Chapter 5 describes the actual planning process for developing and integrating the core values into the corporate culture. It is called *parallel planning* because the effects of alternative plans on both the corporate objectives and the organization's many environments are considered at the same time. This approach eliminates the problems occurring when social responsibility and ethics are considered only after the planning is completed. The parallel planning process also helps the organization identify core values that will be directed toward the very issues that either are problems, or are likely to become problems, for the company. A creative group of individuals could easily suggest hundreds of potential core values, but only a few such values can actually be incorporated into the organizational culture. It is therefore important that these values be selected with care, and that is part of the output of the parallel planning process.

In Chapter 6, specific tools for helping to perform the parallel planning process are presented. Here the traditional tools of strategic planning are adapted to accommodate a concern for the corporate environmental output as well as the corporate objectives. Very specific suggestions are made and an extensive example is used to help the executive implement the parallel planning process.

Chapter 7 further develops the process for implementing and controlling the parallel planning system. These subjects are introduced in Chapter 6 as part of the planning process, but in this chapter, the special problems and techniques of implementation and control are presented. Many things can go wrong at this stage of the process, and it is necessary to understand why they occur and how they can be prevented. Chapter 7 is devoted to that goal.

At this point the reader should have enough understanding of ethics and social responsibility to make sound judgments and a methodology which can help him or her incorporate these judgments into the strategic planning process and corporate culture. That is the goal of this book. Reading this book will not produce ethical managers if those managers do not want to be ethical. At most, it will make them think about the appropriateness and potential outcomes of their actions. Instead, this book is written for those managers and organizations that want to be ethical and are looking for a realistic and workable approach.

Exercises for Chapter 2

The Challenger Space Shuttle Explosion
(January 28, 1986)

The following events preceded the explosion of the space shuttle *Challenger:*

- On the morning of January 28, 1986, NASA management officials OKed the launch of the space shuttle *Challenger.*
- Allan J. McDonald, a senior engineer from Morton Thiokol, Inc., who was in charge of the solid rocket boosters for the space shuttle, argued strongly against launch of the *Challenger* only hours before lift off.
- McDonald, and another engineer named Roger Boisjoly, claimed that the "O" rings, which seal parts of the solid rocket booster, were dangerous at temperatures below 53 degrees Fahrenheit.
- Engineers at Rockwell International, another contractor on the space shuttle, also warned about the problems that cold weather causes on the space shuttle's reentry tiles.
- McDonald and Boisjoly's objections to the launch were overruled by their bosses, perhaps due to pressure from NASA officials at the Marshall Space Flight Center.
- Temperatures on the booster rocket's exterior on January 28 were recorded to be below 10 degrees Fahrenheit at one point prior to launch and remained below 53 degrees.
- The decision to launch *Challenger* was reached by polling certain managers, but not engineers.

After the space shuttle explosion, McDonald and Boisjoly demonstrated to the presidential commission investigating the disaster that the "O" rings had dangerously eroded in prior flights and were a problem when the launch occurred below 53 degrees. After their testimony, both McDonald and Boisjoly were shifted to apparently lesser jobs in Morton Thiokol. Their original positions were later restored after public pressure ensued.

Questions

1. The "Parable of the Sadhu" discussed in this chapter talked about the role of pressure for performance. Obviously, pressure to perform played a role in the *Challenger* disaster; what

other parallels can be drawn between the parable and this disaster?

2. Using this situation as a specific example, discuss the following thesis: American business has failed to develop general methods or approaches for solving ethical problems within individual companies or industries.

CODES OF ETHICS

All of the following statements have been abstracted from the codes of conduct of some of the largest product and service organizations in the United States. The statements have been grouped to illustrate certain organizational concerns that they seem to represent and labels have been suggested for those groups.*

Evaluate the capacity for these items and groups of items to deal with external ethical threats and opportunities that might occur for a given business. Begin by constructing a list of such potential threats and opportunities for an organization of your choice. Use the categories generated for the code items to determine if employees who were familiar with them could adequately respond to those threats and opportunities.

SELECTED DIRECT QUOTES FROM CODES

Cluster 1:
"Be a dependable organization citizen."

Examples
"Demonstrate courtesy, respect, honesty, fairness, and decency in all relationships with customers, competitors, the general public, and with other employees." —Bank of Boston.

*This grouping process was not done casually, but rather it represents the results of statistical grouping techniques on more than 80 codes of ethics.

"If an employee reports for work improperly dressed or groomed, the employee will be instructed to return home to change clothes or to take other appropriate corrective action." —Bank South.

"Wachovia will not tolerate any alcohol or drug use or abuse which is or may be detrimental to your job performance or the reputation of Wachovia." —The Wachovia Corporation.

"All employees of the Company are expected to perform efficient work and service at all times and avoid any activities which might compromise or conflict with the best interests of the Company." —Atlantic City Electric Company.

Cluster 2:
"Don't do anything unlawful or improper
that will harm the organization."

Examples
"It is the policy of Exxon Corporation that all of its directors and employees shall, in carrying out their duties to the Corporation, rigidly comply with the antitrust laws of the United States and with those of any other country or group of countries which are applicable to the Corporation's business." —Exxon Corporation.

"Employees of R. J. Reynolds shall avoid situations where their personal interest could conflict with, or even appear to conflict with, the interests of the corporation and its stockholders." —R. J. Reynolds Industries.

"All Company activities are to be conducted in compliance with all applicable federal, state, and local laws, regulations, and judicial decrees." —Northeast Utilities.

"No bribes of any type may be paid to anyone." —Texas Instruments.

"A payment is prohibited if: (A) It is illegal, (B) No record of its disbursement or receipt is entered into the accounting records of the Company, or (C) It is entered into the accounting records of the Company in a manner which is false or misleading." —Hercules.

Cluster 3:
"Be good to our customers."

Examples

"Manage our human, capital, and other resources to achieve excellence in service to our customers at the lowest attainable cost, consistent with reliability, quality, safety, and environmental standards." —Arizona Public Service Company.

"To deliver to customers only products of proven high quality at fair prices and to serve them in such a manner as to earn their continuing respect, confidence, and loyalty, both before and after the sale." —Texaco.

"Advertising used by the Company is legally required to be true and not deceptive in any manner." —J. C. Penny Company.

Chapter 3

Social Responsibility and Business Ethics: Tools for Decision Making

This chapter is divided into two parts. The first part describes the similarities and differences of social responsibility and business ethics while the second part suggests how these concepts can be more easily used by business people.[1]

UNDERSTANDING THE SIMILARITIES AND DIFFERENCES OF SOCIAL RESPONSIBILITY AND BUSINESS ETHICS

The two concepts, corporate social responsibility and business ethics, have essentially different meanings. Corporate social responsibility is related to the social contract between business and the society in which it operates.[2] Business ethics, in contrast, requires that the organization or individual behave in accordance with the carefully thought-out rules of moral philosophy. Though these two behavioral criteria often lead to the same conclusion, in many situations they do not. For example, actions that any given society defines as "responsible" in its social contract with business may be found by moral philosophers to be ethically neutral or even ethically unsound. Similarly, actions that would be dictated by moral philosophy could be seen as socially unacceptable. These inconsistencies are part of the problem faced by managers when a decision must be made. Therefore, the character of these two concepts must be explored in greater depth.

1. Much of the material comes directly from or is adapted from an article by Donald P. Robin, and R. Eric Reidenbach, "Social Responsibility, Ethics, and Marketing Strategy: Closing the Gap Between Concept and Application," *Journal of Marketing* (January 1987), pp. 44–58.
2. George A. Steiner, "Social Policies for Business," *California Management Review* (Winter 1972), pp. 17–24.

Social Responsibility

An observation by Steiner sets the basis for understanding the meaning of corporate social responsibility.

> At any one time in any society, there is a set of generally accepted relationships, obligations, and duties between the major institutions and the people. Philosophers and political theorists have called this set of common understandings "the social contract."[3]

The social responsibility of business is a substantial part of this social contract. It is the set of "generally accepted relationships, obligations, and duties" that relate to the corporate impact on the welfare of society. What becomes generally accepted is likely to be different for any two societies and is also likely to change within any society over time. In their book, *Business and Society*, Davis and Frederick note that in the United States

> . . . the trend since the 1960s has been toward more social involvement by business. . . . The public expects business to be part of the community and to act responsibly therein. This trend does not change the basic economic mission of business, because society still expects business to provide economic goods and services efficiently.[4]

In addition to differences between societies and within a society over time, subcultures with diametrically opposed expectations are part of most major cultures. Almost any response to a call for "socially responsible" behavior by one group is likely to produce complaints by another group. The result seems to be a kind of paralysis fostered by the implicit suggestion that inaction is the safest response. However, inaction, or the failure to consider the social responsibility of certain outcomes, is often repugnant to much

---

3. Ibid., p. 18.
4. Keith Davis and William C. Frederick, *Business and Society: Management, Public Policy, Ethics*, 5th ed. (New York: McGraw-Hill Book Company, 1984), pp. 41–42.

of society. A sense of frustration with "the system" is thus the fare of business managers at all levels in an organization.

Many individuals have observed and reported on the state of social responsibility in business. Glueck, in his book on policy and strategic management, reviews several studies as examples of organizational objectives and comments:

> Note that there was no mention of social responsibility in the list of major objectives in the studies above. Although much has been written about how firms ought to be more socially responsible, there is little evidence that social responsibility is a significant objective of most business, in spite of a good deal of pressure from some societal groups.[5]

This lack of involvement in social responsibility at a strategic level seems to have occurred in spite of recognition of the need for it and the seeming willingness of executives to incorporate it. Even a decade ago, 81 percent of 248 corporate executives surveyed believed that wealth maximization and social involvement were not contradictory concepts.[6] In this last decade, business has responded to social needs in a variety of ways. Areas such as employee welfare, support for minorities, consumer satisfaction, community improvement, and environmental protection all have been targets for business support in varying degrees.[7] However, these efforts seem to lack a unified collective impact on public opinion. One suggested reason for this lack of impact is that the objectives of such efforts are often inexplicit and *do not fit an overall plan.*[8]

The lack of a central theme and specific objectives is perhaps understandable because of the varied and changing societal expectations, but it is intolerable if business is to fulfill its role as an important and productive element of society.

5. William F. Glueck, *Business Policy and Strategic Management*, 3rd ed. (New York: McGraw-Hill Book Company, 1980).

6. Charles P. Edmonds, III and John H. Hand, "What are the Real Long-Run Objectives of Business?" *Business Horizons*, 19 (December 1976), pp. 75–81.

7. Galdwin Hill, "The New Dimension," in *Participation III* (Los Angeles: Atlantic Richfield Co, 1982).

8. Ibid., p. 87.

Ethics

Because it is an organized discipline, business ethics presents more coherent demands than does the concept of social responsibility; therefore, it provides a solid foundation from which to operate. Even so, the study of business ethics is not without problems of interpretation. Major ethical philosophies are sometimes in conflict with one another as to how a single issue may be resolved.

The two major traditions that dominate current thinking in moral philosophy are deontology and utilitarianism. One other tradition, virtue ethics, is used to help understand how much the organization ought to do to be ethical.

Of the two dominant traditions, deontology is favored by many moral philosophers today. Further, deontological reasoning offers many people who are critical of business an approach for justifying their attacks. Utilitarianism, the other major tradition, has been attacked by moral philosophers because it seems to suggest certain untenable outcomes when applied to particular hypothetical situations. Utilitarian arguments are used historically to provide much of the ethical justification for the modern economic systems of capitalistic democracies.

Deontology. The reasoning found in deontological analyses suggests that there are prima facie ideals that can direct our thinking. Modern interpretations of these ideals suggest that they may be considered "universal" in character but not necessarily "absolute." The difference between absolute and universal is simply the recognition that situations sometimes arise in which one or more universal statements of "right" and "wrong" might be inappropriate. The absolutism of early deontological thinking would not admit to the nonabsolute character of rules, but more modern versions such as that put forth by Ross perceive these statements as prima facie universal in character and allow exceptions.[9] In general, the concept is simply that these rules or duties are required, and a burden of proof lies with any exception to them.

9. William D. Ross, *The Right and the Good* (Oxford: Oxford University Press, 1930).

Kant provided much of the reasoning that underlies modern deontology.[10] His conclusions are based on two concepts. One is simply that the only possible basis for establishing a moral tradition is human reason or logic. The second concept is whether an action can be universalized. For example, one statement of his "categorical imperative" is that "one ought never to act unless one is willing to have the maxim on which one acts become a universal law." His reasoning is simply that good will, and only good will, can be universalized. Thus, a reasonable test for exceptions to universal rules is whether they can meet the criterion of universalized good will. For example, business people could ask whether it is morally acceptable to market a product known to be potentially harmful to some individuals, such as A. H. Robins' Dalkon Shield, an intrauterine contraceptive device, or more recently G. D. Seale's Copper 7 IUD. The Kantian approach would force the business person to ask whether he or she would be willing to live in a world where all producers were making a product known to be harmful to some people in its normal use. The prima facie response would likely be, "No." Thus, the burden of proof for treating the product as an exception is on the producer of the IUD.

Rawls provides an approach called contract theory that is similar to deontological thinking and has had considerable impact on modern moral philosophy. His major work, *A Theory of Justice*, has as its initial position the placing of all people behind a "veil of ignorance."[11] Basically, people then are asked what kind of society they would want to live in, given they know nothing about their own capabilities and potentialities. From this initial egalitarian position, Rawls develops two principles of justice. One is that "each person is to have an equal right to the most extensive basic liberty compatible with similar liberty for others."[12] The second principle has two parts and can be stated, "social and economic inequalities are to be arranged so that they are both (a) reasonably expected to be to everyone's advantage, and (b) attached to positions and of-

10. Immanuel Kant, *Groundwork of the Metaphysics of Morals*, translation by H. J. Paton (New York: Harper and Row Publishers, 1964).

11. John Rawls, *A Theory of Justice* (Cambridge, MA: Harvard University Press, 1971).

12. Ibid., p. 60.

fices open to all."[13] The first principle and the latter part of the second principle are generally accepted by moral philosophers. The former part of the second principle has an undeniable egalitarian trust which is perhaps not surprising given the initial "veil of ignorance" condition. Thus, the deontologist might define an activity as ethical if it involved true freedom of choice and action, were available to all, injured no one, and were a benefit to some. Obviously, price fixing, bribery, and marketing products that harm people are practices that are morally questionable to deontologists.

It is the egalitarian character of deontology, based on universalizing concepts, that provides the foundation for criticisms of the second major tradition in moral philosophy—utilitarianism.

Utilitarianism. The utilitarian ideal can be summarized by the phrase, "the greatest good for the greatest number." There are many variations of utilitarianism, as there are variations of deontology, and only a brief overview of the major ideas is presented here. The primary way of assessing "the greatest good for the greatest number" is by performing a social cost/benefit analysis and acting on it. All benefits and all costs of a particular act are considered to the degree possible and summarized as the net of all benefits *minus* all costs. If the net result is positive, the act is morally acceptable; if the net result is negative, the act is not.

Utilitarianism seems to have been accepted readily by business, in part because of its tradition in economics. Adam Smith (1776) and much of the ensuing economic philosophy of capitalism provide a rich traditional heritage for the utilitarian concepts. Capitalistic systems, by providing the greatest material good for the greatest number, are considered ethical from a perspective of economic philosophy. It should be noted that the utilitarian analyses of moral philosophers extend beyond material good to the much broader concept of utility from which the term is derived (Smart and Williams).[14]

Several technical criticisms of utilitarianism such as the problems of quantifying goodness and requiring superogatory acts

13. Ibid., p. 60.
14. J. J. C. Smart, and Bernard Williams, *Utilitarianism: For & Against* (Cambridge: Cambridge University Press, 1973).

(see Beauchamp;[15] Smart and Williams[16]) are of little interest in the context of this book. However, two criticisms are relevant to the discussion. One is the problem of unjust distribution of utility. Summarizing the costs and benefits as previously described can conceal major negative occurrences to people in small social segments by allowing them to be offset by relatively minor increases in utility to larger segments of society. Though one version of utilitarianism (i.e., rule utilitarianism) would allow constraints so that negative outcomes could be eliminated, the criticism is still valid. For example, most of the arguments in support of the continued sale of infant formula by Nestlé to third world countries were utilitarian (Miller).[17] In this case, it was suggested that the greatest good to society was derived from the continued sale of the product. Other arguments, primarily deontological, seem to have prevailed because Nestlé agreed to severe business restrictions (World Health Organization's *International Code of Marketing of Breast-Milk Substitutes*).[18]

An additional problem for utilitarianism is concern for individual acts. If each act is judged solely on its own cost/benefit outcome, there is a lack of consistency and ability to generalize. Business people may argue that fraudulent advertising is all right if no one is worse off, and a rule against such practices becomes less tenable. However, in spite of the weaknesses of utilitarianism, it is still a major tradition in moral philosophy and maintains substantial support.

A concluding point about the two major traditions is necessary. Deontology has the individual as its major concern and unit of analysis whereas utilitarianism is decidedly social in character and focuses on the welfare of society as a unit. This focus can, in a number of situations, put the two traditions at odds with each other, as in the Nestlé case. There is no totally accepted, absolute statement

15. Tom L. Beauchamp, *Philosophical Ethics* (New York: McGraw-Hill Book Company, 1982)

16. Smart and Williams, *Utilitarianism*.

17. Fred D. Miller, *Out of the Mouths of Babes: The Infant Formula Controversy*. Bowling Green, OH: Social Philosophy and Policy Center, 1983.

18. World Health Organization, *International Code of Marketing of Breast-Milk Substitutes*, Geneva, Switzerland, 1981.

of what is ethical and what is not ethical—only important and care-fully reasoned traditions.

MAKING SOCIAL RESPONSIBILITY AND BUSINESS ETHICS MEANINGFUL IN DECISION MAKING

The central criterion for making these concepts useful in a decision-making setting is for the business person to be concerned about the impact of such decisions on all involved parties. Without that interest and intent, nothing that is presented can be useful or even meaningful. Given that one criterion, there is a way of thinking about the material presented so far in this chapter that can help.

A Business Ethics Perspective

The concept of the business organization has been created by society and its agents, and it must meet the expectations of that society or pay the price in consumerist and antibusiness legislation. If those expectations can be formulated in terms of ethical theory, they can be used in the development and testing of organizational values. Thus, it is appropriate to ask how two of the most popular ethical traditions, deontology and utilitarianism, are used in capitalistic democracies so that values in a business organization can be tested against them.

Many social systems seem to capture aspects of both deontol-ogy and utilitarianism in their laws and social policies. In the United States, cost/benefit analysis, a principal component of utilitarianism, is a tool of major importance in policy making at the national, state, and local levels. Further, the concept of capitalism has strong roots in utilitarianism. However, many individual rights are also protected at all levels of government. For example, the *Dec-laration of Independence* talks about "inalienable rights" and the *U.S. Constitution* has the *Bill of Rights*. The United States, like many capitalistic democracies, can be viewed as adopting a blend of the two philosophies. Even so, the political, legal, and cultural environ-

71

ments of the United States and other capitalistic democracies have changed radically over the last century, with the business community being both a positive and negative agent in causing some of these changes. The blend of the two philosophies that is perceived as appropriate in a given society is subject to change. We believe such changes are often evolutionary rather than revolutionary in most capitalistic democracies.

One problem is to determine how to treat this blend of philosophies. The language of deontology, a term derived from "duty," is fundamentally concerned with the individual and tends to dominate our thinking when the plight of individuals is deemed serious. Even when reasonably sound arguments about the greatest good for the greatest number can be made on one side of an issue, the deontological arguments on the other side tend to dominate if individuals' rights are seriously impaired. An excellent example is the case of Nestlé's sale of infant formula in third world countries. A recent book summarizes the utilitarian arguments made in the case,[19] but the final resolution of the issue occurred when Nestlé agreed to follow the dictates of the World Health Organization (WHO) Code.[20] This code severely restricts even traditional marketing practices in an effort to protect individuals, and typical deontological arguments dominated the case made by its proponents. Thus, one theme that seems appropriate for business people is: *Business activities that have a foreseeable and potentially serious impact on individuals ought to be regulated by the values of deontological reasoning.*

A positive example occurred when Procter & Gamble removed its Rely tampon product from the market. As reported by the *Wall Street Journal*, P&G went through the short initial defensive reaction to protect the product.[21] However, within a three-month period, as evidence connecting toxic shock with the tampon product increased, P&G agreed to do what it could to protect the public. Its actions included proposing a warning label, voluntarily halting

19. Miller.

20. World Health Organization.

21. Dean Rotbart, and John A. Prestbo, "Killing a product," the *Wall Street Journal* 1980 (Novermber 3), p. 21.

production, removing the product from store shelves, offering to buy back all the unused product, pledging research for further study, and agreeing to finance and direct an educational program including a warning not to use Rely.

It is important to note two parallels between the Rely and Nestlé cases. First, in both situations, many of the problems can be attributed to a "natural" consumer misuse of the product. Rely was used for extended time periods beyond that deemed appropriate. Nestlé infant formula was overdiluted to save money and diluted with contaminated water in underdeveloped areas. In both cases, blame for the problems could have been directed partly toward the buyer, a tactic used by Firestone in defending the Firestone 500 product.[22] Second, utilitarian arguments could be developed in favor of retaining both products, and Nestlé supporters did generate such arguments. However, as seen with Nestlé, deontological arguments tend to prevail and it seems reasonable to suggest that P&G's actions with Rely were appropriate.

Alternatively, many and perhaps most business actions do not involve a "potentially serious impact on individuals." In those cases a second theme seems appropriate:

> For all business actions that do not have foreseeable serious consequences for individuals, the arguments of utilitarianism seem appropriate within capitalistic democracies.

Thus, such issues as environmental concerns, import and export restrictions, competitive practices, and relations with supranational organizations such as the European Economic Community or OPEC all seem to be analyzed satisfactorily by means of utilitarian arguments. Though elements of society may argue differently (e.g., environmental groups), sound utilitarian arguments seem to satisfy or at least be understood by most of society. Business values addressing these issues can be developed and tested satisfactorily by means of the utilitarian model.

22. Elizabeth Gatewood and Archie B. Carroll, "The Anatomy of Corporate Social Response: The Rely, Firestone 500, and Pinto Cases," *Business Horizons.* 24 (September-October) 1981, pp. 9-16.

Moral philosophers also have analyzed the level of performance problem. The approach we suggest is borrowed from an older but still respected branch of moral philosophy called virtue ethics. Aristotle proposed an ethics of prudence in his *Nichomachean Ethics*.[23] Though a full description of this philosophical tradition is beyond the scope of our book, a brief presentation of how Aristotelian ethics can help solve the level of performance problem is warranted. The following abstracted statements describe how Aristotle perceived moral virtue:

> Virtue is concerned with emotions and actions, where excess is wrong, as is deficiency, but the mean is praised and is right . . . . Virtue, then is disposition involving choice. It consists in a mean, relative to us, defined by reason and as the reasonable man would define it. It is a mean between two vices—one of excess, the other of deficiency.[24]

Thus, moderation or prudence is appropriate in the way we behave. The following examples of Aristotle's "mean" come from Fuller:

> . . . courage is the right or mean amount of the same activity as in deficiency constitutes cowardice, in excess, rashness. Temperance is a moderate love and pursuit of the physical pleasures; insensibility is too little interest in them, and self-indulgence or sensuality, too great a one; liberality is the golden mean between stinginess and prodigality; magnificence, between ostentarious and niggardly living; greatness of soul, between humility and vain glory; and so the list goes. Acts like theft, adultery, murder, and the like, and emotions like shamelessness, envy, and spite, Aristotle deals with by pointing out that they are in themselves already either excesses or defects, and therefore cannot exist in moderation.[25]

23. Aritstotle, *Nichomachean Ethics*, in *The Works of Aristotle*, William D. Ross, ed. and trans. Oxford: Clarendon Press, especially Books I-V, X, 1925.

24. Beauchamp, p. 161.

25. B. A. G. Fuller, *A History of Ancient and Medieval Philosophy*, 3rd ed., revised by Sterling M. McMurrin. New York: Holt, Rinehart and Winston, 1961.

We suggest that this same concept of moderation be applied to the system of values adopted by business people. Neither excessiveness nor deficiency in performance would be acceptable. Rather, a "golden mean" of performance should be sought. For example, in the Rely tampon case, P&G might have been judged deficient by Aristotle had it adopted the approach of doing as little as possible. The company could have "held back," much like Ford Motor did with the Pinto or Firestone did with the 500 radial tire, and reacted only to the FDA and the Centers for Disease Control pressure, doing the minimum required in each case. However, P&G did *not* use that approach. It is important to recognize that under this recommendation, extreme measures that could ruin the company are not required. Such extremes are outside the "golden mean" of performance. Thus, the level of P&G's performance in this case could be found acceptable.

A Social Responsibility Perspective

In addressing demands to be socially responsible, the business organization is faced with the variety of meanings discussed previously. However, an organized response is possible. We suggest that the organization build a parallel between its problems and the problems of an average family. This image of an average family using central values to solve family problems provides a benchmark for developing values within a business organization.

The parallels between the family and the business organization are *not* isomorphic. The sociology of the family identifies a number of family functions that are not relevant to the organization such as procreation, sexual relationships, and a religious function. Nevertheless, by using the culturally estimated values of an average family as a guide in determining what its reaction to society ought to be, an organization can develop reasonable standards.

The lack of an absolute relationship between the concept of the average family and the social responsibilities of an organization affords some flexibility in choosing the values to be adopted. We used United States cultural patterns as a basis for developing the set of potential parallels in Table 3-1. The average U.S. family is nuclear (i.e., husband, wife, and children) and Table 3-1 is constructed ac-

Table 3-1
PARALLELS BETWEEN BASIC SOCIAL RESPONSIBILITY
VALUES OF THE FAMILY AND THE ORGANIZATION

Basic Family Values	Basic Organization Values
Caring for nuclear family members (i.e., husband, wife, children if any)	Caring for organizational family (i.e., employees, management, stockholders)
Caring for close relatives (i.e., grandparents, aunts, uncles)	Caring for integral publics (i.e., customers, creditors)
Being a helpful and friendly neighbor	Being a helpful and friendly corporate neighbor
Obeying the law	Obeying the law
Being a "good" citizen in the community	Being a "good" citizen in the community, the nation, and the world
A portion of the family budget is allocated for philanthropic purposes	A portion of the organizational budget is allocated for philanthropic purposes
Protecting and caring for the family's home and land	Protecting and caring for the physical environment on which the organization has an impact

cordingly. The first relationship listed follows the Japanese model and suggests a nuclear family type of caring for the organization's employees, management, and stockholders. Many firms have not adopted this type of relationship with their employees, whereas others (e.g., Delta Airlines, Pepsico, and IBM) have moved in this direction. The slowly increasing use of organizationally sponsored daycare centers is an example of such a caring relationship.

Customers are placed in a relationship parallel to that of close relatives. In a society where the nuclear family dominates, the caring for close relatives is great but not of the order of the caring for nuclear family members. However, such caring does go substantially beyond caring for neighbors and friends. Thus, customers should receive considerable concern and attention that goes beyond simply not harming them. Some organizations seem to have adopted the value of treating customers like nuclear family members. For example, the Ronald McDonald Houses for families of sick children might be considered to represent more caring than is ordinarily required for customers or potential customers. Such deviations are usually noted with special interest by society and can produce very positive reactions.

The other parallels in Table 3-1 are not meant to be a complete list, but are examples of relationships that could be used. In all of these cases, the parallels drawn are very close or exact analogies and need no elaboration.

The most obvious question about the average-person approach arises from the nonhuman character of the organization. Because the organization is a creation of society and not a person, is it not reasonable to expect a *better* ethical performance than might be expected from a single average family? The problem with such an expectation is that the organization is a mythical creation, operating only through its human agents. Is it realistic to expect those people to have a higher level of moral performance as agents of the organization than in their personal lives? It seems more reasonable to expect a distribution of socially responsible performance for organizations that parallels the performance of the individual families of society. Hence, the mean or average family performance can be a reasonable guide in establishing organizational values. Individual organizations may choose to strive for higher standards, and some undoubtedly might achieve lower ones, but the concept of the average person can provide at least a reasonably acceptable and understandable measuring device.

Another application of the concept is in establishing levels of performance for socially responsible activities. Even after marketers have created a system of values, the level of performance with respect to each value still can be questioned. For example, if a neighbor or employee were in trouble, how much help should the friend, neighbor, or organization be expected to give? Again, the concept of what the average family would do, combined with priorities in the system of values, can provide guidance. We are not *required* to threaten our own existence to help an employee or neighbor because the value of personal survival has a higher priority. Further, it is not something the average person would be expected to do. Thus, in questions pertaining to social responsibility, the selection of values and their level of performance can be analyzed by using the test of the average person. Carlyle, in *Past and Present*, said, "In the long run every Government is the exact symbol of its people, with their wisdom and unwisdom."[26] It is this sentiment, applied to the concept of corporate social responsibility, that we are suggesting.

APPLICATION AND ANALYSIS

In order to further understand the concepts presented in this chapter, let's go back to Chapter 2 and analyze the Ford Pinto and Johns-Manville cases. First, could Ford have predicted the kind of negative public reaction it received? This question focuses on a threat *from* the environment. How much should it have done in order to be considered ethical and socially responsible? This question focuses on a threat *to* the environment (customers). In order to respond to these two questions in a nonsuperficial manner, we must analyze the impacts that Ford could have had at any of several points during the problem period.

The impact of the action taken (i.e., placement of the tank and fuel system) on the company is well documented. Could Ford have anticipated it? Hindsight is so much better than foresight that we

26. Thomas Carlyle, *Past and Present*. New York: Harper & Brothers, 1855.

must be careful not to answer too quickly. Still the answer to the question is that "They probably could have done better." Why? How? The first point to note from the material on business ethics is that the problem with the fuel system directly affects individuals. As such, society is likely to apply deontological analysis to the problem. Severely burned individuals are likely to elicit emotional reactions about Ford's lack of caring and juries are likely to listen. At this point, readers may be thinking that these results are intuitively obvious and that they didn't need a background in moral philosophy to recognize them. They would probably be right if they initially took the time to think the process through in detail. The moral philosophies provide us with a tool that can be used to structure our thinking about any business action and therein may lie their greatest benefit.

The other question raised earlier concerns how much Ford should have done, and this too, is easier to answer using hindsight. Our objective is to illustrate how foresight might have been applied using the tools developed in this chapter. To set the stage, it is important to understand a major difference between the information and capacity of business and the consumer. In this case, it would be easy to say that auto safety isn't important to consumers because they almost never ask about it or check on it when they buy a vehicle. If said, however, you would be wrong! When auto safety problems are called to the attention of consumers, they react angrily. Remember the Corvair? The problem is that auto consumers don't know what questions to ask about auto safety, and even if they did, they wouldn't understand the answers. So overtly or covertly (probably the latter for most consumers), they assume that major producers of autos provide roughly the same level of safety in vehicles. Basically, they don't have the time, desire, or capacity to evaluate all of the products they buy for all of the things that are important to them. They therefore place considerable trust in producers. When this bond of trust is broken, consumers act hurt and mad. Their response is often emotional and sometimes even irrational.

Business firms often have a chance to use this trust and lack of information against the consumer. It is frequently possible for the consumer to remain ignorant of the problem virtually forever. A person can drive an unsafe vehicle and never understand that a problem exists. However, if the problem ever becomes known, the producer is in for a potentially major exposé with the damage that usually goes along with it. When Robert Chote called breakfast cereals a "nutritional wasteland" to a Senate Subcommittee in the early 1970s, the cereals cited appeared in newspapers and sales dropped accordingly. To prevent such exposés, business must understand the assumptions made by its consumers and attempt to satisfy their trust.

As suggested previously, if the product or action can produce substantial (especially physical) harm to individuals, then deontological reasoning should be used. Business people must ask themselves whether they would want to live in a world where everyone was acting in the same way. Otherwise an analysis of the greatest net good for the greatest number should point the way. In the case of the Pinto, either analysis would produce the same result—more concern for the buyer is appropriate. It is often true that the two philosophies produce the same results, and only in those cases where they do not are the guidelines for selecting them important.

Continuing with our analysis using ethical philosophy, a question still remains concerning how much should have been done. The answer is straightforward in this case. Ford should have corrected the fuel system problems either before the Pinto was released, or at least as soon as the problem became apparent. The "golden mean" of performance would seem to require it. The problem arose during the normal practice of business and could be corrected in the same way. To do nothing or to actively resist such correction would put the company in performance deficit using Aristotelian terms. Making the correction is not beyond what normally can be expected after considering the previous analysis.

Repairing and redesigning the fuel system also passes the tests for social responsibility. If consumers are to be treated as close family, we certainly wouldn't want them in an auto that is less safe than it should be. Neither would we want to take advantage of their trust and lack of knowledge in getting them to buy this product. Further, the average American family would not undertake such activities. Thus, the conclusion is the same under social responsibility analysis as it is under ethical analysis.

An analysis of the Johns-Manville case produces similar results. The major difference between it and the Pinto case is the use of worker ignorance, as well as user ignorance, of the dangers involved in order to help the short-run profitability of the organization. Deontological analysis suggests that individuals should have been protected, and social responsibility toward nuclear and other close family members demands the same thing. Perhaps the only question that arises concerns the level of performance problem since protecting the workers and users meant getting out of the business and a major disruption to all employees, stockholders, and even the users involved. Nevertheless, the level of performance measures tell us that it's expected. If a spouse or child is in a life-threatening situation and the cost of protecting them is primarily financial, the golden mean of performance, as well as what is expected of the average family, is to pay the price and protect the family member.

One other interesting point is what would happen if utilitarian analysis were used instead of deontological reasoning, the obvious choice in this case. Because of the huge financial losses that could occur, as well as the loss of jobs to employees, it might be tempting to argue that the greatest good for the greatest number was to continue production—perhaps with warnings and attempt to protect all handlers of the asbestos. One of the criticisms of utilitarian analysis is that it does not do well measuring all of the benefits and harm occurring from an action, and this is an example of that problem at work. However, most responsible people who honestly analyze the impact of the potential pain, suffering, and death still remaining to employees, installers, and customers who live and work around the product will come to the conclusion that the net greatest good is to stop production. In addition, we know from our other analysis that society is likely to shut us down (and they have) if we don't do it ourselves.

It is hoped that these analyses provide some assistance in understanding how to use the tools presented in this chapter. However, the full integration of these tools into the corporate culture and the strategic planning process has yet to be developed. This integration must occur if we are to make the greatest possible use of these tools. This process is developed in the chapters which follow.

Exercises for Chapter 3

Kellogg Cereals and Children's Television Advertising*

History of Concern and Attacks—Children's Breakfast Cereal and Its Advertising

Circa 1970. A U.S. Senate consumer subcommittee opened hearings on the nutritional value of ready-to-eat cereals in 1970 that reflected a growing national concern about nutrition. Two separate issues were then under discussion that set the context of later debate: First, does the food industry have an obligation to market a nutritious product? Second, even if a product is highly nutritious, what limits should be placed on advertising this product to children?

Robert Choate, Jr., President of the Council on Children, Media, and Merchandising, figured prominently in the 1970 hearings. He made headlines with his nutritional ranking of 60 leading cold cereals. Although his criteria for ranking the nutritional value of cereals rested on vitamin fortification and not on sugar content (later a central concern), his ranking system may have had significant impact. Top executives of the cereal companies consulted their technologists, who had long advocated nutritionally improved formulae. Within 18 months of Choate's first Senate testimony, 26 of 40 criticized cereals had been reformulated.

At these 1970 Senate cereal hearings, Dr. Frederick Stare, chairman of the Department of Nutrition, Harvard University School of Public Health, and Dr. W. H. Sebrell, Jr. of the Institute of Human Nutrition at Columbia University gave testimony. They agreed with the cereal industry that cereal with "milk and sugar" is a nutritionally adequate food and that evaluating the nutritional content of cereal without milk is unfair.[1]

*This case was prepared by Linda Kern, Martha W. Elliot, and Tom L. Beauchamp. Not to be duplicated without permission of the holder of the copyright, © 1989, Tom L. Beauchamp. Used with permission.

1. Molander, "Marketing Ready-to-Eat Breakfast Cereals at the Kellogg Company" p. 130.

1973–77. In 1973, a second Congressional investigation focused on children's presweetened, ready-to-eat cereals. This time the Senate Select Committee on Nutrition and Human Needs addressed the twin issues of nutritional value and advertising fairness. Some of the 1970 testimonies were simply reiterated. Action for Children's Television presented evidence that a child watching a particular Boston station from 7:00 A.M. to 2:00 P.M. on Saturday, October 28, 1972, would have seen 67 commercials for sugary foods, including ready-to-eat cereals.

In March 1973, the FDA introduced the U.S. RDA standards (recommended daily allowance), replacing the older minimum daily requirement (MDR). The cereal companies had to reset their standards at this more stringent level. Also in 1973, FTC chairman Louis Engman set up a task force in the Division of Special Projects to investigate the issues of children's advertising further. During his term of office, the FTC staff was granted the use of a compulsory process that gave them the right to subpoena cereal companies for access to their market research data, and thus to examine their advertising strategies.

1977–78. A broad-based attack on children's advertising was triggered by a petition with a specific intent. In 1977, Action for Children's Television (ACT) and the Center for Science in the Public Interest (CSPI) jointly petitioned the FTC. They proposed a ban on the advertising of sugary, in-between-meal (snack) food to children. ACT and CSPI got more than they bargained for when a 1978 FTC staff report called for a ban on *all* children's advertising.

> It is both unfair and deceptive . . . to address televised advertising for *any* product to young children who are still too young to understand the selling purpose of, or otherwise comprehend or evaluate, the advertising. . . . The classical justification for a free market, and for the advertising that goes with it, assumes at least a rough balance of information, sophistication and power between buyer and seller. . . . In the present situation, it is ludicrous to suggest that any such balance exists between an advertiser who is willing to spend many thousands of dollars for a single 30-second spot, and a child who is incapable of understanding that the spot has a selling intent, and instead trust-

ingly believes that the spot merely provides advice about one of the good things in life.[2]

The preceding quotation from a 1978 Federal Trade Commission (FTC) staff report presents the heart of an argument advanced by the FTC staff and others against televised advertising directed to children for presweetened, ready-to-eat cereals. This report accompanied a set of proposed regulatory rules that would:

(a) Ban all televised advertising for any product which is directed to, or seen by, audiences composed of a significant proportion of children who are too young to understand the selling purpose of, or otherwise comprehend or evaluate, the advertising;
(b) Ban televised advertising directed to, or seen by, audiences composed of a significant proportion of older children for sugared food products, the consumption of which poses the most serious dental health risks;
(c) Require that televised advertising directed to, or seen by, audiences composed of a significant proportion of older children for sugared food products not included in paragraph (b) be balanced by nutritional and/or health disclosures funded by advertisers.[3]

1981. For "practical" reasons, however, the FTC recommended that "the proceedings be terminated." The "practical matter" that prohibited the FTC from banning children's advertising was twofold. First, dental research is sufficiently primitive so that one cannot positively identify which foods are cariogenic, or cavity producing. There are too many unknown factors involved in cavity formation to place a ban on any particular product or set of products. Second, although children *under* six cannot understand the intent of a commercial message, children *over* six often can. To ban the advertising to one group would automatically affect the other older group. For these "practical" reasons, then, the FTC ter-

2. FTC, "Staff Report on Television Advertising to Children," (February 1978), pp. 27, 29.
3. Ibid., pp. 345–46.

minated all investigative proceedings associated with children's advertising.

Perhaps an even more practical reason for inaction by the FTC was a change in the presidency. The 1978 FTC report was developed under the Carter administration, but Ronald Reagan took office in 1980.

Kellogg's Response To Complaints About Nutrition and Advertising of Children's Cereals

Kellogg is the nation's largest manufacturer of ready-to-eat cereals, with more than 40 percent of U.S. sales and over $1.7 billion in 1978 annual sales (38.9 percent in 1982, with over $3.2 billion in sales).

The Nutritional Value of Kellogg Cereals. As early as 1971, the Kellogg Company formally published an ambitious corporate nutrition policy; however, it cautioned as part of the policy itself that "Consumer acceptability of our products in flavor, texture and appearance is essential if they are to make any nutritional contribution." In early 1973 the Kellogg Company, along with General Mills, testified before the Senate Select Committee on Nutrition and Human Needs. Dr. Gary Costley, Kellogg's Director of Nutrition, argued that (1) "only a small part of a child's sugar intake comes from sweetened breakfast cereals"; (2) that "a normal serving of most canned fruits contained far more sugar" than a serving of cereal; (3) that presweetened cereals do not cause a child to become "hooked" on sugar; and (4) that "research studies show no correlation between new dental cavities and the amount of pre-sweetened cereal consumed."[4]

In October 1981, the Consumer Service Department at Kellogg printed and distributed a pamphlet entitled "Cereal Fortification," which followed their 1980 monograph, "Ready-to-Eat Cereals and

---

4. Molander, "Marketing Ready-to-Eat Breakfast Cereals at the Kellogg Company," p. 136.

Nutrition."[5] The pamphlet provided a detailed analysis or "nutrient profile" of their "Corn Flakes" and "Sugar Frosted Flakes." The pamphlet's purpose was to prove that Kellogg cereals, as presented fortified and when used with milk, easily provide the daily nutrient intake recommended by nutritionists.

Kellogg's Advertising Practices. The Kellogg Company has worked to refute charges that their advertising makes false nutritional claims. Kellogg issued a pamphlet on "Advertising" in late 1979. In this pamphlet the company argued as follows:

> Kellogg's has been recognized an unprecedented seven times by *Family Health Magazine* for excellence in nutritional advertising. . . .

> For years we have placed great emphasis on creating honest and tasteful advertising for youngsters with messages that convey the inherent nutritional value of our products. We present these messages in a way that is not only informative and interesting, but also appropriate for a child's level of understanding.

> Our advertising serves not only as a product selling tool, it also stresses the importance of starting the day with a nutritious breakfast. Since 1973 Kellogg cereal advertisements for both children and adults have shown cereal and milk being eaten as a part of a complete breakfast. Our advertising improves a child's awareness of the need for a complete, nutritious breakfast.[6]

Kellogg believes that the products in question are nutritious and that children would be worse off if they were not available and not advertised. William E. LaMothe, president of Kellogg at the time of the proposed FTC ban on advertising, commented:

> We try to construct our commercials so that they can be entertaining, and have a message. We're convinced that if we could

5. The pamphlet argued that in 1955, Kellogg's "Special K" was introduced to provide higher levels of essential nutrients and in 1966 "Product 19" had been introduced for the same reason.

6. FTC, "Staff Report in Television Advertising to Children," (February 1978).

get every youngster in the country to eat a ready-to-eat cereal—the nutritional information we have says they would have a better diet than the mix of things they have now with high cholesterol and high fat, or no breakfast at all. We are almost evangelistic in our thrust to try to convince youngsters to be interested in breakfast.[7]

Questions

1. Evaluate both the attacks on cereal makers and Kellogg's response from deontological, utilitarian, and social responsibility perspectives. Specifically, evaluate the concerns of Robert Chote, Jr., Action for Children's Television (ACT), Center for Science in the Public Interest (CSPI), and the people who wrote the 1978 FTC staff report. Then evaluate the response of Drs. Frederick Stare and W. H. Sebrell, Jr. of Harvard, Dr. Gary Costley of Kellogg, the 1971–72 Kellogg response, Kellogg's 1979 pamphlet, and William E. LaMothe's (then president of Kellogg) comments on the proposed FTC ban on advertising.

2. Suppose it would be shown that *some* children (albeit a limited number) suffered moderate harm from nutrition-advertising problems of breakfast cereals, but following President LaMothe's comments, the social sum of the impacts on children was positive. How should the industry and its critics react? How are they likely to react? Are there similarities between this case and the Nestlé case cited in the chapter? Explain.

7. Molander, "Marketing Ready-to-Eat Breakfast Cereals at the Kellogg Company," p. 138.

Chapter 4

Culture: the Key to Managing an Ethical Corporation

Because corporate culture plays such a pivotal role in our premise that the ethical posture of any organization can be managed, we have included a chapter on some of the more basic propositions governing the concept and idea of corporate culture. While the idea of a corporate culture is not new, the notion that it can be managed is. For a long time management had merely accepted the existence of a corporate culture as a given and tried to work within the framework established by that culture. We would suggest that any attempt to manage the ethical output of an organization depends on having the proper corporate culture in which to plan, implement, and control an organization's activities.

Moreover, the relationship between an organization's culture and its activities is not as casual as some writers would suggest. Jay Lorsch, a well-known student of organizational behavior, posits a tight linkage between culture and resultant strategy. According to Lorsch, "Culture affects not only the way managers believe within an organization, but also decisions they make about the organization's relationships with its environment and its strategy. In fact, my central argument is that culture has a major impact on corporate strategy."[1]

We agree and would hasten to add that culture has a major impact on corporate ethics. As indicated earlier, this fundamental linkage between culture and strategy is axiomatic to our model and forms the basis of what we have called the parallel planning system which is discussed in the next chapter. We begin with a discussion of what culture is and how it can be managed to effect a more ethical corporate posture.

1. Jay W. Lorsch, "Managing Culture: The Invisible Barrier to Strategic Change," *California Management Review*, 28, no. 2 (Winter 1986), 95–109.

WHAT IS CORPORATE CULTURE?

As one would suspect with such a conceptual notion as corporate culture, definitions and descriptons abound. Several such definitions and descriptions capture what we believe are the essential managerial elements inherent in the concept.

Jay Lorsch offers the following on corporate culture: "By culture I mean the shared beliefs top managers have in a company about how they should manage themselves and other employees, and how they should conduct their business(es). These beliefs are often invisible to the top managers but have a major impact on their thoughts and actions."[2]

Stanley M. Davis argues that "culture is the pattern of shared values and beliefs that give members of an institution meaning and provide them with rules for behavior in their organization."[3]

William F. Kieschnick, President of Atlantic Richfield Company, defines the concept more concisely saying that corporate culture "usually refers to a company's business style and sometimes also to its values."[4]

Finally, W. Brooke Tunstall, Assistant Vice President and Director of Corporate Planning of AT&T, describes corporate culture as "a general constellation of beliefs, mores, customs, value systems, behavioral norms, and ways of doing business that are unique to each corporation, that set a pattern for corporate activities and actions, and that describe the implicit and emergent patterns of behavior and emotions characterizing life in the organization."[5]

Embedded within these descriptions and definitions of corporate culture are several component ideas crucial to the develop-

2. Ibid.

3. Stanley M. Davis, quoted by Alyse Lynn Booth, "Who Are We?" *Public Relations Journal,* (July 1985), pp. 14–44.

4. William F. Kieschnick, "A Corporate Culture for a Competitive World," a speech presented at the Executive Forum at California Institute of Technology, June 20, 1983.

5. W. Brooke Tunstall, "Cultural Transition at AT&T," *Sloan Management Review,* (Fall 1983), pp. 15–26.

ment of a more ethical management system. First is the idea that corporate culture involves norms, customs, beliefs, standards, and so on. Each of these concepts performs certain regulating and guiding duties. Norms, customs, and beliefs, for example, establish guidelines for behavior. In the same sense these regulators and directors of behavior can be established to guide actions with respect to what the company says is ethical, right, and moral.

Second, these guidelines are shared to greater or lesser extent. To the degree that an organization has been successful in instilling these guidelines over time through a socialization process, these norms, beliefs, and standards will be more effective in providing direction to employee behavior. Too often top management thinks one set of values, beliefs, and norms exists when in fact, a completely different set of guidelines is operative. Instances of company sabotage are good examples where top management believes one set of guidelines is working when the workers have evolved their own. The same is true of ethics. While top management may believe that ethical values have permeated the organization, the degree to which these values are actually shared may be somewhat less than thought.

Corporate culture may be both explicit and implicit; that is, management may believe that an explicit culture has been developed when a more implicit culture is actually operating. Competing cultures arise when management is inattentive to what the actual culture is. In those instances where cultural values have not been explicitly enumerated and the socialization process is incomplete or ineffective, the organization will evolve its own, usually in response to the reward system. Employees will value and use as guidelines those activities for which they will be rewarded. When a behavior that is rewarded comes into conflict with an unstated and unmonitored ethical value, usually the rewarded behavior wins out.

The importance of an organization's culture to its stability and sense of purpose is made exceptionally clear in the following description of the Catholic Church.

> ...how has the Roman Catholic Church maintained its sway for
> so many centuries? Not by strategic planning systems. Not by

layers upon layers of middle managers. But through one of the strongest and most durable cultures ever created. It is a culture rich in rituals and ceremonies of all kinds: white smoke from the chimney in the Sistine Chapel; a pope's blessing from the small balcony; masses and other religious rituals that govern the behavior of millions around the world. It is a culture that is rich with heroes, stories, and mythologies; martyrs; missionaries; saints; a Polish freedom-fighting pope; heroes to identify with day-to-day. And finally, whether you agree with it or not, it is a culture founded on the bedrock of a set of meaningful (to its followers) beliefs and values.[6]

MULTIPLE CULTURES

The concept of an organization's corporate culture is not as neat and tidy as is generally portrayed. More typical is the existence of multiple and overlapping cultures within an organization. Just as a country may have a dominant culture, it is just as likely to have subcultures. This condition can and does exist in most organizations.

Basic to most organizations is the existence of a formal and an informal culture. The formal culture usually is comprised of idealized statements of those values, beliefs, norms, and behaviors that should exist in an organization. It is a normative as opposed to a positive condition. Informal culture, on the other hand, may reflect the positive or actual culture. This subculture is composed of those values, beliefs, and behaviors that actually do exist and guide behavior.

It is relatively easy to see the problem from an ethics management standpoint that emerges when the formal culture which embodies those ethical core values that top management thinks are operative conflicts or does not coincide with what the informal culture prescribes as ethical behavior. The translation of strategic initiatives through the chain of command can become distorted and

6. Terrence E. Deal and Allan A. Kennedy, *Corporate Cultures: The Rites and Rituals of Corporate Life* (Reading, Mass.: Addison-Wesley Publishing Company, Inc., 1982), p. 22.

the best intentioned plans of a concerned management may become perverted through the informal culture. The reverse is equally likely to occur. Top management pressures to get a job out below cost may subvert the ethical values of individuals at lower organizational levels. Such was the case at B. F. Goodrich where top management pressured engineers to approve substandard and potentially dangerous aircraft braking systems.[7]

Multiple cultures can emerge in any organization because of the existence of several factors. These factors include different employee populations, different tasks, inconsistent reward systems, and significant cultural changes external to the organization.

When an organization recruits employees from different populations, the likelihood that subcultures will emerge is high. For example, organizations that involve both military and civilian workers may exhibit characteristics of both systems. Other factors such as social class or race may also contribute to the emergence of subcultures, especially if management fosters the separation of groups based on task or locational assignments.

Individuals from differing populations may bring varying ideas of what is right and what is wrong. This is particularly true and most likely to occur in multinational organizations.

Different tasks can contribute to the development of different subcultures within the same organization. Workers who are employed on the production line may evolve a system of values, beliefs, and norms that is distinct from employees in research and development.

Probably one of the more insidious contributors to subculture evolution is the system of rewards and sanctions that an organization has developed. The reward system has the capacity for reinforcing values, beliefs, and norms. When this reward system is arbitrarily applied or, if it is applied in an inconsistent manner so that for one group of people it rewards a certain behavior and for another group of individuals it ignores that same behavior, different subcultures that embrace different value systems are likely

7. Kermit Vandivier, "Why Should My Conscience Bother Me?" in *The Name of Profit*, eds. Robert Heilbroner, et al. (New York: Doubleday & Company, 1972).

to emerge. This is an extremely important factor when applied to the management of corporate ethics.

Finally, environmental forces exogenous to the organization can be reflected in subcultural differences within an organization. Natural divisions between the "young Turks" and the "old guard" may reflect a different social and cultural ethos not under the control of the organization. Through the need to recruit new workers to replace retiring or leaving workers, these social and cultural influences may be incorporated within the organization.

Such an occurrence is common in academic organizations where older established professors are slowly replaced by younger more ambitious Ph.Ds. Departments which had been characterized as complacent, nonproductive, or full of "dead wood" are eventually transformed into dynamic productive departments turning out research and actively engaging in consulting work. New Ph.Ds bring a set of values that includes a strong desire to get ahead, a desire to develop a reputation, and a need for success. Sometimes too these values are not controlled by a sufficiently strong ethical value system which can have a deleterious effect, not only on the individual, but also on the department, the college, and the university.

The potential existence of subcultures within an organization points out two important managerial consequences of culture management. First, the culture of an organization needs to be monitored and managed. Subcultural differences are not necessarily dysfunctional. On the contrary, if properly managed, they can be useful for identity, pride, and motivation. However, we are concerned about the dysfunctional aspects of multiple subcultures and to the extent that these subcultures embrace different visions of what is ethical, right, and moral they increase the probability that management decisions and corporate actions may not reflect what was intended.

Second, the potential existence of subcultures points out the need for a solid and effective socialization process so that one dominant corporate culture exists. Subcultural systems may exist but must be subservient to the dominance of the formal corporate culture. This is particularly true when the formal culture is the main vehicle for communicating, teaching, and enforcing ethical values and standards.

ASSESSING CORPORATE CULTURE

The first step in managing an organization's corporate culture is to understand the one that is currently operating. This involves an assessment procedure and conducting a culture audit. Such an audit can point out those areas that need reinforcing and those aspects of the culture that may require change.

As a precursor to the actual audit, top management must develop a well-defined sense of what the organization's culture should be. With this in mind, Lorsch suggests that top management answer a series of question such as those presented in Table 4-1.[8]

Noticeably absent from this list of questions are those dealing with the ethical values of the organization. Consequently, to this list we would add a series of questions such as those shown in Table 4-2.

A more detailed and elaborate audit framework is offered by Deal and Kennedy. Their approach involves an external evaluation, an internal evaluation and an identification of major cultural problems. Some of the more salient aspects of this approach are excerpted and shown in Table 4-3.[9]

Once top management has reached a consensus decision on what the proper culture should be, this consensus becomes the value system that guides the formal culture. This consensus is based on the development of a number of core values or those values which are critical to the culture, similar to those discussed in Chapter 3.

Now an assessment of the belief and value system of the rest of the organization is necessary. This audit will indicate the extant operating culture in different departments and at different operating levels within the organization. To the extent that there exists a significant difference between the audits, the socialization process becomes more important and the objective of the process becomes one of changing the culture rather than reinforcing it.

8. Jay W. Lorsch, "Managing Culture: The Invisible Barrier to Strategic Change."

9. Terrence E. Deal and Allan A. Kennedy, *Corporate Cultures: The Rites and Rituals of Corporate Life.*

Table 4-1
AN EXAMPLE OF A CULTURAL AUDIT

	Questions	Examples
Beliefs about Goals	About what financial objectives do we have strong beliefs based on traditions and history?	Return on assets Rate of growth Debt/equity ratio Bond rating Dividend policies
	How, if at all, are those beliefs about financial goals related to each other?	Growth should be financed internally, which means no long-term debt and limited dividends.
	What other goals do we believe to be important?	To be in the top quartile of Fortune 500 companies. To be the best in our country. To be a responsible corporate citizen. To be an "all-weather" company.
Beliefs about Distinctive Competences	What do we believe to be the appropriate scope of our competitive activity?	We can manage any business. We can succeed in domestic consumer products. We can succeed with products based upon our technological expertise. We can only succeed in the paper industry. We can manage our business worldwide.
	To what earlier experience can we trace these beliefs? Do they reflect a realistic assessment of the competence of management and the company?	

Table 4-2

AN EXTENSION OF THE CULTURAL AUDIT
TO INCLUDE CONSIDERATION
FOR ETHICAL CASE VALUES

	Questions	Examples
Beliefs about Ethical Core Values	About what ethical values do we have strong beliefs?	Caring for the organizational family. Caring about the health and welfare of our customers. Being a helpful and friendly corporate neighbor. Caring about the managerial environment.
	What beliefs do we have concerning the relationship between ethics and profits?	Profits should be the result of ethical activity. Walk from deals which are unethical. We can market a quality product and still make money.

Changing the Culture through Socialization

The principal process in which values, beliefs, and norms are transmitted throughout the organization is by a process called socialization. This is a process by which an employee learns about the organization, its people, and its culture. It can be a very potent shaper of behavior and as such can be an important tool for developing the ethical culture.

There are a number of factors involved in the socialization process including reinforcement, social modeling, and direct instruction. Each of these is discussed as it pertains to the socialization of ethical cultures.

Table 4-3
IDENTIFYING CULTURES

I. External Evaluation

A. *Physical Setting:* (Bricks and Mortar) Pride in the company is reflected in its buildings and their location. Look at more than corporate headquarters. Also look for facility consistency across classes of employees to identify attitudes toward those different classes. Strong culture companies care about people (all of them) and see that they are treated appropriately.

B. *What The Company Says About Its Culture:* (annual reports and quarterly statements, press releases, comments to financial analysts) Companies with strong cultures recoganize the importance of values and people and continually report this to the world. Companies with weak or fragmented cultures focus on business and its performance with almost nothing about the human side. However, be wary—often management says it believes things but other clues suggest otherwise.

C. *How Does The Company Greet Strangers?* The Reception Area (formal/informal, relaxed/busy, elegant/nondescript) reflects the values of the company's culture. The style of the receptionist (attitude and service) also provide a clue. What are visitor procedures (elaborate/casual)? Are they consistent for everyone? Companies with strong cultures take rituals very seriously.

D. *Interview Company People:*
   1. What is the company like? Is it a good place to work? The *character* of the answer (enthusiasm and degree of support—few will speak negatively) is important.
   2. Tell me about the history of the company. What were its beginnings? Answers communicate the mythology of the company (Note: Facts are often wrong).
   3. Why is the company a success? What explains its growth? Answer tells what they think is important in the company. They may not be substantively correct but reflect their impressions of the company's values.

Table 4-3 (cont.)

4. What kind of people work here? Who really gets ahead in the long term? People will characterize fellow workers and especially the hero in the culture.
5. What kind of place is this to work in? What is an average day like? How do things get done? Answers will characterize important rituals, meetings, or bureaucratic procedures. If the response is hierarchical ("The boss is a good person to work for.") assume that this bet-your-company aspect of cultural life is important.

E. *Observe How People Spend Their Time:* What people do is determined by what they value and what is valued by the organization. Comparisons between what people say and what they do is a good measure of cultural cohesion.

F. *Interpretation of Findings:* Look for internal/external orientation of organization. Is the culture focused inward (all beliefs, heroes, and rituals relate to internal matters and political debates)? If so, you can project a slowness to respond to external threats and opportunities.

II. Internal Evaluation Of Culture

(Note that the major problem with this approach is objectivity.)

A. *Understand Career Path Progression of Employees:* Which divisions or activities in the organization tend to move people up the ladder? What does an employee have to do to get promoted? (e.g., competence in key skills, objective criteria, tenure, loyalty)

B. *How Long Do People Stay in Jobs*—particularly middle-management jobs? Tenure is critical in assessing culture.

C. *Look at the Content of What Is Being Discussed or Written About:* The culture spends its time on what it values most, therefore tabulate what's in your (and other) in-boxes, and track how much time is being spent on each subject in meetings.

Table 4-3 (cont.)

D. *Pay Particular Attention to the Anecdotes and Stories that Pass Through the Cultural Network:* Stories that are repeated by several people are especially important. What is the point of the story? What are they about (e.g., customers, political infighting, individual initiative that was rewarded or punished)?
E. *Interpretation of Findings:* Weak cultures
   1. have no clear values or beliefs about how to succeed in their business.
   2. or have many such beliefs but they are not congruent. Different parts of the organization have fundamentally different beliefs.
   3. have heroes who are destructive or disruptive. They don't build on any common understanding of what is important.
   4. have day-to-day rituals which are either disorganized or even contradictory in nature.

III. Major Cultural Problems

A. *Inward Focus:* Organizations often get into trouble when they stop paying attention to what's going on in the outside world. Examples include: a focus on satisfying the boss rather than meeting external problems like customers, competitors, etc.; overemphasis on internal budgets, financial analysis or sales quotas without mention of customers, competitors, trends, etc.; focus on internal politics.
B. *Short-Term Focus:* How much time is spent in the culture on short-term results? How much on long-term survival?
C. *Morale Problems:* Are key people or just many people chronically unhappy? Degree of turnover is a clue, but remember some turnover is inevitable. Look for upward trends in divisions or across the company. Signals may be subtle and apparent only in lack of enthusiasm.

Table 4-3 (cont.)

D. *Fragmentation/Inconsistency:* Often these differences within a culture are visible: dress and speech standards, physical settings, different work habits and rituals. Such fragmentation of values and beliefs do not pull together well when they need to. The cultures of the parts are not integrated into a coherent whole and there is a lot of lost energy.

E. *Emotional Outbursts:* The final *and most serious symptom* of a culture in trouble is increased and rampant emotionalism. The culture is a security blanket that directs behavior and when the culture is weak in transition, or in trouble, people get frightened. This state takes the form of emotional outbursts against the organization. It may also influence personal affairs such as increased number of divorces or drinking problems.

F. *Strong Subcultures:* Some strong subcultures are natural for an organization. Risk-taking marketing types versus conservative financial types and different age cohorts within the company are examples.

  1. If no commerce exists between these subcultures, they can become ingrown and detrimental. Try to determine if there is regular and open access to these different subcultures.

  2. A clear sign of trouble between subcultures is when open "warfare" begins to occur between them. Some tension between subcultures is desirable, but it must be tempered (not pronounced or destructive) to be useful.

  3. When subcultures become exclusive a potential problem exists because organizations work best when all employees pull together—not when some put their collective interests above others.

  4. When subculture values preempt shared company values (i.e., when subcultures tout their values and beliefs as superior to the organization), the tail is wagging the dog.

Adapted from T. Deal and A. Kennedy, *Corporate Cultures,* © 1982, Addison-Wesley Publishing Co., Inc., Reading, Massachusetts. Reprinted with permission.

Reinforcement

The psychological literature is replete with discussions concerning the value of reinforcement as a shaper of behavior. It has been proven that human behavior can be significantly directed and shaped when the proper conditions of reinforcement have been applied. This is a key aspect of the socialization process. When an individual exhibits a behavior that is congruent with a desired corporate value and that behavior is rewarded, the likelihood of continued desired behavior is increased. Thus, if an employee brings to his or her superior's attention an action that has ethical consequence for the department or organization, that behavior should be rewarded. To do so is to increase the probability that such an occurrence will take place in the future. Not to do so is to inculcate an attitude that the ethical conduct of employees is unimportant at best and, at worse, is to instill the notion that it does not matter how things are done in the company.

Of course, this process cannot take place unless the organization has identified what it considers the desired corporate values and has communicated these values to all levels of the organization. Moreover, reinforcement does not always have to be positive. If a superior finds that a behavior of an employee has not been congruent with the desired value system, that behavior must be sanctioned. While many management gurus will debate the nature of the sanction system, suffice it to say that any reinforcement system must be developed with a clear understanding of the organizational social system.

It is important to point out that not all individuals respond to the same type of rewards. For some individuals money may be highly prized, while for others a simple pat on the back is sufficient. For others, such social factors as recognition, praise, and acceptance may be much stronger motivators than money. The point is the use of reinforcers must be organizational and, in some cases, individual specific if they are to be effective shapers of behavior.

As was mentioned earlier, it is of extreme importance to be aware of the desired corporate values in order for the proper socialization process to take place. We use the word "proper" in the sense that under most reinforcement processes some learning will take place. However, it is important that the *correct* learning take place. This process involves management communicating what is to be learned.

One of the problems we feel that impedes the socialization process more than any other problem is that too often the wrong behaviors are rewarded. There are two aspects to this problem.

First, if desired values and consequent valued behaviors are not made overt by management, typically the culture will evolve its own. And, more than likely, the resultant behaviors will be those that are positively rewarded. In some organizations, those values which result in behaviors leading to advancement, promotion, or raises are the values that emerge. In many cases when individuals are forced to choose between a behavior that is ethical and one that results in a desired reward, the behavior which is rewarded will be chosen. If ethical actions are not valued and rewarded by an organization, the organization will evolve its own valued behaviors. It is therefore crucial, if the socialization process is to work, that management make explicit those values which are desired by the organization.

A second aspect is that these values must be transmitted and communicated throughout the organization and those behaviors congruent with these values rewarded. Those behaviors that are not congruent must be sanctioned. When management is blind to certain behaviors, this intentional ignoring of incongruent behavior has the effect of rewarding it. Over a period of time this process instills that kind of behavior and elevates it to the status of a norm. Subsequent efforts at changing the norm are made even more difficult because of these rewards. This appeared to be the situation at Southern Methodist University where not only university officials were aware of cheating by the athletic department, they actually participated in the cheating. With this type of support there is little wonder that the system became corrupt and was finally discovered.

How rewards are meted out, when they are administered and in what form will depend on the particular subculture, the department or the organization level, as well as the prevailing social system. Reinforcement can be a powerful tool for socializing specific values, beliefs, and standards of behavior throughout the organization if management will take the time to understand what the organization prizes.

Social Models

It is a well-documented finding in social research that individuals rely on other individuals for cues as to how to behave in certain settings. The use of role models in business is equally extensive and can be useful in the development of the valued culture.

There are several aspects of role models that can make the socialization process even more effective. First is the notion that individuals do not blindly imitate the behavior of just any other individual. There is a choice involved. Individuals choose whom they wish to imitate. Often this choice is based on the perception that in imitating another individual's behavior, the imitated behavior will lead to a desired and valued outcome. To the extent that this condition prevails, the probability of imitative behavior is increased. To the extent that imitation does not lead to a desired outcome, future likelihood of imitation is decreased.

When attempting to instill a set of values and desired ethical behavior within an organization, management should recognize that at all levels and within different operating departments, there are individuals that act as role models. Co-opting these individuals into the socialization process as role models can provide an effective means of achieving the desired behaviors. When an individual who is respected and admired by fellow workers blows the whistle on an unethical practice or action, he or she sets a pattern of behavior to be imitated by other workers. When the other workers act in a similar fashion and are recognized by the role model, the probability of future actions congruent with desired behaviors has been increased.

This increased probability is strengthened when the role model has the ability to reward an individual for engaging in a desired behavior. This is why it is so important to get management involved in the development of an ethical culture. Top management has the ability to reward more quickly and more substantially than other levels of management within the organization.

Not all models have to be live models. Individuals learn vicariously as well as from firsthand experiences. Filmed sequences of model behavior may be effective in teaching desired behaviors. Some companies use a film of the CEO or other very visible top management person to communicate organizational value systems.

Organizational heroes can also be positive models. Those individuals in the organization's history who did the right thing can be used as examples of desired organizational behavior after which employees can pattern their behavior.

Direct Teaching

Face-to-face exchanges between individuals is still another way in which values can be communicated and learned. This type of instruction can be particularly effective for the new recruit. Training sessions in which other workers tell new workers about the way things are done can be useful. A potential problem with this type of socialization process is that if the values have not been adequately socialized throughout the organization, once the new recruit starts to work in his or her assigned department, co-workers may subvert much of the learning. If the learning in a direct training session is not reinforced through models and employee support for the value system, that learning will be replaced by a more informal learning process. Often, the informal learning process conducted by peers is much stronger.

BARRIERS TO CHANGING
ORGANIZATIONAL CULTURES

Plans for changing the organizational culture must incorporate plans for dealing with the different barriers that individuals and the organization itself have already erected. In order to overcome the natural resistance to change, it is first necessary to understand what these potential barriers are. Essentially there are two types of resistance: that which springs from the individual and that which is often endemic to the organization.

Individual Barriers

Individuals will resist change for a variety of reasons.[10] These include:

1. *Habit.* That to which one is accustomed is usually more comfortable. Individuals grow comfortable with a particular culture in large part because they have contributed to it and are reinforced by it. Changing the value system within the culture may mean changing the individual, a potentially difficult task. In fact, in many instances of cultural change, the resulting culture may be so uncomfortable to certain individuals that they will choose to leave the organization rather than to have to work in such a setting.

2. *Selective attention and retention.* Changing the culture involves a learning process. New values have to be taught by top management and new values learned by subordinates. Preestablished values and attitudes act as filters through which individuals may distort noncongruent information or facts. In addition, individuals may not remember things which are at odds with their preestablished attitudinal and value systems. Finally, they may selectively ignore those things in the new cultural system which are incongruent with their former belief systems. This selective attention and retention places a heavy burden on communication, reward systems, and information flows when attempting to change the organization's culture.

3. *Dependence.* Many individuals will rely on significant others within the organization as role models. Nonadoption of new cultural system components is likely until they have diffused throughout the organization and have been adopted by these role models. It may take longer to change the organization's culture than expected while the change is diffusing throughout the organization.

4. *Fear of the unknown.* A changed culture means a new way of doing things and this can be a formidable situation for some individuals. Fear makes people anxious and less certain about the nature and effects of the change.

10. Don Hellriegel, John W. Slocum, Jr. and Richard W. Woodman, *Organizational Behavior* (St. Paul, Minn.: West Publishing Company, 1983); Gerald R. Faltman and R. Duncan, *Strategies for Planned Change* (New York: Wiley Interscience, 1977).

5. *Economics*. Changing the culture may actually impact the pocketbooks of some employees. This is especially true with respect to instituting a more ethical culture. Walking away from seemingly good deals because those deals are unethical may cause an individual to actually lose money. Padding expense accounts and accepting gifts are two other examples of economic loss which may make change difficult. This can be a significant barrier to accepting a new, more ethical value system.

Organizational Factors

Two factors dominate the list of organizational barriers to change.[11]

1. *Power and territory*. Power and territory are derived from the control of certain resources. These might include money, information, and certain activities to name but a few. Any change in the organization's culture which threatens a dimunition of power and territory for a group or department will certainly raise barriers to change.

2. *Organization structure*. Organizations develop structures to achieve certain strategic goals. In those organizations in which the structure is characteristically rigid with narrowly defined jobs and tightly defined communication flows, change can be retarded. To the extent that departments differ and the change calls for freer and greater communication which is essential in an organization that embraces an ethical value system, this change can be slowed.

EFFECTING CULTURAL CHANGE

Given these potential barriers to developing a more ethical culture, how can change be effected? Several models exist but

11. Don Hellriegel, John W. Slocum, Jr. and Richard W. Woodman, *Organizational Behavior*.

Beckhard offers the following summary models which contains many of the change propositions found in other models.[12]

1. The organization must recognize a need to change its culture. In the case of adopting a more active ethical posture, this impetus for change is found on the front pages of most newspapers. Typically, the major change agent is the president or CEO. Without his or her recognition for the need to change and subsequent backing of the effort, efforts at change are likely to fail. More about recognizing this need for change is discussed in the next chapter.

2. Once a commitment has been made at the top level, this same commitment must be sold throughout the entire organization. Many experts recommend coopting recognized significant others within the organization in the planning phases of the change. Letting these individuals develop and establish appropriate core values and standards will give them more commitment in selling these values to other individuals. When this approach is reinforced

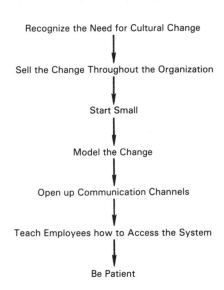

Figure 4-1 A Flow Chart for Effecting Cultural Change

Adapted from: Danny R. Arnold, Louis M. Capella and Delia M. Sumrall, "Hospital Challenge: Using Change Theory and Processes to Adopt and Implement the Marketing Concept," *Journal of Health Care Marketing*, 7, no. 2 (June 1987), 15–24.

Recognize the Need for Cultural Change

Sell the Change Throughout the Organization

Start Small

Model the Change

Open up Communication Channels

Teach Employees how to Access the System

Be Patient

12. Richard Beckhard, *Organization Development: Strategies and Models* (Reading, Mass.: Addison-Wesley Publishing Company, 1973).

by the active participation of top management, the selling job is much easier.

3. Start with minor changes instead of trying to induce a broad sweeping change. Early success will go far toward introducing other aspects of the change. When an individual acts in an ethically notable manner, make a hero out of him or her and this will tell the rest of the organization that management is serious about the change.

4. Using other organizations as models can help effect the change. Doing so provides concrete examples of how organizational behavior ought to be.

5. Free flowing communication with numerous open channels is a must. In a subsequent chapter we point out that companies which have multiple means of communicating and dealing with ethical problems seem to be the companies most comfortable with their new ethical postures. When a channel is used to identify an ethical problem, make sure that something is done about it. This assures the individual who is attempting to follow the proper procedure that the organization really means what it says. Not to establish these communication channels is to retard if not condemn the change process.

6. Employees must know how to activate any new procedures associated with the change. If employees are encouraged to talk about potential or actual ethical dilemmas with an ombudsman or an ethics committee, he or she must know how to do it. This involves a certain degree of training for the individual.

7. As was mentioned earlier, this change will take some time. Confidence and trust have to be developed and the new system tested. Management must realize that an organization cannot develop a new culture overnight. It will take time and a consistent effort on the part of those directing the change. In some instances, this cultural change may take years to effect.

Exercises for Chapter 4

Bank of Boston's Code of Conduct*

"The only true and useful secret (of success) is to conduct the business so as to acquire the fullest confidence of your fellow citizens and neighbors."

This advice was given to our founders early in the Corporation's history. Over the years, we have grown from a single bank to an international holding company. Yet that advice maintains its usefulness as a guiding principle.

Inspiring confidence requires that all employees uphold a rigorous standard of integrity. Accordingly, the Corporation has established this Code of Conduct and expects each and every individual employee to honor the letter and spirit of its provisions.

Integrity

Exhibit standards of personal integrity and professional conduct that reflect positively on your association with the Corporation.

Confidentiality

Maintain strict confidentiality of customer, employee and corporate records and information.

Quality

Strive to provide products and service of the highest quality.

Compliance

Conduct personal and business dealings in compliance with the letter, spirit and intent of all relevant laws, regulations, and policies.

Conflict of Interest

Refrain from using the Corporation's reputation or resources for personal gain, and avoid outside activities or influences which conflict with, compete with, or impair the performance of your duties or which give the appearance of doing so.

Objectivity

Make decisions and allocate resources objectively without regard to friendship or personal taste.

*Distributed to Bank of Boston's employees in 1985.

Personal Finances

Manage personal finances, including investments, in a manner consistent with your employment by a fiduciary institution.

Social Responsibility

Seek opportunities to participate and, if possible, to play a leadership role in addressing issues of concern to the communities we serve.

Decency

Demonstrate courtesy, respect, honesty, fairness, and decency in all relationships with customers, competitors, the general public and with other employees.

Accountability

Report questionable, unethical or illegal activity to your manager without delay.

Under a Cloud*

Bank of Boston Faces Image Problem Likely to Linger for Years

It Pleads Guilty to a Felony, Admits Handling Money for Alleged Mob Leaders Poor Judgment, Chief Says

Because 1983 was a mediocre year at Bank of Boston Corp., with profit before securities transactions up only 5 percent, the management-incentive plan offered what was considered a mediocre reward for the top 54 officers: a bonus averaging 20 percent.

Then, after what the bank says was a suggestion from the board, William L. Brown, ending his first year as the $350,000-a-year chairman and chief executive, arranged to double the reward—but only for himself and three others.

Richard A. Smith, the head of the board's compensation committee and the chairman of General Cinema Corp. (on whose com-

*David Wessell and Bob Davis, *Wall Street Journal,* March 7, 1985, pp. 1, 29. Used with permission.

pensation committee Mr. Brown himself sits) defends the bonus, "Those with the greatest responsibility get...the greatest reward," he says.

The incident shows something of the style of Mr. Brown, who now is disclaiming responsibility for a controversy that is humbling the company's First National Bank of Boston, the nation's sixteenth-largest bank. In the past month, the bank has pleaded guilty to a felony and paid a $500,000 fine. It has admitted handling millions of dollars in cash for reputed organized-crime leaders without alerting the government. Federal officials trying to stop money laundering have made an example of it, and three congressional committees plan hearings into its cash operations.

What went wrong at Bank of Boston, which in many respects has a reputation as solid as the red granite of its headquarters building? "The record shows a lot of lack of judgment," Mr. Brown has admitted. It also shows surprisingly sloppy controls for a $22 billion bank and a devastating inability to deal with a public crisis. And it shows an aggressiveness that has helped the bank grow larger than its three nearest Boston competitors combined but also seems to have bred arrogance that has become a corporate hallmark.

The upshot: an image problem likely to shadow Bank of Boston for years. And in banking, a business based on trust and good judgment, such a shadow can make new corporate customers, talented young managers and government regulators skittish. Citing the recent problems, for instance, Rhode Island officials are reopening hearings into Bank of Boston's plan to acquire a Providence bank.

How It Began

The controversy began with a Justice Department investigation of Gennaro J. Angiulo, who is alleged to be the head of organized crime in Boston and who has been charged with racketeering and loan-sharking. For at least seven years, the bank says, Mr. Angiulo and his associates walked into a small branch in Boston's Italian North End with paper bags full of cash and walked out with cashier's checks—163 of them worth $2.2 million between 1980 and 1983 alone. Federal regulations, enacted in 1972 and toughened in 1980 to combat money laundering, require reports on such transactions.

But the bank exempted the Angiulos from the requirement.

Mr. Brown, who refused to be interviewed for this article, has blamed the omission on "poor judgment" by some employees. Neither the bank nor any employee has been charged with a crime in connection with the Angiulos.

While tracking the Angiulos' cash, federal investigators discovered that the bank also wasn't reporting shipments of U.S. currency to and from Swiss banks, in violation of a 1980 federal requirement. Describing the problems as "a systems failure," the bank last month pleaded guilty to "knowingly and willfully" failing to report $1.22 billion in shipments between 1980 and 1984, despite official letters and at least one phone call with a senior Treasury official alerting the bank to the requirement.

Bank's Position

"There weren't any broad failures, in our opinion. There were a series of isolated situations," insists Barry Allen, the bank's vice president for communications.

Even so, the admissions were startling, coming from a bank that has dominated New England for generations. John Hancock signed its charter in 1784. Bank of Boston was the first U.S. bank to offer commercial loans running more than 90 days. By following its wool, textile and shipping customers overseas in the nineteenth century, it cultivated an international business unusual for a bank its size. (Equally unusual, the bank outsmarted Fidel Castro in 1959. Says Donald L. Miller, a retired executive vice president: "When Castro was at Harvard stadium speaking as the liberator of Cuba, the bank was figuring out how to get its assets out of the country." Unlike a lot of banks, it managed to do so.)

Because the bank's lending policies were—and remain—bolder than those of other Yankee bankers, Bank of Boston fueled New England's recovery from the demise of its textile industry. Its loans to infant high-technology companies such as Data General Corp. and Wang Laboratories Inc. helped make them two of the region's economic mainstays. "The bank has been more reliable, imaginative, aggressive and innovative than any bank we have ever dealt with," says Daniel E. Hogan, the chairman and chief executive of Standex International Corp., who says his Salem, N.H. diversified manufacturing company wouldn't have grown forty-fold in 25 years without Bank of Boston's aid.

The bank, of course, benefited as well. In 20 years, its loan portfolio has expanded to $14.6 billion from $1.5 billion. It has avoided the disastrous loan losses that have plagued some other big banks recently, and it generally is slightly more profitable than its competitors. Last year's operating income was $118.9 million, off about 12 percent, but net income, after nonrecurring items, rose 21 percent to $164.1 million. "A lot of banks would like to be in our position financially," says Mr. Allen, the bank spokesman.

Some of the bank's innovations, and its freewheeling ways, are the legacy of the late Serge Semenenko, a Russian-born Harvard M.B.A. who joined it as a clerk in 1926 and resigned as vice chairman in 1967 amid controversy over his investments in companies to which the bank was lending money. Mr. Semenenko, who headed a "special industries" lending unit, extended loans to some companies that other banks shunned, including movie studios and the ailing *Saturday Evening Post*. John Chequers, who worked for Mr. Semenenko, recalls: "Serge would come back after his three-month summer vacation and say, 'I did the following eight deals on my boat.' "

Mr. Semenenko encouraged loan officers to make daring loans, often backed by unconventional, though solid, collateral, and he dispensed with the traditional bank loan committees. Although his unit had exceptional freedom, most Bank of Boston loan officers were on longer leashes than were those at other banks.

"There was a joke that ran around the bank that any loan officer could lend to the bank's legal limit," says Robert Nyere, who retired in 1979 as the head of retail banking. In the mid-1960s, a single loan officer could lend money to a "research-based" company, but it took two to turn one down, adds Mr. Miller, who oversaw commercial lending from 1966 to 1982. After the bank was forced to double its loan-loss provision in 1974, however, it finally established a formal credit committee, Mr. Miller says.

One such incident occurred ten years ago, when the city faced its worst fiscal crisis since the Depression. According to James Young, a former deputy mayor, Mr. Hill spent days conferring with city officials and the bank eventually did buy city notes, but its heavy-handed demands—including an unsuccessful call for a state guarantee of certain city debts—angered some officials.

"We came out of it not wanting any institution to have as much power as the First (National Bank) had during that period," Mr. Young recalls. For the next few years, the city pointedly chose a New York bank, Morgan Guaranty Trust Co., as its lead underwriter (a position now held by Kidder, Peabody & Co.).

Last year, Bank of Boston's top officers were publicly forced to back off their refusal to discuss local lending practices with leaders of a watchdog group that had met with the chief executives of other Boston banks. "If all they're asking is to sit down and have a cup of coffee with the president or chairman, it's not an unreasonable request," said the state bank commissioner, Paul Bulman, who delayed action on a pending acquisition to underline his displeasure. The bank's president, Ira Stepanian, but not Mr. Brown, later met with the group.

So, few supporters rushed to Bank of Boston's defense when its problems surfaced—indeed, a few small towns withdrew their deposits. And in the past few weeks, the bank has demonstrated an almost tragic capacity to make a bad situation worse.

Needing a big law firm to represent it before congressional committees, it hired Covington & Burling, which is suing 222 Democratic congressmen over a disputed Indiana seat. The bank spent months negotiating with federal prosecutors for an indictment that omitted any mention of the Angiulo family—and, just four days after the indictment, found itself unprepared to answer questions about the family's cash transactions. It called a press conference to explain its guilty plea—and argued that a fine of even $1 was excessive, although it had allowed 1,163 international cash transactions to go unreported. It summoned reporters again ten days later to explain its relationship with the Angiulos—and, though taping the session itself, attempted unsuccessfully to bar reporters' tape recorders.

116

The bank says its business hasn't been harmed, but the pending congressional hearings and the continuing investigation into the Angiulos' finances promise to keep it on the defensive.

One Embarrassment

Still, loan officers retained enormous freedom, which at least once brought ignominy to the bank. In 1978, a bank loan officer initiated and helped finance the purchase of World Jai Alai Inc., a Miami-based legalized-gambling company, by Roger Wheeler, then the chairman of Telex Corp. (The $30 million loan was one of few that the bank made to gambling concerns.) World Jai Alai's former president, John B. Callahan, was an occasional consultant to the bank and an alleged associate of organized-crime figures.

Florida investigators questioned the bank's "moral character" and its ties to Mr. Callahan after they learned that the loan officer had tacitly offered Mr. Callahan his old job at World Jai Alai back if anything happened to the company's chief executive. In 1981, Mr. Wheeler was murdered and, a year later, so was Mr. Callahan. Neither crime has been solved.

For years, the bank has been trying to rein in its loan officers—without fully succeeding. William F. Thompson, who took over the special-industries unit in 1972, lacked Mr. Semenenko's flamboyance, but he retained much of his influence in Hollywood and expanded special industries into cable television and venture capital.

Unit Split Up

After Mr. Thompson quit to form a venture-capital company in 1983, Bank of Boston broke up the unit and split its operations between two executive vice presidents. Movie lending was buried deep in the bank's bureaucracy, but the present chief movie lender, Martha Croninshield, retains considerable autonomy. She makes loan commitments fast, movie executives say, and though only a vice president, she has ready access to Mr. Brown. Says Geoffrey

Holmes, a vice president of Warner Communications Inc.: "First National (Bank of Boston) is at least as aggressive as before."

But it is the bank's management style, rather than its lending practices, that lies behind the current embarrassment. Until retiring in 1983, Richard D. Hill, the bank's personable chief executive for 11 years, spent much of his time outside the office as a director of five large local companies, a trustee of Dartmouth College and a leader of such groups as the Reserve City Bankers Association.

"He wanted to be on a lot of boards," says Mr. Miller, the retired executive. "He never wanted anything to do with operations. To be in operations, you have to be in the bank all the time."

Still Aloof

Mr. Brown, just two years younger than Mr. Hill, largely ran the bank—but was nearly invisible to community leaders. He gave only his second interview, on the occasion of the bank's 200th anniversary. The change in chairmen two years ago changed the atmosphere inside the bank, employees say, by emphasizing the distance between top managers and those below. Mr. Brown, for instance, has stopped showing up at the daily morning coffee hour, once a morale-boosting occasion for junior loan officers to talk with senior executives. Instead, coffee now is delivered to the bank's second-floor executive suite.

What hasn't changed, though, is the bank's aloofness, which has generated resentment locally and caused sometimes sticky relations with Boston's city hall.

Questions

1. From the information presented in the *Wall Street Journal,* prepare a culture audit on the Bank of Boston. What core values emerge from the description of the Bank of Boston's corporate history?

2. How does the informal culture of the Bank of Boston differ from the formal culture implicit in their Codes of Conduct?
3. Do you see any subcultural influences at the Bank of Boston? If so, what are they?
4. How has the history of the Bank of Boston influenced their actual corporate culture?
5. Is their problem, in your opinion, really "a systems failure"?

Chapter 5

Parallel Planning— an Overview

Thus far we have suggested that in order to develop corporate social responsibility and ethical behavior, strong organizational values must be established. These values must be reinforced enough to occasionally overcome personal values that would direct employees to behave unethically. It has also been suggested that the most effective way of establishing strong corporate values is through the corporate culture, but so far we have only hinted at the process for determining and incorporating these values. This chapter provides an overview to such an approach with subsequent chapters scanning key aspects to the process.

INTEGRATING SOCIAL RESPONSIBILITY AND ETHICS INTO THE STRATEGIC PLANNING PROCESS

The preceding chapter provides a view of corporate culture that is instrumental in the integration of social responsibility and ethics into the strategic planning process. The basis of this integration process is the idea of ethical core values acting as guidelines for the development of corporate plans.

Without the integration of concerns about ethics and social responsibility at the very beginning of the planning process, as well as throughout the process, the organizational culture may not provide the checks and balances needed to develop ethical and socially responsible business programs. Corporate values of profit and efficiency tend to dominate most organizational cultures, particularly in the absence of the overt addition of ethical and socially responsible values. This situation arises because the organization reinforces its members at all levels on the basis of achieving profitability or efficiency objectives. *Though profit and efficiency must remain central values within the culture, they must be balanced by other values that help define the types and limits of activities designed to achieve those objectives and by values describing other important ethical and socially responsible behaviors.*

Figure 5-1 depicts the suggested parallel planning approach by which ethical and socially responsible core values can be introduced into the organizational culture.[1] It applies to the development of a new set of core values and corporate strategy. However, the development of one when the other already exists follows a similar pattern.

Two Inputs and Two Outputs of the Planning Process

Figure 5-1 contains two inputs to the system and two outputs from it. Both the inputs and the outputs have been divided into human and nonhuman considerations. This approach is needed because ethics is a uniquely human topic, and ethical problems occur only when a human system (individual, group, or organization) interacts with either a human or nonhuman system. The split is also appropriate because of the use of the human corporate culture to direct and control behavior within the organization.

Elements of what is meant by the two inputs should be familiar to individuals who understand the strategic planning process. Part of the environmental input is the traditional threats and opportunities to the organization *from* the environment. Further, part of the corporate input is the traditional analysis of organizational strengths and weaknesses for attaining business objectives. However, another crucial aspect of this analysis is now an attempt to empathize, or clearly understand, the meaning of these inputs to the supplier of them. Unfortunately, this latter step seems to be omitted by most of the current management literature. Without understanding the meaning of the inputs to the parties involved, it will be impossible to analyze the effects of subsequent actions on them.

1. Some of the ideas that follow are adapted from an article by Donald P. Robin and R. Eric Reidenbach, "Social Responsibility, Ethics, and Marketing Strategy: Closing the Gap Between Concept and Application," *Journal of Marketing* (January 1987), pp. 44–58.

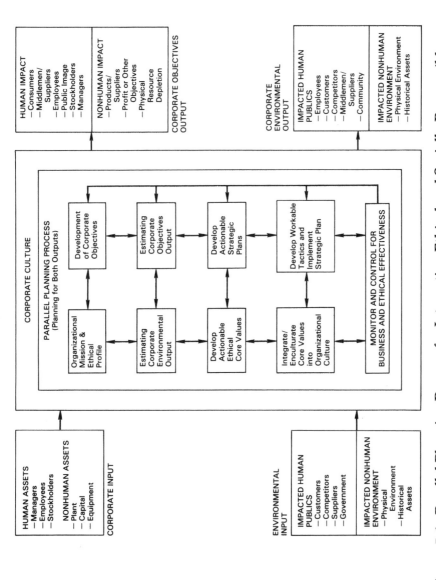

Figure 5-1 Parallel Planning Process for Integrating Ethical and Socially Responsible Analysis into the Strategic Planning Process.

Figure 5-1 also recognizes two outputs. Part of the corporate output will be recognized as a traditional consideration in the strategic planning process. Achieving corporate profit, along with the impacts on all of the other listed outputs related to that corporate economic objective, are all part of the strategic planning analysis. Of course, primary noneconomic objectives in the not-for-profit sector also follow the same pattern, with only slight changes in wording necessary to make the "corporate objectives output" appropriate for them. Obviously, this output is central to the success of the organization and is analyzed in detail in the strategic planning literature.

The "corporate environmental output" is seldom treated in the planning literature, and if it is mentioned at all, it is usually treated as an ancillary issue. It is almost never integrated into the strategic planning process, and that is unfortunate. This output must be understood and to do so requires that the planners develop empathy or careful understanding for the effects of each planned action on each impacted party. Thus, the analysis of consumers considers not only whether they will buy the product, but also whether there are unknown but important impacts on them. Similar concerns for employees are also appropriate. Wages and benefits are one output that is part of the corporate objective, but if there are unknown damaging effects from the work, that is part of the environmental output as well. Similar impacts on all of the publics listed in Figure 5-1 are often either unanalyzed or are conveniently pushed aside. Conveniently forgetting or simply not bothering to deal with these tough issues seems to be an unfortunately common approach when confronted with them. Specifically requiring an analysis of these issues is the first step in reducing the probability of unethical practices.

It is the purpose of the parallel planning process to plan for both outputs. The process must be parallel for the effects on the environment to be fully integrated into the strategic plan. Doing so produces a second step for reducing the probability of unethical behavior due to conveniently not dealing with these tough problems. Further, parallel planning for both outputs allows the planners to (1) anticipate ethical problems, (2) apply social responsibility and ethical analysis tools, (3) determine those corporate values that are most important to the organization, and (4) integrate them into the corporate culture.

Role of the Corporate Culture

The corporate culture is shown in Figure 5-1 as surrounding the entire planning process. It both influences the process and is influenced by it. One of the first tasks of top management is to understand this culture, or the influence exerted by it may go unnoticed causing the planning to be less effective. Understanding the corporate culture is also necessary since our intention is to influence and change it. Chapter 4 provided the general background and tools for such analysis and change, and this chapter focuses on the specific process for integrating these changes.

In the absence of an overt, coherent, consistent, and integrated set of ethical core values, the organization must develop its own. The set of assumptions constituting the organization's value system comes from the leadership of the organization and the experiences of its employees. Two assumptions tend to thrive in most organizations' culture—profits and efficiency. Management preaches these twin values, and employees know they will be rewarded for practicing them. *When profits and efficiency dominate the culture without the balancing effects of ethical core values, strategic planning and other behaviors are directed principally, if not solely, by those values.* An example that was discussed in Chapter 2 is Ford Motor Company's response to their defective fuel system problem in the Pinto. Ford's planners conducted a cost/benefit analysis and concluded that it would be more profitable to settle any claims resulting from the fuel system problem out of court than to make the design change that would have eliminated the problem. An integrated set of ethical core values might have tempered their purely economic response with ethical considerations.

A second aspect important to the enculturation process is the positive impact from the integration of socially responsible and ethical core values throughout the activities of organizations. For ethical core values to have a positive effect on planning, the integration of the values must follow the same pattern as the strategic planning function. They must become part and parcel of the same planning procedure. To be most effective, these core values should become part of the mission and the organization's culture. They should be tested against the external environment and the internal publics and monitored for their appropriateness in light of organizational environmental change. Once achieved, these core values give ethical direction to the business activities of the organization. That direction tends to be more uniform and focused toward ends that are desired by top management.

The corporate culture approach, as supported by literature in the United States, has a strong basis in successful Japanese management practices. Deal and Kennedy state:

> A major reason the Japanese have been so successful, we think, is their continuing ability to maintain a very strong and cohesive culture throughout the entire country. Not only do individual businesses have strong cultures, but the links among business, the banking industry, and the government are also cultural and also very powerful. Japan, Inc. is actually an expansion of the corporate culture idea on a national scale. Although this homogenization of values would not fit American culture on a national scale, we do think that it has been very effective for individual companies. In fact, a strong culture has almost always been the driving force behind continuing success in American business.[2]

An example of the corporate culture approach in American business is seen in Cummins Engine.[3] Historically, the company has had close relations with an independent local union and a special concern for the community in which it is located. Further, the company has emphasized extraordinary service to its customers. Both of these activities represent core values of the company that were planned by top management, are communicated clearly to the employees, and are presented as logically consistent with other goals and values of the organization.

2. Terrence E. Deal and Allan A. Kennedy, *Corporate Cultures* (Reading, MA: Addison-Wesley Publishing Company, 1982), p. 5.

3. Vijay Sathe, "How to Decipher and Change Organizational Culture," in *Managing Corporate Cultures*, ed. R. H. Kilman and Associates (San Francisco: Jossey-Bass, Inc., 1986).

When the corporate culture approach is successful, there is a substantial amount of openness in the organization. People know what's happening and why. Only through such openness can the organization benefit from all of the capabilities of its employees. For example, in Robert Waterman's book, *The Renewal Factor,* he seems to stress this openness in several ways.[4] Five of his eight major themes deal directly with openness and flexibility based on freedom to information.

If openness in the corporate culture is essential to success in attaining business objectives, it is absolutely critical to achieving socially responsible and ethical performance. In an "ethics prize winner" article in the *Harvard Business Review,* Sir Adrian Cadbury notes that "...openness and ethics go together and...actions are unethical if they won't stand scrutiny."[5] This simple rule of thumb by itself can prevent a considerable amount of unethical behavior. The idea that "everyone will know" in an open culture with carefully planned ethical values can be an effective deterrent.

Mission Statement and Ethical Profile as Guides for Corporate Objectives

The organizational mission statement and ethical profile guide the development of corporate objectives. As these objectives are being developed, however, a feedback function also occurs, whereby the mission statement and the ethical profile are questioned, elaborated, and clarified. The corporate objectives anticipate the two corporate outputs, and as alternative objectives are considered, the expected outputs from each are tested against the predetermined mission and profile. As real objectives are tested in this manner, certain aspects of the corporate mission and ethical profile may seem to be unrealistic and need to be adapted. For example, part of the ethical profile may include continuous growth in employment. However, after testing the realistic corporate objec-

4. Robert Waterman, *The Renewal Factor: How to Get and Keep the Competitive Edge* (New York: Bantam Books, Inc., 1987).

5. Sir Adrian Cadbury, "Ethical Managers Make Their Own Rules," *Harvard Business Review* (September–October 1987), pp. 69–73.

tives available to the organization, it may become apparent that this aspect of the profile is unattainable. The process could also suggest other options such as the possibility of expanded benefits for existing employees. Thus, feedback becomes two directional and the process becomes iterative. Tools to aid in this process are discussed in the next chapter.

Just as the organization's mission statement guides the entire planning process, it also guides the development of the organization's desired ethical profile. The profile is a projection to external publics with whom the organization interacts, identifying how the organization chooses to interact with those publics. Its importance and function are similar to those of the mission statement in that it provides broad, general guidelines for identifying relevant ethical opportunities and developing more specific objectives.

Profile Sources

There are numerous sources of ideas for aiding the organization's management in developing an ethical and socially responsible profile. These sources parallel the ones that would be suggested for establishing any organizational mission. However, the application of these sources has a somewhat different connotation than that typically found in the management literature. Specific ideas for a socially responsible and ethical profile can come from threats, opportunities, organizational history and mission, current corporate image, personal preferences of management and owners, plus special organizational resources and competences. In fact, ethical profiles can be generated from any combination of these sources particularly in conjunction with the ideas of social responsibility and ethics discussed in Chapter 3. Further, and perhaps even more important, these ideas come from the empathy and understanding of the corporate and environmental inputs.

For example, threats to the organization can come from any of the publics affected by the basic business of the firm, as well as any one of the uncontrollable environments. In this context, threats can be anything that might discredit the organization in the eyes of the general public or their representatives, or something that might be deemed unethical in the sense already described. Phillips 66 has reacted to a potential threat in the form of perceived environmental damage to areas in which it operates by promoting environmental concern. The company's positive record in this regard gives substance to this dimension of its profile.

Opportunities also provide a means of developing the ethical profile of the organization. The social problems or needs of all elements of society are a beginning point for analysis. In addition, the problems of directly affected publics such as buyers, competitors, and employees should receive special attention in the search for opportunities. McDonald's concern for the needs of families of children who are chronically or terminally ill was the impetus for Ronald McDonald Houses, which were established near treatment centers to enable the family to stay together during the child's care. In this case, McDonald's is responding to an opportunity in a portion of its market.

The organization's history, mission, and current image may provide some of the dimensions of the ethical profile. The financial industry typically relies on history and tradition as a source of its ethical profile to establish a sense of trust between an organization and investing publics. This profile has been tarnished somewhat by the actions of such financial firms as E. F. Hutton, cited for a check kiting operation, and The Bank of Boston, charged with the laundering of drug money. Personal preferences of top management or owners are a similar source of an ethical profile because these individuals provide its necessary support and enforcement.

Finally, the special resources and competences that organizations use to satisfy and facilitate their design, production, and marketing of products and services can be applied to project ethical and socially responsible profiles to the different publics. For example, Procter & Gamble loaned some of its special resource expertise to the Centers for Disease Control for investigation of toxic shock syndrome linked to the Rely tampon product.[6] A creative look at such competences and resources can be useful in suggesting dimensions of an ethical profile.

6. Dean Rotbart, and John A. Prestbo, "Killing a Product," *Wall Street Journal*, November 3, 1980, p. 21.

The corporate mission and ethical profile act as standards with which corporate objectives can be compared to determine whether their *anticipated* impacts on the corporate environmental or objectives output will be incongruent with the mission or the profile. The word "anticipated" is stressed because it is not always possible to predict either the corporate objectives output or the corporate environmental output. Nevertheless, basic corporate objectives are directly influenced by the newly developed ethical profile as well as the more traditional mission statement.

Specific profile dimensions might include such ideas as customer orientation, environmental concern and involvement, product reliability, job growth, progressive/innovative aid to local communities, and concern for quality. It is important to note that it is the total profile rather than the individual dimensions that should be the focus of attention at this stage. All of the parts must fit together to produce a logical, internally consistent, and easily communicated ethical profile. The benefit of such coherence is similar to the benefit accruing from internally consistent individual behavior. Without a consistent profile and mission statement, the organization projects a split personality to its external environment, as well as to its own stockholders, managers, and employees.

Anticipating the Corporate Environmental and Objectives Output

In the process of deciding on corporate objectives an estimate of the environmental and objectives output was developed. However, once the objectives are in place a thorough business and environmental analysis is necessary. The traditional business analysis focuses on the items in the corporate objectives output and considers alternative strategic plans for attaining them. During this process, one- to five-year projections on sales and profits are typical.

At the same time that the organization is projecting the corporate objectives output from alternative strategies, projections of the corporate environmental output should also occur. In fact, the two efforts should be united for maximum efficiency and are only separated in Figure 5-1 for emphasis. The same zeal and level of analysis that is expended on the business analysis should be part of identifying and analyzing the impacted environments. This analysis focuses on the positive and negative impacts of each alternative strategy on each of the human and nonhuman environments. In the case of the human publics, primary attention should be centered on their perceptions of the effects of the strategy rather than speculations by other parties.

The identification and analysis of these potentially affected publics enable the strategic planner to fine-tune the profile dimensions into specific core values that will be used in the enculturation stage. It is at this second stage, however, that the concern for the organization's impact on these identified publics is combined with the traditional management concern for the impact of the environment on the effectiveness of the alternative strategic plans and resultant profit expectations. This concern for the dual impacts (those of the environment on the organization and of the organization on the environment) represents a significant departure from typical planning processes in which the focus is generally one way. Moreover, this dual focus differentiates the concern for ethical and socially responsible planning from issue management, which is typically concerned with controlling the harmful effects of negative publicity (see Gatewood and Carroll,[7] Policano,[8] Sherrell et al.[9]).

Each identified environmental output must be analyzed carefully to determine the potential impact of corporate action. Specifically, the broad ethical profile and its constituent dimensions are used as the basis for judgment in this analysis. If the corporate activity appears to be incongruent with the desired ethical profile, the activity must be reconsidered.

7. Elizabeth Gatewood and Archie B. Carroll, "The Anatomy of Corporate Social Response: The Rely, Firestone 500, and Pinto Cases," *Business Horizons*, 24 (September–October 1981), 9–16.

8. Christopher Policano, "Case Study: A. H. Robbins and the Dalkon Shield," *Public Relations Journal*, 41, no. 3 (1985) 16–19, 21.

9. Daniel Sherrell, R. Eric Reidenbach, Ellen Moore, Jay Wagle, and Thaddeus Spratlin, "Exploring Consumer Response to Negative Publicity," *Public Relations Review*, 6, no. 1 (1985) 13–29.

An Example of the Analysis Process

As an extended example of this analysis process, suppose that we consider the controversial but topical situation that occurred between Nestlé S.A. and infant formula buyers in less developed countries (LDCs). Examples of the literature on this subject include: Higgens,[10] *Newsweek,*[11] Adleman,[12] Miller,[13] *Wall Street Journal,*[14] Barovick,[15] Pagan, [16] *World Health Organization,*[17] Gerlach,[18] Nichel,[19] Minus,[20] and *Business Week.*[21]

The controversy began about 1974 when a group in Germany singled out Nestlé from a number of infant formula producers and accused them of "killing babies,"—a lack of respect for human rights and an obvious ethical problem particularly when viewed from a deontological perspective. The concern voiced by the group came from the belief that Nestlé was encouraging third world mothers to give up breast-feeding in favor of the infant formula. The arguments suggested that two significant negative impacts fol-

10. Kevin Higgens, "Nestlé Gains Formula Accord: Product Boycott is Suspended," *Marketing News,* February 17, 1984, pp. 5, 7.

11. "Nestlé's Costly Accord," *Newsweek,* 103, February 6, 1984, 52.

12. Carol Adleman, "Infant Formula, Science, and Politics," *Policy Review,* (Winter 1983), p. 15.

13. Fred D. Miller, Jr., *Out of the Mouths of Babes: The Infant Formula Controversy* (Bowling Green, OH: Social Philosophy and Policy Center, 1983).

14. "Why Are Babies Dying?" the *Wall Street Journal,* February 9, 1983, p. 26.

15. Richard L. Barovick, "Activism on a Global Scale," *Public Relations Journal,* (June 1982), p. 32.

16. Rafael D. Pagan, Jr., *Nestlé Announces Its Implementation of the WHO Code on Infant Formula,* (Washington, D.C.: Nestlé Coordination Center for Nutrition, March 16, 1982).

17. World Health Organization, *International Code of Marketing of Breast-Milk Substitutes,* (Geneva: World Health Organization, 1981).

18. Luther P. Gerlach, "The Flea and The Elephant: Infant Formula Controversy," *Society,* 17 (September/October 1980), 51–57.

19. Hermann Nichel, "The Corporation Haters," *Fortune,* 101, June 16, 1980, 126–36.

20. Paul M. Minus, "The Infant Formula Issue: Other Perspectives," *The Christian Century,* 96, June 20–27, 1979, 662–64.

21. "A Boycott Over Infant Formula," *Business Week,* April 23, 1979, pp. 137, 140.

lowed from the use of the Nestlé formula in such a situation. First, breast milk dried up which (1) eliminated it as a feeding option, and (2) because women are less likely to conceive when breast-feeding, they lost its contraceptive effects. Second, and perhaps more important to the controversy, the infant formula was either being excessively diluted or mixed with impure water. The results were malnutrition, diarrhea, and in some cases death for the infants.

While other firms pulled out of the market, Nestlé continued to market their product to LDCs in the face of protests and boycotts. Nestlé's defense included a substantial volume of facts and figures attesting to benefits of the infant formula—even in developing countries (e.g., for an organized summary of these arguments see Miller 1983). These figures seem to show that the social benefits outweighed the social costs—a utilitarian based defense, and one which is traditionally invoked by organizations.

The decision could have been analyzed from a dual perspective using both philosophies which, in turn, could have produced a more acceptable marketing decision from Nestlé. The discussion in Chapter 3 suggested that a problem of this type should use a deontological analysis. Thus, Nestlé's utilitarian defense could have been expected to produce an unsympathetic response, as it indeed did. It is arguable whether a utilitarian analysis of the situation which included an adequate value for the suffering of the most influenced individuals would have produced the same conclusion suggested by deontological arguments. However, the language of those parties that attacked Nestlé for their marketing practices was decidedly deontological in character.

A number of the involved groups and organizations focused their attention on the ethical problems which they perceived were produced by the marketing practices. INFACT (Infant Formula Action Coalition) was the group that organized the boycott against Nestlé, and at one time it listed 44 groups or organizations which endorsed the boycott. Others that were heavily involved included the INBC (International Nestlé Boycott Committee), the United Methodist Task Force on Infant Formula, and the ICCR (Interfaith Center on Corporate Responsibility, an agency of the National Council of Churches). Eventually, the governments of the LDCs became involved in the controversy. However, the final settlement of the controversy occurred when agent organizations of the United Nations, specifically the World Health Organization (WHO) and UNICEF, became involved. The boycott of Nestlé was generally lifted when it agreed to follow the WHO's *International Code of Marketing Breast Milk Substitutes.*[22]

While it may not be reasonable to expect Nestlé to have anticipated the misuse of its formula, focusing on the nature of what might occur with consumer use could have provided insight into the potential ethical problems of marketing this product in LDCs. Better directions, less manipulative promotions, better selling techniques and educational programs might have been developed as contingency plans in the event of a problem.

No real ethical problem existed until Nestlé refused to alter its marketing programs. Nestlé's ethical culpability arises not so much from children dying from a misuse of the formula but from their ethical rationalization of the deaths. At this point the feedback of information had occurred as would normally take place in the monitoring and control function (Figure 5-1), but the company did not use it to make corrective actions. In effect, their utilitarian justification inflamed their opposition and increased the scale of the ethical issue. The information presented in Chapter 3 is simply a suggestion of how organizations can expect their behavior to be evaluated. If they don't respond using the same method of analysis as their critics, the results can easily follow a path similar to the one outlined in this example.

In analyzing this marketing strategy for its impact on consumers as one element of the corporate environmental output, Nestlé might have partially anticipated their problem. If they had, then the ethical profile and corporate objectives could have been adjusted to account for appropriate treatment of consumers. Also, ethical core values in the sales and marketing organization could have been created to satisfy this profile—the next step in the process.

One of the things that makes the Nestlé case a good example is that it illustrates the need for flexibility. As suggested, it is entirely possible that Nestlé could have missed the negative impact of its

22. World Health Organization, *International Code of Marketing of Breast-Milk Substitutes.*

product on LDC consumers. However, a monitor and control function as in Figure 5-1 would have provided feedback that an ethical reevaluation was needed when a problem became obvious. At that time, another analysis should have occurred. Then applying the ethical analysis learned in Chapter 3, Nestlé could have anticipated what actually followed.

Develop Actionable Ethical Core Values and Strategic Plans

The ethical profile developed in the first stage is the ethical "face" of the organization that it presents to all its relevant *external* publics. Figure 5-2 illustrates that ethical core values are constructed directly from this profile and are the *internal* guidelines for maintaining and supporting the ethical profile. Each core value flows directly from discussions on ethics and social responsibility as well as projected impacts on the corporate environmental output. Deon-

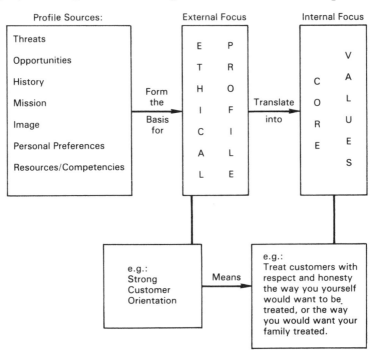

Figure 5-2 Extracting Slope Values for the Ethical Profile.

tological concern for the individual and utilitarian concern for the "greatest good" are combined in the construction of core values. Further, the family analogy described in Chapter 3 is another ingredient in the design of an ethical value system. The content of each value is intended to direct the behavior of organizational members in both the level and nature of performance. These core values are combined with the economic and efficiency values of the organization.

Some of the profile dimensions identified before provide examples of how core values can be extracted and developed from the profile. One dimension is the idea of a strong customer orientation. The problem with such a profile dimension is that without appropriate core values, employees of the organization may not know how to implement it. An appropriate core value must be actionable and easily understood. Thus, an appropriate statement of a core value to support the profile dimension of customer orientation might be:

> Treat customers with respect, concern, and honesty, the way you yourself would want to be treated or the way you would want your family treated.

A profile dimension of quality orientation for products and services might be translated into:

> Make and market products you would feel comfortable and safe having your own family use.

Similarly, a societal core value toward being environmentally concerned and involved might become:

> Treat the environment as though it were your own property.

Once developed, these core values have a controlling function in the design of specific tactics and operate as guides in developing the strategies. In another sense, the development of these core values is analogous to the development of a strategy. Though there may be several ways in which an organization can be customer oriented, the approach identified through the development of the core values reflects the method or strategy selected by the organization. This selection of core values is governed by the idea that there is a limitation to the number of core values that can be assimilated effectively. Alternative core values should be developed to satisfy the needs of the affected environmental and objectives output, and each should be tested to determine the fit between the core values and the affected public's concerns. In addition, the selected core values should be examined in light of their internal consistency. If they are inconsistent, management must return to the alternatives to find values that are consistent with each other and the profile. The process is iterative until the core values and the profile achieve the desired results.

Actionable strategic plans flow from establishing the corporate objectives. The latter process was described as considering alternative strategies in order to select acceptable objectives. At the second stage of estimating corporate objectives and environmental output, a thorough business analysis was suggested. In this business analysis projections of sales and profits for alternative strategic plans were developed. At the current stage of developing actionable strategic plans, these projections provide the basis for selection and further development of actionable strategic plans. Details concerning exactly what is meant by a strategic alternative are established at this stage and problems are fed back to earlier stages of the process. Attention to the two outputs continues in this stage. As the details of the strategic plan are developed it is possible that previously unforeseen outputs will be recognized, and as this occurs, the planners must take appropriate actions.

Core values become the day-to-day guidelines for developing and implementing the strategic plans. They are a filter of sorts through which plans are passed to ensure their ethical content. They balance profit and efficiency values with a concern for ethical and socially responsible conduct. That several firms have let the values of profitability and efficiency dictate their marketing activities is evident in a number of well-known examples.

Ford Motor Company's reaction to the fuel system problem in the Pinto reviewed in Chapter 2, is a good example of business plans conceived in the absence of well-developed ethical core values. If the core value for safe products, as has been suggested, had been adopted by Ford, then the Pinto problem should never have developed. Figure 5-3 is an illustration of this process. With the proposed core value, the altered policy decision should have occurred.

Johnson & Johnson demonstrates the type of response that would be expected from an organization that has a well-developed system of ethical core values. After the deaths of seven individuals who had consumed contaminated Tylenol capsules, Johnson & Johnson, within the week, had instituted a total product recall costing an estimated $50 million after taxes.[23] This action was taken even though the deaths were not the fault of the company but were

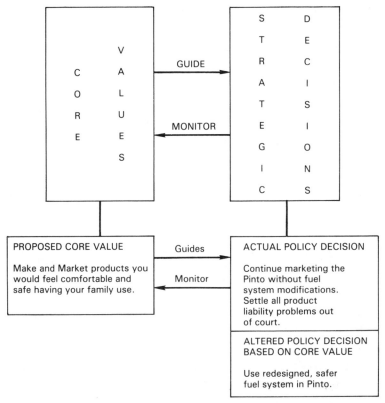

Figure 5-3 The Use of Core Values to Guide and Monitor Planning—the Pinto Example

23. Judith B. Gardner, "When a Brand Name Gets Hit by Bad News," *U.S. News and World Report,* November 8, 1982, p. 71.

attributable to the actions of some unknown individual outside the company. In addition, Johnson & Johnson spearheaded an industry move to develop more effective packaging to prevent tampering in the future. The company's behavior was reaffirmed when, after further tampering occurred, it quit producing capsules entirely. This action suggests that Johnson & Johnson considers the well-being of the customer to be as important as profitability in direct contrast to the response made by Ford Motor Company.

IMPLEMENTATION AND CONTROL

The Enculturation Process

Core values such as those suggested in the last section are also the principal tool for *implementing* the kind of ethical behavior desired. They are the major objectives of the enculturation of personnel. (See Pascale for insight into the enculturation process.)[24] This enculturation process instills the core values into each individual and integrates ethical and socially responsible concerns into the planning process. Ideally, each member of the organization would adopt those values when operating in his or her role of employee. Realistically, the process will not be perfect but should reach most employees if carefully implemented. While Chapter 7 discusses the implementation process in greater detail, several examples may add meaning to the current discussion.

Several companies that have experience with the enculturation of ethical values provide guidelines for how this process can be accomplished. General Dynamics, in the wake of the controversy about overcharging the U.S. government on military contracts, invested heavily in a program to increase the probability of future ethical behavior. General Dynamics uses seminars to communicate top management's concern for ethical behavior to its 100,000

24. Richard Pascale, "Fitting New Employees into the Company Culture," *Fortune,* May 18, 1984, pp. 28ff.

employees.[25] Backing up the seminars is a so-called "squeal clause" that not only protects whistleblowers who bring unethical behavior to the attention of the proper individuals, but also rewards them. Each division of General Dynamics has an ethics program director who is approachable when employees feel it is inappropriate to go to their immediate supervisor with a complaint. Over the ethics program director is a steering committee headed by two vice presidents whose responsibility it is to ensure implementation of the program. Changes in late 1988 against General Dynamics suggest that the enculturation process may not be complete or has been less than successful.

E. F. Hutton chairman Robert Fomon suggested that effective enculturation involves education, training, and compliance. He goes so far as to say their program "…will have teeth and systems of enforcement."[26] Robert V. Krikorian, chairman of Rexnord, has videotaped a speech on ethics to be shown to all employees in which he tells them to "walk away from business when it means doing anything unethical or illegal."[27]

Educationally, projecting a total mission statement and ethical profile is extremely difficult because it is couched in broad, general terms. Core values, in contrast, are more concrete and easier to understand, and hence are the primary vehicle for enculturation. With the selection of the core values, their communication, enculturation, and enforcement within the organization, top-level management has begun a process conducive to ethical and socially responsible decision making at all levels of the organization. Further, much of the frustration that has accompanied traditional efforts in these areas because of a lack of well-planned, logically consistent, and integrated efforts should be eliminated.

The enculturation process can take several years, and actually never ends as long as new members are added to the organization. There is a continual need to monitor behavior to determine whether the enculturation process is working. If the progress is too slow or if the core values are not producing anticipated behavior, the

25. Daniel B. Moskowitz, and John A. Byrne, "Where Business Goes to Stock Up on Ethics," *Business Week*, October 14, 1985, pp. 63, 66.

26. Ibid., p. 66.

27. Ibid., p. 66.

reasons for these problems should be identified. Once understood, the(se) cause(s) may force a complete reevaluation of the process beginning with the first step in Figure 5-1. Alternatively, a slight change in the manner of enforcing the core values or in the way they are stated may be all that is needed. Generalization is not possible, but a careful analysis of the reasons for the problem should be suggestive of its solution. Chapter 6 provides tools that should help managers in their analysis.

The successful enculturation of core values provides an overseeing function on not only the implementation of programs but also the planning of subsequent programs. It is at this point that the integration of ethical and social responsibility concerns into the parallel planning process is complete.

One other point is important. In addition to internal enculturation or behavior problems, unexpected external reactions from affected publics can arise. For example, customers may misuse a product in ways no one would reasonably expect as in the Nestlé case. When unanticipated and unintended ethical issues arise, moral excusing conditions might apply. DeGeorge lists three categories of excusing conditions:

> ...those conditions that preclude the possibility of the action; those conditions that preclude or diminish the required knowledge; and those conditions that preclude or diminish the required freedom.[28]

Thus, in the Nestlé example, if it were unreasonable for Nestlé management to know the consequences of marketing infant formula in third world countries, they might be excused from moral responsibility. However, once they did know, they should be held responsible. Clearly, this is not the case with Ford Motor Company and its marketing of the Pinto. Ford management knowingly marketed a defective and dangerous product and should not receive the benefit of the excusing argument.

With the radically changing environment facing corporate management, the addition of new employees with their personal

28. Richard R. DeGeorge, *Business Ethics*, 2nd ed. (New York: Macmillan Publishing Company, 1986), p. 83.

values, the constant innovation of products and services, and the changing public ethos concerning the practice of business, the process of developing core values and their enculturation must be ongoing. Just as personal value systems evolve and change in a society, so too must the core values that guide an organization's planning change. In both situations the value changes are reactions to shifts in the needs of society and its members.

AN EXAMPLE: PUTTING IT ALL TOGETHER

Suppose that you were CEO of a moderate-sized public utility located in the southeastern United States in late 1974. The company operates its own construction division that has been very successful in terms of costs and quality of work. The decade of the 1960s had seen more than a doubling of demand for your service, and the construction division had expanded accordingly. However, the cost of fuel in the early 1970s jumped radically and with the Arab oil embargo of 1973, and prices skyrocketed. Other problems included a substantial rate of inflation and the high costs of newly required anti-pollution equipment. It should be noted that much of this paragraph outlines the historical environmental impacts. The remainder of this section follows Figure 5-1, and in order to simplify reading the example, only the most relevant facts are presented in outline form.

Corporate Input

1. Well-trained and capable employees exist in the construction division.
2. Previous boom years have necessitated hiring large numbers of employees into the construction division and a large proportion of these employees are still working in the division.
3. Substantial affirmative action progress has been achieved over the last few years, but current proportions of black workers still don't match the number in the geographic area.

143

4. Reasonable borrowing limits have been reached and the current cost of debt is substantial.
5. Current stock prices are depressed below book value.
6. Since the company is a regulated monopoly, stockholders tend to seek secure income and growth.

Environmental Input

1. Federal agencies have been interested and active in the past concerning the company's hiring of minorities.
2. Consumer usage of the service has leveled off and is anticipated to remain about level for the near future.
3. The utility commission that regulates the price of the service has not allowed revenues to keep up with the rapidly increasing costs.
4. The company is in a moderately depressed (economically) area.

Corporate Culture

1. Operations throughout the company have been run informally with major decisions agreed upon with just a handshake.
2. A substantial trust developed between managers and other employees to use their capabilities in the best and most creative ways possible to solve problems.
3. Decentralized decision making is used throughout the company with the impact of the decision determining how high in the corporation it is made.
4. In the past, hiring and firing had been based solely on ability and performance.
5. Previous attempts at unionization of the construction division had failed by substantial margins.
6. No ethical profile or core values existed with respect to minority hiring except that the company met the legal equal opportunity requirements and hired as indicated (No. 4).

Parallel Planning Process

The organizational mission of the utility was to provide quality service in an efficient way so that stock and bondholders could receive reasonable rewards. While no ethical profile had been developed, the company seemed concerned about its public image and was upset by the recent federal agency actions concerning the hiring of blacks.

Because of its lack of any type of policy, mission, or profile for handling the obviously required cutbacks in construction division personnel, the CEO is left with a dilemma. Due to the required large size of needed layoff, the recency of black hirings, and the relative lack of training of black recruits, any approach that used seniority, value to the company, or a performance criteria would heavily act against blacks. The gains in affirmative action would be wiped out. This is the first potential environmental output. The other half of the dilemma is that if the company doesn't use its traditional performance standards for hiring and firing, the quality of the service supplied by the utility could deteriorate and white workers, who make up the majority of the construction division employees, could vote to unionize. In such a case, the successful informal corporate culture might be destroyed or at least damaged.

It is appropriate for the CEO to start to develop an ethical profile that includes this affirmative action dimension. Obviously, the profile would include many other dimensions, but for the purposes of this example, only affirmative action is considered in conjunction with the mission of the company.

Ethical analysis: deontology.   Probably the best approach for using deontological analysis is to attempt to place yourself behind a "veil of ignorance" and ask how you would feel in the place of the involved employees. The approach simply forces you to empathize with each employee. Suppose you were to instantly swap places with one of the employees in the construction division. You were to end up with only their skills, their history, their family, their attitudes and emotions, and their opportunity for employment elsewhere. The "veil" implies that you don't know which of these employees you will become, but before the switch, you get to make the rules about who is to be fired. How would you decide? Would you protect those workers who have done a good job but are least able to recover from the firing? Another approach?

Ethical analysis: utilitarianism. Calculating the greatest good for the greatest number, considering all effects now and in the future, is obviously a very difficult task. Even when the calculation process is at a detailed intuitive level instead of a numeric level, it is a considerable task. At the minimum it requires a substantial amount of empathy for each employee. Without this depth of understanding for the plight of each individual it is impossible, even at an intuitive level, to understand the effects of one approach over another. Once you have made a valid attempt to understand the impact on each individual, then a mental summing process must occur to estimate which action will produce the minimum harm. One tendency which should be warned against is discounting the future. Financial concepts like time adjusted return, in addition to the natural tendency to discount that which is more difficult to determine, makes it natural for business people to minimize the future effects of an action. Avoid doing so because it is discounting our future and the future of our children. The group favored in this type of analysis would depend on the individuals involved but if blacks as a group would experience greater injury, then this analysis would favor protecting them.

Social responsibility analysis. In Chapter 3 it was suggested that employees be treated as family, and in this company elements of that idea had already been adopted. The problem would seem to be that all of the people involved are employees. However, just as we would hope the family would adapt to the strengths and weaknesses of each family member, the analogy can be extended to do the same thing. This approach implies that we have real concern for all of our employees that we must dismiss, possibly to the point of trying to help them find other employment. Do we send the ones with special problems out and continue supporting those most able to help us? Or do we send out the most able and keep those most in need of our support? Or is there another approach that is a compromise of these two?

146

Results of analysis. Suppose that the initial analysis by the CEO favors strongly supporting the black minority and making affirmative action a core value of the company.

Objectives and Follow Through

At this stage we must evaluate the output of alternative strategies. Suppose that there are two initial strategies: (1) protect all black employees and then fire based on performance, and (2) fire employees based on performance only. In addition, we can assume that all released employees will be aided by a special task force to find new jobs. The first strategy reduces the quality of workforce performance, increases the likelihood of union activities, and may create some divisiveness between whites and blacks. However, it does protect affirmative action gains and supports the new core value. The second strategy produces a higher quality workforce and continues an existing policy, but it does not match the core value or profile and may discourage blacks if they are fired in large numbers.

Here the mission and the ethical profile seem to be in conflict. Now is the time for compromise and feedback. In Chapter 3, Aristotle was referenced as suggesting a golden mean of performance, and it was also suggested that the organization was not required to severely damage itself in attempting to be socially responsible. In searching for a "golden mean" type compromise perhaps a reasonable strategy would be to release a group of the weakest performers without regard to race, then protect the remainder of the blacks. The ethical profile and core value would then be adapted to account for this minimal performance level.

If accepted, this amended core value would then be integrated into the organization's culture. The very action of top management in this situation would be a strong beginning of the enculturation process. Some monitoring and correcting or controlling would have to occur especially during the early stage of the process. As the evaluations of impacts became clearer, adjustment may be necessary. However, the company would now have an *ethically reasoned* core value to help in solving future problems of this type. The "ethically reasoned" is important because now all participants know *why* the company value exists rather than having it appear as a dictate based on a whim of top management.

Exercises for Chapter 5

Jerold W. "Bill" Brown (a&b)*

The Dilemma

Bill Brown sat at his desk pondering his uncertain future. In front of him lay the weekly sales report dated December 12, 1975. There remained only two weeks in the fiscal year, and from Bill's vantage point, it looked as if the affiliate would not even surpass last year's sales. The year had started out so successfully, and the home office had been very impressed by the affiliate's performance. He thought, "Why did I boast to Mr. Arnold (V. P. Region) that I would be able to better last year's sales?"

Background

Bill was happily married, with three children. The family lived comfortably on his salary with the help of company scholarships for his two sons in college. Bill's career ambitions were motivated by his desire to better his family's style of living, as well as his personal ambitions.

*This case was prepared by August E. Doskey, Abel A. Lopez, and Paul Vauden Geyden, under the supervision of Professor Jeffery A. Barach, as a basis for class discussion and not to illustrate either effective or ineffective administrative practices. Adapted and used with permission. The events described herein do not apply in their entirety to a specific company, but come to the attention of the case researchers from various sources. Some of the events depicted are fictional, but the writers believe them adequately close to reality to be useful for class discussion. Copyright © by J. Barach, A.B. Freeman School of Business, Tulane University.

Bill Brown had moved up the corporate ranks through various marketing positions, establishing a good record. He had worked for a number of firms in an attempt to find the fastest track to an upper-management position. At 40, his dreams had failed to materialize. At that point in time, he was offered a position with a large multinational firm, which he believed would provide the fast track he had so eagerly searched for. In taking this job, he had to enter at one level lower than his previous position. In his new position, he was marketing manager for the company's largest affiliate in Latin America. Within two years, a problem arose in a smaller but more promising affiliate. John Arnold decided that Bill Brown was the man to turn the troubled affiliate around, because of his success in increasing sales and market share in his present position. The troubled affiliate was located in Puerto Rico.

Bill Brown was promoted in October 1974 to Marketing Manager–Caribbean and Managing Director–Puerto Rico. He believed this would be a stepping stone to area manager as the current area manager was near retirement. When Brown arrived in Puerto Rico, he found a very unprofessional marketing department, plagued by older, unaggressive employees.

Brown faced several other problems in turning around Puerto Rican sales. One of these was the company's advertising strategy. Headquarters demanded that all affiliates use the standard advertising campaign. The campaign was not culturally geared to Puerto Rico and, in effect, proved detrimental to their marketing strategy.

Faced with these problems contributing to declining sales, Brown took three basic steps in attempting to turn around the situation. First, he initiated a wholesale pricing strategy which called for a 2 percent discount to all wholesalers over and above the existing industry discount. Furthermore, in an effort to sidestep the Robinson-Patman Act, Brown gave free merchandise to selected large wholesalers who could instantly increase sales. The effect of this free merchandise was to give large wholesalers an additional discount of 4 percent.

Second, Brown initiated a shelf-space strategy in major chain-supermarkets which called for more eye-level shelf space. Sales had been found to be positively correlated with the use of eye-level shelf space. In his mind, the quickest way to obtain the extra shelf space was through a questionable payment to the general manager of the chain. This payment proved ineffective because in the course of the year Brown did not receive all of the shelf space agreed upon.

Brown's third step was to open another channel for distribution of his products by convincing a local distributor to set up a ship-chandlering operation. This distributor represented 20 percent of the total sales of the affiliate. A ship chandler sells duty-free merchandise to oceangoing vessels, both passenger and cargo. The only drawback to this type of operation was, according to the distributor, that in order to get the business a ship chandler would have to comply with many ship stewards' demands for kickbacks.

John Arnold, the vice president of the region, climbed the corporate ladder through dealings in the export markets. These dealings included bona fide transactions as well as dubious operations with reputed smugglers. However, he had a reputation within the company as a discreet manager who accomplished results. The corporation felt that he was the right man for this region. Furthermore, it was Arnold's job to decide who would be promoted to be area manager.

Considering the adverse conditions he had faced throughout the year, sales were better than could have been expected; however, Brown felt that he must better last year's sales in order to get his promotion.

Caldwell, the sales manager, knew of Brown's predicament. He felt that he had to protect Brown in order to protect himself. Caldwell knew that the ship chandler, a friend of his, could be induced to purchase enough merchandise to put the affiliate's sales figures over last year's. The catch was that the ship chandler would not sell the product to oceangoing vessels. Instead, the merchandise would be sold in another Latin American country outside of Brown's designated territory. This action would have infringed upon the territory of another area manager within the region. As a result, company sales overall would not have improved, but this ploy would have made Brown and his affiliates shine. The company could even be hurt by this action as Mr. Francisco Diaz, the licensed distributor for the area where the excess product would be pushed, had a larger contribution to overall company sales than Brown's whole area.

Brown told Caldwell that he would have to think it over and would let him know in half an hour. Bill was telling himself that at his age he needed the promotion immediately. He felt there was a low probability of being caught. In fact, he had heard through the grapevine that such maneuvers were being practiced elsewhere in the company. However, he thought upper management could not condone this action if the facts became publicly known. He based his belief on headquarters' newly released form to be signed by all management personnel regarding knowledge of questionable dealings by company employees. Brown reasoned that there were several options before him, and he had to make a decision quickly.

On February 18, 1976, Arnold received an emotional phone call from his long-time friend, Francisco Diaz. Diaz was extremely upset. He related to Arnold that merchandise not sold by Diaz's outfit was being retailed in his area. Diaz wanted to know why this situation was allowed to occur and insinuated that if strong remedial action was not taken promptly, he would take his business elsewhere. Arnold promised a thorough investigation of the facts and a prompt reply.

Arnold was extremely concerned. He knew that he could not afford to lose Diaz's business. Arnold felt that Diaz would demand more than a simple assurance that the situation would not reoccur; he could even expect the defranchising of a distributor or the dismissal of an employee found involved in the matter. He was told by Diaz that the merchandise in question was produced in the U.S. and not by one of the Latin American affiliates. This probably meant that it was supplied from a U.S. possession or exported by a ship chandler within his region.

It has been brought to my attention by Mr. Francisco Diaz that merchandise is being sold to retailers in his area through irregular channels. Mr. Diaz is very distraught about this state of affairs, and I have promised him a thorough investigation and a complete report. Mr. Diaz insinuated that if our answer is not satisfactory to him he may take his business elsewhere. Please look into this matter and report to me personally no later than March 2, 1976.

Bill Brown sat at his newly acquired mahogany desk mulling over the recent memo from Arnold. His heart began to palpitate as he pondered his situation.

Questions

1. Could a parallel planning approach have prevented the actions that occurred in this case? How?
2. Develop an appropriate core value (or values) for the company described in this case using both inputs and both outputs of the company in your deliberations.
3. Describe what you believe would be the biggest problems in implementing the core value(s) you developed in Question 2.

Chapter 6

*Tools
to Make
Parallel
Planning Work*

In an effort to help make the parallel planning system work as smoothly as possible, this chapter presents a discussion of accepted ideas, adapted for use in this planning effort, and a new measuring tool that can be used to understand the ethical perceptions of others. The accepted ideas include the variety of strategy planning techniques that have been popularized in strategic management and business policy books and articles. The addition of the corporate environmental output (see Figure 5-1) to the strategic planning process calls for some variations to the steps normally used. The new measuring tool is focused specifically on the corporate environmental output. It provides an important additional means of measuring perceptions of the various publics who will pass judgment on the company. Both discussions should help the practitioners who use the parallel planning process.

ADAPTING THE IDEAS OF STRATEGIC PLANNING TO THE PARALLEL PLANNING PROCESS

Figure 6-1 is a replication of the parallel planning model in Figure 5-1 with many of the details omitted for clarity. The figure is reproduced here because of the need for frequent reference to it. This presentation provides only limited advice on the corporate objectives output since such advice is available elsewhere, and instead, it focuses on using strategic planning in the parallel planning process. That new focus occurs because of the importance of the corporate environmental output in the parallel planning process.

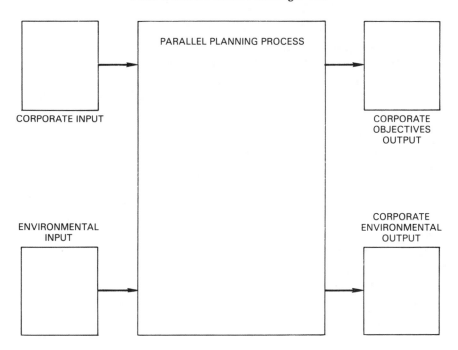

Figure 6-1 Parallel Planning Process.

SWOT Analysis

SWOT stands for Strengths—Weaknesses—Opportunities—Threats and is usually the starting point for strategic planning. Threats and opportunities come from the environmental input while strengths and weaknesses are part of the corporate input (see Figure 6-1). Thus, SWOT analysis is an effort to determine the potential impacts of the various inputs to the organization. Those impacts are also potential outputs—corporate objectives and/or corporate environmental. It is from this analysis that the alternative strategies discussed in the last chapter are developed. Sometimes a threat or opportunity acts on an organization and there is little that the company can do to react. In such *fait accomplis*, the organization must either endure or enjoy the outcome as it occurs. The more interesting cases from a management point of view are those in which the organization can influence the outputs stimulated by the threats or opportunities. It is this type situation that will occupy our attention for the rest of this analysis.

Of the four parts of SWOT, the environmental inputs must be the true beginning point. The opportunities and threats provide the menu and the organization reacts by developing plans for them. Obviously, many organizations act without much planning, and in those cases outputs are far less predictable. However, since this book is an aid to better planning, such cases will be ignored. The role of the other half of SWOT analysis (strengths and weaknesses) is subject to the environmental input. A strength or weakness is important to an organization only as it can be applied to a current or *potential* threat or opportunity. The search for potential as well as current threats and opportunities is not always discussed in the strategic planning literature, but since reaction time is often short, and since environmental scans usually are not performed as frequently as needed, potential as well as current occurences should be considered.

Table 6-1 is an idealized SWOT matrix. It allows the strategic analyst to match the relevant strengths and weaknesses. If a matrix is used to analyze more than one threat or opportunity, the list of strengths and weaknesses may surprise the analyst. For example, it is possible for a corporate strength in taking advantage of one environmental opportunity to be a corporate weakness in meeting an environmental threat. For example, a strong, independent corporate culture among employees might be a major strength in meeting an opportunity involving additional orders, but that same independent culture might turn against the company if layoffs are required. One approach to the SWOT matrix is to use one per threat or opportunity because of the complexity that is likely to develop. Table 6-1 contains several threats and opportunities only for illustrative purposes.

One helpful addition to the matrix approach is to include an estimate of the relative importance of the strength or weakness to its threat or opportunity. In Table 6-1, a one to five weight appears after each strength and weakness. This system uses a value of one to represent a strength or weakness of minor importance, and a

Table 6-1
STRENGTHS—WEAKNESSES—OPPORTUNITIES— THREATS (SWOT) MATRIX: CORPORATE AND ENVIRONMENTAL INPUTS

Environment

	Existing Or Potential Threats (T)	Existing Or Potential Opportunities (O)
Corporate — Weaknesses (W)	W1 for T1[1] (#)[2] W2 for T1 (#) W3 for T1 (#) etc. W1 for T2 (#) W2 for T2 (#) W3 for T2 (#) W4 for T2 (#) etc.	W1 for O1 (#) W2 for O1 (#) etc. W1 for O2 (#) W2 for O2 (#) W3 for O2 (#) W4 for O2 (#) etc. W1 for O3 (#) W2 for O3 (#) etc.
Corporate — Strengths (S)	S1 for T1 (#) S2 for T1 (#) S3 for T1 (#) S4 for T2 (#) etc. S1 for T2 (#) S2 for T2 (#) S3 for T2 (#) etc.	S1 for O1 (#) S2 for O1 (#) S3 for O1 (#) etc. S1 for O2 (#) etc. S1 for O3 (#) S2 for O3 (#) S3 for O3 (#) etc.

[1]W1 = First weakness, W2 = second weakness, etc. T1 = first threat, T2 = second threat, etc. S1 = first strength, S2 = second strength, etc. O1 = first opportunity, O2 = second opportunity, etc.

[2](#) = an estimate of the importance of the strength or weakness. # can be 1 to 5 with 1 = minor importance and 5 = major importance.

value of five to represent one of major importance. Values from two to four represent equal, increasing increments of importance. The reason for estimating a weight or relative importance of each strength and weakness is to provide perspective. A large number of entries that are low in importance may seem to offset one or two very important items when listed without the weights, but with the weights, those important strengths or weaknesses should stand out. For those people preferring graphical presentations, each strength and weakness could be represented by a bar, whose length is a measure of importance, in a bar chart which runs vertically down the page. Then the relative importance of each entry could be determined at a glance.

Estimating the Impact on Outputs

One or more alternative plans should be developed for each threat and opportunity. The development of these alternative plans requires creativity, but the comparisons made in the SWOT matrix ought to help in providing ideas. A close look at the strengths and weaknesses of the company as they relate to each threat and opportunity should aid the planner in developing viable alternative plans. All reasonable alternatives should be considered and unsuitable ones eliminated in a later analysis.

At this stage each alternative strategic plan for meeting each threat or opportunity is considered separately, a tedious but necessary task. It is also at this stage that the parallel outputs become important. Figure 6-2 is a suggested format for a form that might be used in analyzing each alternative plan. The form has a place to identify the (current or potential) threat or opportunity, as well as the alternative under consideration for dealing with it. Parallel lists that identify the corporate objectives output and the corporate environmental output follow the identification portion of the sheet.

Once again, a one to five weighting system which estimates the relative impact of each output is suggested for each entry in each column. This weighting system is an aid in determining the overall impact of the alternative, but it should only be used as a guide. For

Threats or Opportunity: Current ( )   Potential ( )
(Briefly Describe)_____

Alternative Plan: (Briefly Describe)_____
_____
_____

Corporate Objectives Output   Environmental Output

Output 1 (#)[1]   Output 1 (#)
Output 2 (#)   Output 2 (#)
Output 3 (#)   Output 3 (#)
etc.   etc.

[1](#) = an estimate of the importance of the output. (#) can be 1 to 5 with 1 =
minor importance and 5 = major importance.

Figure 6-2 ANALYSIS OF PARALLEL OUTPUTS

example, the weights should *not* be summed to make an overall
determination of the impact. To do so would cause the evaluator to
miss the effects of any interactions between the alternatives in both
columns. Instead, the combined impact of both outputs must be
considered as a whole, and the weights should be used only as
reminders in making that overall evaluation.

If there are, say, three alternative plans for reacting to a single
threat or opportunity, then the three overall evaluations must be
considered together. Each of these evaluations are compared to the
corporate mission and ethical profile to establish their relative
value, and one is selected for implementation. If the outputs of these
alternatives seem to conflict with the mission or ethical profile of
the organization, two options are possible. First, the search for alternatives that would better match the mission or profile can be continued. Second, if the mission or profile can be improved in a way
that has not been previously considered, an adjustment can be made
to either or both. This approach incorporates the concept of feedback discussed in the last chapter.

A Step-by-Step Approach for Applying the Parallel Planning Process

Table 6-2 is a step-by-step presentation of the ideas in this section. In Step One the planner attempts to identify all current or potential threats and opportunities. Scans of all human and non-human environmental inputs are necessary. Ideally, a continuing scanning process would be established that at least used secondary sources (e.g., newspapers, magazines, government publications, and so on) to create a list of potential threats and opportunities. This process could be combined with periodic evaluations using primary data gathering techniques (e.g., interviews and surveys). Once identified, a threat or opportunity should suggest initial responses or plans of actions (Step Two). These alternative strategies may be somewhat superficial initially and the number of alternatives may be limited. Nevertheless, they provide a beginning point.

In Step Three, the planner lists the strengths, weaknesses, and relevant facts appropriate for each threat and opportunity. The addition of relevant facts to the traditional listings is a simple aid to the decision maker. Also part of this listing are estimated importance figures for each strength and weakness. As the lists are created other alternative strategies may become apparent, and a separate list of strengths, weaknesses, and relevant facts must be developed for them (Step Four).

Step Five requires another listing. Here the outputs or effects of following an alternative are itemized and weighted with their anticipated importance. At this stage as well, new alternatives may become apparent (Step Six). As important, or perhaps more important, existing alternatives should be able to be extended and developed beyond their initial statement as outputs are analyzed. As this occurs, new or modified lists of strengths, weaknesses, relevant facts, corporate objectives output, and environmental output should be developed.

In Step Seven, the outputs of all alternative strategies are compared with the organizational mission and ethical profile. Such a comparison should suggest the appropriateness of one alternative

160

Table 6-2
STEP-BY-STEP FLOW OF EVENTS
IN THE PARALLEL PLANNING PROCESS

Step One: Identify a threat or opportunity.
Step Two: Identify the basic alternative strategies.
Step Three: List and weight (1) strengths, (2) weaknesses, and (3) relevant facts important to each alternative for each threat and opportunity.
Step Four: Were other alternative strategies identified during Step Three? If so, repeat Step Three for the new alternative strategies.
Step Five: List and weight the corporate objective outputs and the environmental outputs for each alternative strategy.
Step Six: Were other alternative strategies identified during Step Five? If so, repeat Steps Three through Five for the new alternatives.
Step Seven: Compare output analysis of all alternatives with the organizational mission and ethical profile.
Step Eight: Select an alternative strategy, *or*
Step Nine: Continue search for alternative strategies or adjust company mission and/or ethical profile, and repeat Steps Two through Eight if necessary.

over the others. If not, the planner may wish to (1) continue the search for alternative strategies, or (2) may find it necessary to adjust the company mission and/or ethical profile.

The constant feedback process becomes very apparent in this step-by-step approach. While it is tedious and frustrating, it is also very important. This feedback allows the planners to develop their plans based on the information as it develops, rather than prematurely locking-in on an alternative. When the process is completed, the best alternative strategy should have developed and been selected.

An Example of the Process

Many of the ideas for this example come from a *Business Week* article entitled "Bank of America's Blueprint for a Policy on AIDS."[1] However, additional conditions and extrapolations were added to the example that probably do not fit Bank of America's approach. Further, the problem actually existed for the bank, but it is portrayed as a potential threat for another company in this example. The AIDS example was selected because of its currency and real potential as a problem. Specifically, the threat is that one or more of the company's employees would become infected by the AIDS virus and wish to continue to work for as long as they could still be effective.

Table 6-3 is a sketch of the step-by-step approach to plan for this threat. It is a sketch because only the key elements of the process are included in order to illustrate the approach without becoming mired in detail. The threat is again outlined in Step One. As previously stated, the threat is seen as a *potential* problem rather than one that already exists. Two basic alternatives are suggested in Step Two: to keep or to release the employee(s). Little analysis is needed to discover these alternatives, and they illustrate the earlier statement that some alternatives should come immediately to mind.

The strengths, weaknesses, and relevant facts for the alternative strategy of supporting the employee(s) by allowing them to continue working appear in the first part of Table 6-4. It is very likely that other entries could be added, but the one strength, two weaknesses, and two relevant facts are sufficient to illustrate the process. The other alternative strategy of releasing the employee(s) is presented in the second part of Table 6-4. In this case, the strengths in the first alternative become weaknesses for the second alternative and the weaknesses become strengths. The importance levels change, however, because their potential impact varies between the two alternatives.

1. Nancy L. Merritt, "Bank of America's Blueprint for a Policy on AIDS," *Business Week*, March 23, 1987, p. 127

Table 6-3

AN EXAMPLE OF THE STEP-BY-STEP APPROACH
FOR AN EMPLOYEE WITH AIDS

Step One:	Threat = The possibility that one or more of company's employees would contract AIDS and wish to continue work.
Step Two:	Two basic alternatives seem apparent: (1) support the employee(s) by allowing them to continue to work, and (2) release the employee(s) as a threat to the rest of the work force.
Step Three:	The strengths, weaknesses, and relevant facts for one alternative appear in Table 6-4.
Step Four:	Other alternative strategies such as releasing the employee(s) with salary or severance pay are possible.
Step Five:	An example of the corporate objectives and environmental output for one alternative appear in Table 6-5.
Step Six:	At this stage new strategies could develop and/or there could be an elaboration of existing strategic alternatives. For example, the strategy to allow the employee(s) to continue working could be combined with moving the employee(s) to a position with less contact and beginning an extensive education program. Such a program might be even more effective if begun before the threat actually develops.
Step Seven:	In comparing the alternative strategies with the organizational mission and ethical profile we are aided by the material in Chapter 3 on ethics and social responsibility.
Step Eight:	Select the enhanced strategic alternative of retaining the employee(s) and beginning an education program on AIDS.
Step Nine:	No adjustment in mission or ethical profile is needed.

Table 6-4
STRENGTHS, WEAKNESSES, AND RELEVANT FACTS
FOR A THREAT FROM AN AIDS VICTIM*

Alternative Strategy One: Support The Employee(s)
By Allowing Them To Continue Working.

Strengths 1. One dimension of our ethical profile is
that we support employees who are sick
or disabled both temporarily and for
longer periods.
(Importance = 5)

Weaknesses 1. The company's employees exhibit the
same unwarranted concern about the
contagious nature of the disease as is
found in the general public.
(Importance = 5)

2. One dimension of the company's ethical
profile is that the organization is committed to provide a safe work environment
for employees. This commitment could
be used against us in following this
alternative.
(Importance = 3)

Relevant Facts 1. The reality of AIDS transmission is that it
is not a casually contagious disease.

2. A supportive work environment may be
able to prolong the life of an AIDS victim.

Alternative Strategy Two: Release The Employee(s)

Strengths 1. The company's employees exhibit the same
unwarranted concern about the contagious
nature of the disease as is found in the
general public.
(Importance = 5)

*A potential, not current, threat

Table 6-4 (cont.)

	2.	One dimension of the company's ethical profile is that the organization is committed to a safe work environment for employees. (Importance = 5)
Weaknesses	1.	One dimension of our ethical profile is that we support employees who are sick or disabled. This commitment could be used against us in following this alternative. (Importance = 3)
Relevant Facts	1.	The reality of AIDS transmission is that it is not a casually contagious disease.
	2.	A supportive work environment may be able to prolong the life of an AIDS victim. There is some evidence to support that possibility.

Importance levels are independent judgments and may change as perceptions of their impact change. In the alternative of keeping the employee(s), the importance of the strength (supporting sick or disabled employees) has been rated as a five. Any defense of this strategy would probably focus on this strength, and it should therefore receive the highest rating. In the alternative of releasing the employee(s), this same profile dimension, now a weakness, is rated at an importance level of three (moderate). The difference is due to the company's focus when choosing one alternative over the other. This situation could change over time if the released employee(s) make an issue of their firing and focus on this ethical profile, but the initial assumption is that they would not. Similarly, the importance of the other employees' concern about the contagious nature of the disease could be reduced from a five if the level of concern were first reduced, possibly through education. Thus, the perceived importance can change over time.

Evaluating the initial alternatives should suggest the central conflicts involved in the threat or opportunity. As these conflicts become clearer, new alternatives can be developed. The major conflict in this illustration is between the ethical profile dimension of loyalty to all employees and the other employee concerns about providing a safe workplace. In Step Four of Table 6-3, the search for new alternatives begins by analyzing the elements of the conflict. Can one or the other of the elements in conflict be reduced in importance? For example, one option is to support the affected employee(s) monetarily if not allowing them to continue to work. The released employee(s) could be allowed to continue group medical insurance and either provided with a severance bonus or even kept on the payroll. Certainly, this approach would have to be considered as supporting the affected employee(s). However, one of the relevant facts notes that being allowed to work in a supportive environment may be able to prolong the victim's life. Thus, this alternative would provide some support, but not a full measure of support.

Step Five requires a listing of both the corporate objectives output and the environmental output. The listings for the alternative of supporting the employee(s) appears in Table 6-5. Again, other outputs could be considered, but the five listed in this table provide a suitable illustration. The moderate-to-low importance figures attached to these outputs simply represent the probable overall impact of this decision on a large company. In an organization with only a few employees, the decision could become considerably more important. The second environmental output in Table 6-5 assumes an adaptation or extension to this alternative. As the potential conflict from following this alternative is studied, it should become apparent that something would have to be done to reduce the concerns of employees who must work with the AIDS victim. One option may be to move the employee to a position where less contact with others occurs. Further, a program for educating these people about the difficulty of transmitting the disease in a normal work environment seems to be necessary if this alternative is selected. Step Six in Table 6-3 discusses this process.

Step Seven in Table 6-3 requires that we compare the strategic alternatives with the corporate mission and the ethical profile. Since we have made only limited assumptions about either of them, it seems appropriate to test these alternatives using the material dis-

Table 6-5
CORPORATE OBJECTIVES AND ENVIRONMENT
OUTPUT FOR A THREAT FROM AN AIDS VICTIM*

Alternative Strategy One: Support The Employee(s) By Allowing Them To Continue Working.

Corporate Objectives Output	Environmental Output
1. There would be a chance of at least a short-term decrease in productivity if employees quit or become antagonistic toward the company. (Importance = 3)	1. This strategy would reinforce the company's profile of caring for individual employees. (Importance = 3)
2. There would be a small chance of employee lawsuits. (Importance = 1)	2. If this strategy were combined with an education program on AIDS, it could help to reduce the misconceptions about the ease of transmitting the disease. (Importance = 2)
	3. There could be a loss in the belief that the company is maintaining a safe work environment. This situation could produce a negative change in the corporate culture. (Importance = 2)

*A potential, not current, threat

cussed in Chapter 3. One of the conflicts in our choice of alternative strategies is superficially similar to the differences in the analysis between utilitarianism and deontology. The concern for "the greatest good for the greatest number" might lead us to choose one of the alternatives that releases the employee(s) with AIDS. Alternatively, deontological reasoning would ask if we want to live in a world that had a rule which instructed us to release employees with AIDS or similar diseases if we thought that we could be the person with the disease (the veil of ignorance). Actually, depending on all of the real harms and benefits to all parties, the utilitarian approach might suggest that the worker be retained. That would be especially true if worker concerns could be reduced by moving them within the company and with a convincing education program *before the potential problem became a reality.* In this case the concern for employees is at the individual level, and according to the rules in Chapter 3, deontology should dominate the analysis. Thus, retaining and helping the employee(s) would seem to be the most desirable alternative.

Further, in applying the family analogy from the discussion on social responsibility to the employee, how would we react if, say, our child contracted AIDS? In an average family sick or hurt children receive special attention. If, as suggested in Table 6-4, part of our ethical profile is to support employees, and especially if that support is based on the family analogy, then wouldn't the alternative to support the employee(s) be the most desirable? Further, if this core value were effectively made part of the organization's culture, adverse reactions to retaining the employee(s) would more than likely be reduced. Step Eight suggests that this alternative be selected, and Step Nine recognizes that no adjustment is necessary in either corporate mission or ethical profile.

Exercises for Chapter 6

Small Plant Layoff*
Harold Oaklander

Background

The Mountainside name is used locally, but the full name of the operation is Orion-Mountainside. It is the oldest of five body plants that comprise one division of Orion-Diversified Industries Incorporated, a subsidiary of the Orion General Corporation.

*Harold Oaklander, Professor of Management, Pace University, One Pace Plaza, New York, New York, 10438. Used with permission.

Each chassis is moved into the plant to receive careful grafts of panel upon panel, accessory upon accessory, until the particular delivery vehicle has been completed after 120 working hours. The General Motors or Ford chassis is thus made complete with a Mountainside body. It will then be serviced in preparation for its delivery to one of the regional bread companies or motor express companies, or another familiar company whose trade name is colorfully displayed on the finished vehicles. A new type of mass transportation vehicle is being produced by another division of the Orion-Diversified subsidiary. The Annual Report attributes a 10.5 percent decline in earnings to a multimillion dollar pretax loss from "start-up problems in the production" of the new vehicle.

Vehicle body production has been an expanding enterprise for the company ever since it began 30 years ago. Operations were shifted to Rhone in the mid-1950s and over the years four additional plants were established to cater to regional markets as far away as the west coast. Headquarters for the five plants are centrally located 150 miles away from Rhone, and the marketing and purchasing functions are performed there. Design engineering is carried out at the largest of the plants.

Early in July 1980, Mr. Cannon called his staff together to discuss a threatening development, the possibility of having to lay off a number of workers because of looming production and marketing problems affecting all five plants of the vehicle body division.

Business Factors Triggering the Layoff Deliberations

By July 1980, orders had indeed slackened off, but not critically. Consideration was given to anticipating future orders so that more work could be provided. However, a more ominous threat to the maintenance of full work schedules loomed as the months passed—a drop in the supply of chassis.

The supply situation which the general manager and his staff worried about was influenced by events in Detroit. The major automobile and truck manufacturers who supplied their chassis had suffered severely in 1980 and many auto workers had been laid off. Under normal business circumstances, vehicle production lines in Detroit are shut down for model changes for the traditional one- or two-week period.* That year the interruption might be longer.

This spelled trouble for the Rhone plant. Ways of circumventing a layoff were considered during the entire month of July. Mr. Cannon, who has considerable latitude to make locally important decisions such as the decision to layoff, touched bases frequently with division headquarters.

When the plant shutdowns in Detroit started on July 20, Mountainside was informed that chassis production would not resume until September 8. Even if this date were kept it would still mean that chassis would not begin to arrive for another three weeks at the earliest. An overall delay of at least ten weeks loomed ahead.

The situation would worsen if, by September 8, the automobile companies had not accumulated sufficient orders for their own standard trucks and automobiles to be able to start *uninterrupted* production. All truck body plants of the division would suffer from the want of their small share of Detroit's truck chassis output.

The Final Deliberations and the Events that Followed

Mr. Cannon and his staff of managers discussed the evolving situation many times during the month of July. The problem was not discussed with the workers who are not represented by a union. As the month drew to a close with no improvement in Detroit, management came to feel that a layoff would have to be put into effect. A procedure was then agreed upon.

On the last Friday morning of the month, the production manager called all foremen into his office. He told them for the first time that a layoff involving 17 workers would be implemented that afternoon and provided them with the procedure worked out by the plant management. Who was to be laid off was decided strictly by seniority: it was deemed the only fair way. In an effort to give the same picture to everyone, the following message was prepared:

*Truck chassis are built on the same assembly line as automobiles, light trucks, and other vehicles.

> Due to general economic conditions and questionable chassis production start-up of 1981 models, it has become necessary for the plant to have a reduction of employees for an indefinite period. When business conditions so warrant, employees will be recalled as required.

That afternoon the plant manager and his personnel manager called into his office the 15 workers who were present, out of the total of 17 surplus workers. Mr. Cannon estimated that the meeting took five minutes. It was intentionally kept short and was based on the prepared message. The employees were then invited to remain and ask questions. None did so.

Meanwhile, foremen out in the plant were telling the remaining workers of the layoff. They used the prepared message given to them earlier in the day. The message was posted on the plant bulletin boards. The layoff was to take effect immediately.

While instructing the supervisors in preparation for this meeting, questions were anticipated from workers not scheduled for layoff. Some might speculate that they would be next because of their low seniority. Supervisors were instructed to respond that no new layoffs were presently being planned, but that this was not a guarantee against future layoffs.

Why the Layoff was Implemented as it Was

The personnel manager explained, weeks later, that no advance notice was given because it wouldn't do to have workers around the plant after they had been notified. He felt that their attitude towards their work would change.

This was the personnel manager's first experience with a layoff. He was relatively new at the job and had previously been a partner in a small business. His professional education had been in accounting. He was described as one who was interested in taking care of the employees. He expressed his helplessness in this situation with the comments, "We don't have control over the economy," and "We are responsible to the stockholders." His son was among the 17 workers dismissed.

In response to my inquiry as to whether any form of work force adjustment other than layoff was considered—for example, work sharing—Mr. Cannon responded that work sharing had been considered. It was not a new concept for the company. His predecessor had used work sharing in the 1960s but had come to feel that it didn't work. It was resented by the older workers who felt that they had been around long enough to be entitled to job security. For them, job security meant the full pay checks necessary for full bags of groceries on a regular basis. In July 1980, according to Mr. Cannon, there was little talk among the workers about work sharing as an option for avoiding dismissal in the recent layoff.

The plant manager had considered discussing the layoff with the local office of the state labor department prior to its occurrence. Even though this might have expedited the payment of benefits, he did not do so because "It might have given away the layoff plans." He did not want to alarm the workers unnecessarily in case the layoff were to be called off at the last minute. Even with all these precautions, some of the more experienced workers might have suspected an impending layoff, since there was an obvious reduction in the number of chassis in the storage yard.

What of Those Laid Off?

All of the laid-off workers had been hired by Mountainside after September 4, 1979. At most they had accumulated 11 months of experience. Their ages ranged from 19 to 49, with an average age of 24. One woman (from a female work force of 15 to 20 percent of the total) and two black workers (of five on the payroll) were among the dismissed.

Some of the workers lived near the plant, the furthest lived 15 miles away. The group was fairly evenly divided among married and single individuals. The dependent children numbered eight. The average hourly pay at time of layoff was $4.35.

The laid-off workers were the most junior in terms of experience as well as seniority. They would probably still be classified as unskilled by their next employer because of the shortness of their service and because Mountainside had hired them as unskilled. In fact they had learned a lot during their tenure at the body works. All had survived the close scrutiny of a 90-day probationary period.

Six weeks after the layoff, the personnel manager reported that all the dismissed workers were still unemployed. This information was obtained from state unemployment insurance records. Mr. Cannon mentioned that even though he knew of the one-week waiting period before the start of benefits, he was surprised and dismayed when he discovered that it took three weeks for unemployment checks to reach those entitled to them.

Benefits and Services for Those Laid Off

There are several potential sources of assistance for laid-off workers. The company itself is closest to the worker, but various government agencies offer a wider range of services.

I asked the plant manager what benefits and services the 17 displaced workers had received from the company. All had been paid for vacation accrued but not taken; because of their short tenure this amounted to a few days at best. Severance pay is not a fringe benefit in Orion-Mountainside. Even if severance pay were provided, the short service of those dismissed would have entitled them to very little. All other fringe benefits, including group health and other protective benefits, cease with termination of employment. There is a 31-day grace period during which the company group health policy may be transferred to other health insurance. None of those laid off had worked long enough to win vested rights in the pension plan. Even if they had, they would not have realized them until retirement age. Mr. Cannon pointed out that, in general, senior workers receive more in benefits than junior workers, except for health insurance.

The 17 dismissed workers also missed benefitting from a profit-sharing plan by falling short of its one-year waiting period.

The unemployed workers' ultimate concern is to find other jobs. They need all the help they can get, especially in recessionary times. Like practically all other American companies, with the recent exception of the Goodyear Tire Company, Orion-Diversified provides no formal outplacement counseling (systematic placement and search assistance) for blue-collar workers.

The local unemployment service office processed the claims of the dismissed Mountainside workers. While a routine form reporting the layoff to the state was completed, the purpose of such reports is merely informational. The local office takes no special action when groups of individuals are involved in a layoff. Records are kept only by individuals' social security numbers. The average full-week payment to unemployed workers was $79.47 in August 1980, according to state published statistics. The maximum weekly benefit that can be paid, according to current regulations, is $125.00. The average unemployment insurance benefit paid to the dismissed workers was estimated to come close to the state average.

Normally, benefits are paid weekly, up to a maximum of 26 weeks. Under the federal extended benefits program, 13 additional weeks of benefits can be paid when unemployment rises to high levels in the nation or within particular states. Mountainside was located in one of 17 states paying extended benefits in August 1980.

The Layoff in Retrospect

The interviews required to prepare this case gave the management of Mountainside many opportunities to reflect on the events attendant on the layoff. When asked whether a cost/benefits analysis of the layoff had been or might be made, the response was no.* Had they contemplated such an analysis, they would have had to plan it in advance of the layoff. Line supervisors would have had to gather much of the information, which would have jeopardized the secrecy surrounding the layoff.

The layoff appeared to have gone smoothly. As a result of the company's encouragement of skill development and internal job

---

*The overall cost to manufacture vehicles at Mountainside was allocated to materials (60 percent), direct labor (15 percent), and overhead (25 percent).

mobility, intraplant transfers were made as soon as the layoff was implemented. There was no discernible worker resistance. The plant did not experience disruptions, such as the interdepartmental "bumping," which is more likely to occur in unionized plants than in nonunion plants, when plant-wide seniority is applied to a layoff.

As late as three months after the layoff, there was no sign that the company would be able to invite workers to return. Five of the 17 dismissed had found new jobs. After months of reflection over the causes, implementation, and consequences of the layoff, Mr. Cannon was beginning to formulate ideas which he felt might be put into effect to mitigate future work force reductions.

Questions

1. Attempt to establish the corporate values toward employees in effect at the time of the layoff. Evaluate these values using the ethical tools in Chapter 3. For example, the deontological analysis would ask "What, if any, rights do employees have in a situation as described in the case?" and "What duties, if any, does Orion-Mountainside have toward its employees?" Kantian logic or the approach of John Rawls can be used to suggest answers to these questions. The utilitarian analysis would ask if the actions of the company produced the greatest social good, or in this case produced the least social cost possible. The social responsibility analysis would refer to the framework in Chapter 3. Then compare results of these analyses to the list of corporate values you have constructed and come to a conclusion about their appropriateness.

2. Develop a SWOT analysis using the parallel planning approach described in this chapter. Be sure to focus on the ethical "opportunity" in the corporate environmental output.

Du Pont's Policy of Exclusion from the Workplace*

In January 1981 the *New York Times* reviewed a new and startling development in the workplaces of the nation. Some fertile women workers chose to undergo voluntary sterilization rather than give up high-paying jobs that involved exposure to chemicals potentially harmful to a developing fetus. Disclosure of this practice precipitated discussion of a new civil rights issue with "questions...raised about whether a company should be allowed to discriminate against a woman to protect her unborn child, or whether the practice of keeping a woman out of certain well-paying jobs because she was fertile was simply another form of sex discrimination in the workplace."[1]

Some background information is necessary for understanding this issue. The causes of congenital (or "birth") defects in humans are not well understood. Four to six percent are known to be caused by specific drugs and environmental chemicals, but the causes of at least 65 to 70 percent are unknown. It *is* known, however, that of the 28,000 toxic substances listed by the National Institute of Occupational Safety and Health (NIOSH) 56 are known animal mutagens (that is, they cause chromosomal damage to either the ova *or* the sperm cells), and 471 are known animal teratogens (that is, they can damage the developing fetus).[2] As the 1960s' thalidomide tragedy showed, a substance can be perfectly harmless to the mother, while at the same time having devastating effects on the developing fetus. (Doctors prescribed thalidomide for pregnant women as a tranquilizer, but found that the drug caused such fetal defects as severely shortened and often useless arms and legs.)

---

*This case was prepared by Martha W. Elliott and Tom L. Beauchamp and revised by Linda Kern and Anna Pinedo. Not to be duplicated without permission of the holder of the copyright, © 1989, Tom L. Beauchamp. Used with permission.

1. Philip Shabecoff, "Industry and Women Clash over Hazards in the Workplace," *New York Times*, January 3, 1981.

2. Earl A. Molander, "Regulating Reproductive Risks in the Workplace," in his *Responsive Capitalism: Case Studies in Corporate Social Conduct* (New York: McGraw-Hill Book Co., 1980), p. 9.

Exposure to mutagenic or teratogenic substances in the workplace is complicated by the fact that chemicals and other toxic substances usually do not occur singly, but in combination. Also, the average worker does not have knowledge of the chemical makeup of many products. Furthermore, the period of maximum hazard of the developing fetus occurs during the third and fourth weeks of pregnancy, which is often before the woman is even aware of her pregnancy. The United States government (FDA and EPA, in particular) requires animal testing of drugs to insure that any new product to which pregnant women may be exposed is harmless to the fetus.

Industries such as chemical plants and zinc smelters with high concentrations of lead have coped with this potential threat to the fetus in various ways. The most common strategy is simply to make jobs that involve the risk of exposure "off limits" to women "of child-bearing potential." That is, fertile women in their late teens, twenties, thirties, and forties are banned from those particular positions. (Ironically, lead poses an equal danger to the male reproductive system.) Since a woman is assumed fertile until proven otherwise, this sweeping policy affects a large portion of the female workforce.[3] This policy, entitled "protective exclusion," has aroused the ire of the women's movement and civil libertarians, who see these policies as one more form of sex discrimination.

Charges of discrimination are made credible for several reasons. Jobs that *are* open to "women of child-bearing potential" are almost always lower-paying jobs. In addition, women's groups have noted a shortage of well-supported evidence about exposure to certain alleged toxic hazards and a general lack of consensus in government and industry about proper levels of unsafe exposure. The most significant charge of discrimination rests on evidence of the *male's* contribution to birth defects. As noted earlier, mutagenic substances affect the sperm as well as the egg. This can result in sterility for the man, but also can produce mutated sperm and ultimately a malformed fetus. (See Table 1 for chemicals known to affect the male reproductive system.) Thus, any policy designed to protect the fetus must include considerations of the sperm and egg

3. Albert Rosenfeld, "Fertility May be Hazardous to Your Job," *Saturday Review* 6 (9), p. 12.

Table 1
MALE REPRODUCTIVE EFFECTS: ENVIRONMENTAL AGENTS, HUMAN STUDIES

Agent	Exposure Conditions	Species	Type of Study	Effects
Anesthetic gases	Occupational	Male workers	Reproductive history	Increased incidence congenital anomalies offspring
Chloroprene	Occupational	Male workers	Semen analysis; reproductive history	Decreased motility and number of sperm; threefold excess miscarriages in wives
Dibromochloro-propane	Occupational	Male workers	Semen analysis; reproductive history	Decreased sperm count; infertility
High altitude	14,000 ft	Male workers	Semen analysis	Decreased sperm count and motility; increased number abnormal sperm
Hydrocarbons	Occupational	Male workers	Reproductive history	Twofold increased incidence childhood cancer with occupational hydrocarbon exposure of father
Kepone	Environmental	Male workers	Reproductive history	Decreased fertility males
Lead	Occupational	Male workers	Semen analysis	Decreased sperm count and motility; increase abnormally-shaped semen
Microwaves	Occupational	Male workers	Semen analysis; reproductive history	Decreased libido; decreased sperm count and motility; increase abnormally-shaped sperm

Agent	Exposure	Population	Method	Effect
Carbon disulfide	Occupational	Male workers	Semen analysis; reproductive history	Impotence, loss of libido
Irradiation	Occupational	Male workers	Gonadotropic hormone and semen analysis	Depression gonadotropic hormone levels; alterations in spermatogenesis
Oral contraceptives	Occupational manufacture	Male workers	Reproductive history, physical exam, blood analysis	Gynecomastia, decreased libido, infertility
Vinyl chloride	Occupational	Male workers	Reproductive questionnaire	Adverse pregnancy outcome wives; excess fetal loss
Cigarette smoking	Environmental	Male	Semen analysis	Increase in abnormally-shaped sperm
Elevated temperature	Occupational, environmental 30 → 37°C	Male	Semen analysis; histology	Inhibition spermatogenesis, testicular pathology

Source: Vilma Hunt, *Work and the Health of Women* (Boca Raton, Fla.: CRC Press, Inc., 1979), pp. 158–59.

that form it. This would logically include a more expansive protective policy than the mere exclusion of women from the workplace.

Du Pont de Nemours & Co., the largest chemical manufacturer in the United States, has been concerned about these issues since a high incidence of bladder tumors appeared at its large Chambers work plant in Southern New Jersey in the 1930s. Du Pont has issued perhaps the most explicit policy statement about hazards to women and fetuses. If a chemical is found to be or is suspected of being an "embryotoxin" (toxic to the fetus), the first step is to use engineering and administrative procedures to eliminate the risk or to reduce it to an acceptable level. Engineering procedures might, for example, involve special ventilation equipment; administrative procedures might involve management of the length of exposure time or the required use of protective clothing. However, where no "acceptable exposure level" has been determined or where engineering and administrative procedures are inadequate to control exposure, the Du Pont policy reads: "females of childbearing capacity shall be excluded from work areas."[4]

Du Pont has rejected the suggestion that a woman be apprised of the health risk and sign a waiver if she chooses to accept the risk. The Du Pont position is that the exclusionary policy is to protect the fetus, not the woman. Bruce Karrh, medical director of Du Pont, holds that "the primary issue...is not whether the exclusion from the workplace is necessary to protect the adult female or male, but whether it is a necessary step to protect the embryo or fetus."[5] Karrh has developed a specific procedure for management and employees upon determination that a substance presents a risk to the fetus:

1. Employees who may be affected shall be informed of the possible consequences of exposure to such substances and appropriate safe handling procedures shall be established and communicated.

4. Bruce W. Karrh, "A Company's Duty to Report Health Hazards," *Bulletin of the New York Academy of Medicine* 54 (September 1978), esp. pp. 783, 785, and Molander, "Regulating Reproductive Risks," p. 16.

5. Bruce W. Karrh, "Occupational Medicine," (Editorial) *Journal of the American Medical Association* 245 (June 5, 1981), p. 2207; see also his "Evaluation and

2. Engineering controls shall be used to the extent practical to reduce and maintain exposure to embryotoxins to acceptable levels. Such controls shall be augmented by administrative controls as appropriate.
3. Whenever engineering and administrative controls are not practical to keep exposure at or below acceptable levels, personal protective equipment, where appropriate, and training for its proper use shall be provided to and required to be used by employees who may be affected by such compounds.
4. Females of childbearing capability shall be excluded from work areas where:
   a. There is potential for exposure to an embryotoxin for which an acceptable exposure level cannot be set, or
   b. whenever engineering and administrative controls augmented as appropriate by personal protective equipment, are determined to be inadequate to insure acceptable levels of exposure.[6]

Du Pont also holds that "...the waiver of subsequent claims by the female worker would be of no legal significance because the deformed fetus, if born, may have its own rights as a person which could not be waived by the mother."[7]

Women's groups continue, however, to view "protective exclusion" as sex discrimination, especially since there is growing evidence that the reproductive systems of men are also adversely affected by certain industrial chemicals. A discussion between Dr. Donald Whorton, one of the first to study testicular toxins in the workplace, and Dr. William N. Rom illustrates the problem many women's groups find with policies of female exclusion:

DR. WHORTON: ...In a situation in which there is testicular toxicity, why would you be removing the women?

DR. ROM: Because it may affect both sexes.

6. Bruce W. Karrh, "Women in the Workplace," an address on May 2, 1978, as quoted in Molander, "Regulating Reproductive Risks," p. 16.
7. Molander, "Regulating Reproductive Risks," p. 16.

DR. WHORTON: But you would remove the men before the
                women, wouldn't you?
DR. ROM: Somebody has to work there.[8]

The Coalition for the Reproductive Rights of Women, a group organized to fight discrimination against women of childbearing age, points out that exclusionary protections are unusually broad, especially since not all women want or plan to have children. An attorney for the women's rights project of the American Civil Liberties Union has criticized the notion that women should be protected "against their wishes" and states that "we insist that the cost of safety cannot be equality. Another solution should be found."[9]

Du Pont sees the sex of the excluded party as irrelevant, on grounds that the sole issue is that of protecting the susceptible fetus. The company also notes that implementation of the above four-step procedure is far more costly to the company than a policy that would allow women to make their own choices. However, women's advocates take the view that companies such as Du Pont are simply remiss in developing technological solutions for the control of embryotoxins. A common union complaint is that industry makes the worker safe for the workplace, even to the point of exclusion, rather than making the workplace safe for the worker. These women view with suspicion management contentions that acceptable levels of exposure cannot be achieved.

Growing evidence that toxic substances pose a threat to the *future* fetus, as well as to the *existing* one, through mutation of the sperm and egg, indicates that this issue is not likely to prove amenable to simple solution.[10]

8. M. Donald Whorton, "Considerations about Reproductive Hazards," in Jeffrey S. Lee and William N. Rom, eds., *Legal and Ethical Dilemmas in Occupational Health* (Ann Arbor: Butterworth Group), p. 412.

9. Shabecoff, "Industry and Women Clash."

10. Sources: M. Donald Whorton, *et al.*, "Testicular Function among Cabaryl-Exposed Employees," *Journal of Toxicology and Environmental Health* 5 (1979), pp. 929–941; H. Northrop, "Predictive Value of Animal Toxicology," a paper presented at the "Symposium on Reproductive Health Policies in the Workplace," Pittsburgh, Pennsylvania, May 10, 1982; Vilma R. Hunt, "The Reproductive System Sensitivity through the Life Cycle," a paper presented at the American Conference of Governmental Industrial Hygienists, "Symposium: Protection cf the Sensitive Individual," Tucson, Arizona, November 9, 1981.

All these issues are further complicated because information that a chemical may be embryotoxic often is not available well in advance of policy decisions. In the case of a chemical used by Du Pont in some resins and elastomers, Du Pont was informed by a supplier in March 1981 that it was possibly teratogenic. The data was preliminary and needed corroboration by a study designed to show if teratogenicity occurs. Rather than wait for such a study to be completed, Du Pont immediately determined a level of exposure considered to pose "no risk." Du Pont then promptly advised all employees working with the chemical of the preliminary findings and determined that the jobs of about fifty women involved unacceptable levels of exposure. About one-half were found to be of childbearing capability and were excluded. All excluded women were moved to comparable positions without penalty in wages or benefits.

Du Pont's Haskell Laboratory simultaneously instituted an animal study to corroborate the preliminary work. The supplier's follow-up study and the Du Pont study both found no teratogenic effect in the animals studied. The supplier's earlier study results apparently contained experimental error. Du Pont notified its employees of the new findings and no longer excluded women of childbearing capability. Return preference was given to women formerly removed from these jobs. During this period, Du Pont made its plant physicians available for counseling employees and for consultations with the personal physicians of employees.[11]

Questions

1. Evaluate Du Pont's stand on the central issue in the case using the ethical and social responsibility tools developed in Chapter 3. Be sure to consider the role of the rights of the fetus in your analysis. How can your analysis be used to aid the parallel planning process?

11. The final two paragraphs are based on personal correspondence of August 24, 1982, from Nancy K. Tidonia of Du Pont's Public Affairs Department to Tom L. Beauchamp.

2. Use a step-by-step parallel planning approach to develop strategies for dealing with the problem of worker protection/discrimination developed in this case. First, develop a plausible mission statement and ethical profile for Du Pont, given the issues in the case. Second, use the case material to justify a list of company objectives for Du Pont. Then begin with a SWOT analysis and continue the process.

Chapter 7

*Implementing
and Controlling
the Parallel
Planning System*

Chapters 5 and 6 discussed, in detail, the nature and operation of the parallel planning system whereby strategic decisions can be developed with a concern for their ethical content. Planning alone does not guarantee that resultant decisions and actions will be ethical. As the old adage states, "The road to hell is paved with good intentions!" What is needed is a system which will increase the probability that the intended plans will be carried out as they are implemented throughout the differing operating units of the organization.

Individuals at lower management levels must be able to translate plans into actions as they are meant to be interpreted so that the ethical content of the plans is translated into desirable and correct behaviors. When variances between what was intended and what actually occurred are discovered, controlling actions must be put into effect.

What causes variances between intended and actual behaviors of individuals within organizations? An article by William G. Dyer and W. Gibb Dyer identifies six reasons why individuals may violate ethical standards. These include:

1. They do not know the standard or have not learned that compliance with the standard is important.
2. Situational pressures may operate to impel an individual to act unethically.
3. Organizational superiors may be poor or ineffective role models.
4. Peers and colleagues may provide pressure to deviate from the established ethical standards.
5. Management may ignore behavior that is at variance from ethical standards. This has the effect of reinforcing and institutionalizing incorrect behavior.

6. Personal gain or the hope of personal gain may induce behaviors at odds with established ethical standards.[1]

Any system which seeks to reduce the probability of ethical misconduct on the part of its employees must have the capacity to manage these potentially disruptive factors. As we have said earlier, planning is a necessary but nonsufficient condition for increasing the probability of ethical corporate behavior.

THE SOCIALIZATION PROCESS

Socialization, as briefly discussed in Chapter 4, is aimed at the new employee and has the purpose of educating that individual concerning the way in which the organization accomplishes its business. Choosing the right applicant for the job is important but certainly not a foolproof way of insuring compliance with ethical guidelines. Once individuals have been hired, it is incumbent upon the organization to train those individuals not only in the skills needed to perform their jobs but equally important, to offer training in how the company expects them to behave in the conduct of the job. This is the socialization process.

Socialization involves learning the organizational ropes, how things get done within the organization. Typically, this socialization process has focused on developing job-related skills in the more functional sense. We would argue that this socialization process must also involve considerations of the organization's commitment to ethical behavior. Moreover, this socialization process must be effected in such a manner so that the learning of job skills and their application in an ethical manner are not unrelated. Corporate ethics cannot be dealt with on a post hoc, afterthought basis. It is part and parcel of the everyday corporate life, and the successful integration of ethics into the development and execution of job requirements is

1. William G. Dyer and W. Gibb Dyer, "How Organizations Lose Their Integrity," *Exchange*, (Fall 1982), pp. 26–31.

a surefire way to reduce ethical misconduct. Ethics must be made a necessary condition for an individual's personal success within the organization.

The question is "How can ethical training be incorporated within the socialization process?" To understand how this can be done, let's look at what might be considered a typical socialization process. Richard Pascale notes that looking at successful companies such as IBM and P&G produces a picture of a composite or generic socialization process that involves the following seven steps:

1. Heavy emphasis on the candidate selection process.
2. Make candidate question prior beliefs and values.
3. Put the employee in the trenches.
4. Measure operating results and reward accordingly.
5. Promote adherence to transcendent values.
6. Stress company history and tradition.
7. Supply promising individuals with role models.[2]

Step 1: Emphasize Candidate Selection

Screening of applicants for ethical awareness and concern is a necessary first step and one which is often overlooked. Once the applicant has been tested and initially accepted, he or she should be told of the importance that ethics plays within the day-to-day operating system. Many companies will spend a substantial period of time explaining all the demands that the job places not only on the individual but also on friends and family. Their idea is to ask the individuals to eliminate themselves from contention based on an honest appraisal of job demands and candidate capabilities. In these honest face-to-face discussions it is also vital to introduce the importance that ethics plays in the organization's way of doing business. Not only does the organization demand much of the individual's time, effort, and family life, but it also demands that these contributions be made with the highest concern for their ethical consequence.

2. Richard Pascale, "Fitting New Employees into the Company Culture," *Fortune*, May 28, 1984, pp. 28, 30, 34, 38, 42, 44.

Some companies may go so far as to interview spouses and to explain what the job will mean to them as well as to the individual applicant. In keeping with the notion of family developed in the core values of a previous chapter, this is a good time to explain to family members the high value that is placed on ethical behavior. Family members can be a strong shaper of values too.

Step 2: Question Prior Beliefs and Values

Many companies like to put their new recruits under the pressure of hard work and training. The idea is that the pressure induces humility and a questioning of the belief and value system that the individual has brought to the organization. This is typically accomplished by giving the individual more work than he or she can possibly do. When the pressure increases so too does an individual's vulnerability.

We would argue that this is an excellent time to make sure that work assignments include questions about the ethics of a particular action. When individuals are under pressure, as Dyer and Dyer rightfully contend, questions about the ethical ramifications of a decision or action are likely to be relegated to questions about efficiency and effectiveness. This should not happen. Too often individuals will cite the pressure of the situation as the compelling factor in making an unethical decision. Decisions made in the luxury of ample time give the decision maker the opportunity to examine more carefully the potential ethical repercussions. This consideration must be inculcated with the normal decision-making process used at the time the decision is made. Again, our point is that ethical considerations, if made at all, are typically made on a post hoc defensive basis and are not part of the real-time decision-making process.

Moreover, we would contend that many individuals, especially those eager to prove their economic worth to a company, may have difficulty in identifying ethical problems. Individuals may have varying levels of insensitivity to issues of right or wrong, a sensitivity that can be dulled even further by pressure and a focus on productivity, efficiency, and effectiveness. This is an excellent time to exercise and sharpen a new employee's ability to spot ethical pitfalls that might exist in everyday activities.

Step 3: Put the Employee in the Trenches

Humbled recruits are now ready for exposure to one of the key disciplines that is the core of the company's business. This is a carefully monitored process whereby the individual can gain actual work experience. Progress is rewarded by promotion at predictable intervals, with an emphasis on the longer term.

This aspect of the socialization process should not ignore the opportunity for further internalizing organizational ethical values. Individuals who embrace organizational values should be used as models for the new recruit. And of course, these models should exemplify the organization's commitment to ethics. In addition, this is an excellent time to teach the individual how to use company mechanisms for reporting questionable practices. Organizational ombudsmen, ethics committees, and open door policies should be explained and even exercises conducted so that the individual becomes more comfortable with them.

Step 4: Measure Operating Results and Reward Accordingly

For most companies, operating results are measured in terms of market share, profits, and sales volume. No mention is made of how those results were obtained. By ignoring the qualitative nature of these measures, organizational managements may in fact be inadvertently socializing a disregard for ethics. As we pointed out in Chapter 4, the reward system is a powerful shaper of personal values and ultimately a shaper of the organizational culture. All the well-intentioned training and loudly voiced concern for ethical behavior will not stand up to a reward system that penalizes ethical behavior and rewards unethical behavior.

In the socialization process, company managements must make it explicit that in the evaluation of the progress of individuals, their ethical record and reasoning plays an important role in the reward system. During evaluations of individuals, the respective managers must discuss their record with them, not only in terms of economic performance but also in terms of the decision-making process that produced these results. By tying economic and ethical performance to the reward system, the organization is likely to increase the probability that subsequent decisions will be made with a consideration for their ethical consequences.

Reward systems that operate with consistency and speed are also effective shapers of behavior. Individuals who transgress company ethical value systems for the sake of market share or profits must be punished. Not to do so suggests, in the strongest terms, that ethics is a word to be used but has no importance in what really counts in the organization. This punishment should be strong enough to send a potent message that ethics is a principal consideration in any decision made in the organization. Punishments should allow the transgressor the opportunity to learn from the mistake and hopefully serve as signs for other individuals that ethics is indeed an important consideration.

Step 5: Promote Adherence to Transcendent Values

Transcendent values are those values "that connect the organization's purpose to human values of a higher order than just those of the marketplace—values such as serving mankind, providing a first-class product for society, or helping people learn and grow."[3] We have called these core values, descriptive of their location and importance to the corporate culture, and have discussed at some length how they should be incorporated within the strategic planning system. These are the values that are used on a day-to-day basis and become part of the individual's decision-making apparatus. Issues of market share and profitability are guided by a concern for products which the individual would want his or her family to use or considerations about how increasing profitability will affect the environment of the local community. The notion of the organizational family as a guiding principle for doing business suggests that there exists a reciprocal relationship between family sacrifice and family well-being.

3. Ibid.

Step 6: Stress Company History and Tradition

In a recent prize-winning article appearing in *Harvard Business Review*, Sir Adrian Cadbury, chairman of Cadbury Schweppes PLC, recounts how his grandfather reconciled several situations concerning profits and ethical beliefs. On one occasion, Sir Adrian's grandfather, who owned the second largest chocolate company in Britain, was given an order from the British government to send a decorative tin of chocolate to soldiers serving in South Africa. This was the time of the Anglo-Boer War, against which Sir Adrian's grandfather was deeply and publically opposed. How to resolve the conflict between increased business and his ethical views of the war? He did so by accepting the order but carrying it out at cost. This allowed his employees to benefit, the soldiers to receive their royal gift, but made no profit for Sir Adrian's grandfather.[4]

This type of story becomes folklore in a company. It sets the proper tone against which subsequent actions can be compared. These stories become tradition and have the ability to shape current and future behaviors. They are learning experiences in and of themselves and when extolled by management and used as guiding principles can be useful shapers of behavior.

Step 7: Supply New Individuals with Role Models

We have already alluded to the value that role models can bring to the socialization process and their potential impact on behavior and adherence to ethical norms and values. Perhaps no other individual in the organization has greater impact on behavior as a role model than the president and his or her immediate management circle. These people must act as the ultimate role models.

Not all individuals in an organization have access to the top management cadre. Accordingly, it is extremely important for them

---

4. Sir Adrian Cadbury, "Ethical Managers Make Their Own Rules," *Harvard Business Review*, (September–October 1987), pp. 69–73.

to provide this access, either in person or in messages to other organization members. Top managements that feel strongly about ethics can make powerful statements about how the organization regards ethical behavior and can choose specific moments to demonstrate this regard. To state that ethics is important is not sufficient. Top management must take an active role in demonstrating its importance and in rewarding instances in which an individual may have had to sacrifice economic performance for the sake of other ethical concerns.

Some companies use videotaped sessions of the top management people talking about the importance of ethics. These can be useful in the early stages of the socialization process. However, actions speak louder than words, and actual demonstrations of the importance of ethics make a much stronger impression.

Top managements that have a genuine concern for the ethical posture of their companies must make a strong overt effort to insure that new individuals within the organization have every motivation to act in an ethical manner. Not to do so is to provide a filtering device through which all the plans that are developed become distorted in their implementation. Planning, by itself, is not sufficient. Every individual within the organization must be motivated to carry out the *intent* of the plan as well as the *goal* of the plan. No organization will have a perfectly motivated group of employees and no organization will have a completely ethical culture. Problems will occur.

THE COMMUNICATION PROCESS

As was pointed out in the Dyer and Dyer article, ethical misconduct can arise through the noncommunication or miscommunication of plans, standards, and norms. Accordingly, to reduce the potential ethical problems attendant to improper communication, management must develop a set of procedures for handling cases of ethical misconduct. There are several management mechanisms for doing this, some of which involve structural changes as well as additions to or alterations in the formal and informal communication channels.

Ethics codes are not new to corporate experience. Ethics codes that are actually used, however, are. In addition, a study of 202 corporate codes of conduct found that they typically stress items such as relations with the U.S. government, customer/supplier relationships, political contributions, conflicts of interest, and honest books or records. These items all stress infractions against the corporation rather than corporate impacts on the environment. Again, we offer as evidence the one-way thinking discussed in Chapter 2.

Few corporations actually implement and enforce ethics codes once they have been developed. Typically, they are stashed away in a drawer somewhere and their real value as a managerial aid is lost.

Ethics codes which go beyond defining conflicts of interest to include a number of other activities with potential ethical consequence that are specific to the organization can be useful documents. Some companies have gone so far as to turn these written codes into "living codes." Joseph A. Raelin cites two examples of companies which use living codes.[5]

At Norton Company, all managers are expected to maintain an open door policy with respect to the question of ethics, especially those embodied in their "Norton Policy on Business Ethics." They review the policy at least once a year with their supervisors and field representatives and investigate any suspicion that unethical or illegal activities are taking place. Perpetrators of illegal or improper practices are dealt with swiftly but fairly. Corporate officers all sign a letter (perfunctory though it might be for some) affirming their understanding and implementation of the ethics policy, and the company's chief auditor reports on any ethical violations or suspected violations. The Corporate Ethics Committee (of the board) is primarily responsible for this action orientation on ethics; it answers questions about gray areas of the policy, updates the policy when necessary, and monitors and investigates policy compliance.

Raelin notes a variation of this living code idea as it is applied at Motorola.

5. Joseph A. Raelin, "The Professional as the Executive's Ethical Aide-de-Camp," *Executive*, 1, no. 3 (August 1987), 171–82.

At Motorola a similar board committee, the Business Ethics Compliance Committee, meets on an ad hoc basis about six to eight times a year to rule on cases requiring an interpretation of their code. As a result, the code of conduct has been revised three times in the last decade. For example, the committee has implemented a corporate policy on frequent flyer privileges because of the number of cases arising from this relatively recent but controversial travel benefit.

Another communication vehicle for heading off potentially troublesome ethical problems is the development of a formal grievance mechanism. This system allows employees to challenge decisions that have lead to or may lead to ethical misconduct. Such a system would have been useful in preventing the problems at Lockheed, where management was pressuring engineers to approve substandard airplane braking systems. The engineers turned to their supervisors for help but received none. The existence of a formal grievance or appeals procedure would have made the problem known to management in Lockheed who could have initiated an investigation. As it turned out, the engineers who initiated the appeal resigned.

Less formal appellate procedures can also be established. So-called "squeal clauses" that protect corporate whistleblowers from retribution by superiors can increase the flow of communication and head off potentially debilitating ethical dilemmas. Other communication vehicles such as suggestion boxes, employee meetings, survey feedback, and question-and-answer programs have proven effective.[6] In fact, research by David G. Spencer concludes that the more communication processes available to voice complaints, the greater the confidence that employees have that their concerns will be addressed in an effective manner.[7]

Ethics committees, ombudsmen, and ethics task forces are other structural adaptations that can increase the flow of information to head off and correct instances of ethical misconduct. Again, Raelin reports an example of this type of structure instituted at Dow Corning Corporation.

6. Ibid.
7. David G. Spencer, "Employee Voice and Employee Retention," *Academy of Management Journal*, 1986, 29, pp. 488–502.

At Dow Corning Corporation an executive committee, made up of four members, was formed to develop a global system of values, since a significant share of the company's business lies outside the United States. Initially, the committee was charged with learning how the company really operated outside the United States, drafting guidelines and reporting on the legal and ethical business behavior of the company worldwide, and recommending ways to correct questionable practices as they arose. As part of this process, committee members would conduct "face to face audits" of company sites, working with local managers to identify problems and resolve them. Today the face to face audits are still used but in a less adversarial manner, according to company officials, since the company has assured its managers and professionals that ethical standards are taken seriously.[8]

Consider the General Dynamics document shown in Table 7-1.

This document informs employees at General Dynamics Space System Division about their ethics program and how individuals in the corporation can access it.

The success of these types of structures and processes appears to hinge upon the idea that action will be taken. Investigations of specific allegations must be made under considerations of due process. If an instance of ethical misconduct is discovered, appropriate actions must be taken quickly and impersonally.

THE CONTROL SYSTEM

Overlapping some of the ideas behind the development of an appropriate communication process is the idea of controlling actions. Henri Fayol has described the control process as "seeing that everything is being carried out in accordance with the plan which has been adopted, the orders which have been given, and the principles which have been laid down. Its object is to point out mistakes in order that they may be rectified and prevented from occurring again."[9]

8. Joseph A. Raelin, "The Professional as the Executive's Ethical Aide-de-Camp."

9. Henri Fayol, "Industrial and General Administration Game," J. A. Coubrough, (Geneva, Switzerland: International Management Institute, 1929), p. 77.

Table 7-1
GENERAL DYNAMICS ETHICS PROGRAMS*

1. *Who is my Ethics Program Director?* The Ethics Program Director is Dick Neal. His office is located in Century Park, corner of Balboa and Kearny Villa Road, Building 2, second floor.
2. *How can the Ethics Director help me?* He can help by providing advice, counsel, or by just listening to the ethical problems or dilemmas you are trying to solve. The Ethics Director also initiates investigations into violations of the Standards. The Ethics Director will, to the maximum extent possible, conceal the identity of anyone who reports a possible violation. The company is committed to the policy of no retribution as a result of talking with the Ethics Director. He acts as a valuable source of information and will assist you in getting any additional information you need in order to resolve a dilemma.
3. *How can I contact my Ethics Director?* Contacting the Ethics Director can be done in several ways:
   - By calling him on the Hotline (573-8367). The Hotline is answered only by the director. When he is out of the office, an answering machine will ask that you leave a message and the director will call you back as soon as possible.
   - By sending him a letter. The proper mail zone to use is C2-7000. The mail system can also be used to send documents that the director needs to see in order to fully appreciate or act on the problem.
   - By sending an EMOS to Neal, RL. The Ethics Director personally handles his own EMOS account.
   - By personal contact. If possible, make an appointment to ensure the Ethics Director is in the office and available. If it is not possible or feasible for you to leave your workplace, the Ethics Director will gladly come to your area to talk with you.
4. *Do I need my supervisor's permission to talk with the Ethics Director?* No. We do encourage you to talk with your supervisor to get his/her help first in resolving your ethics problems; you are not required to do so prior to talking with the Ethics Director. Of course, you need your supervisor's permission to leave your workplace if you have an appointment in the Ethics Office.
5. *How does the Ethics Hotline work?* The Hotline provides all employees with a ready source of help by providing direct access to the Ethics Director. Your conversation will not be recorded. You do not have to

---

*"Ethics Program: Commonly Asked Questions" published and distributed by General Dynamics Space Systems Division.

Table 7-1 (cont.)

give your name or phone number; however, the director would not be able to get back to you with an answer unless you do. Once again, your identity will be protected, and you also will be protected from retribution for making a Hotline call.

6. *How do I know what General Dynamics' Ethic Standards really are?* By reading the blue booklet entitled, *General Dynamics Standards of Business Ethics and Conduct.* If you have not received a personal copy, please call 7-7447 or 7-7543 and a copy will be sent to you. If you are ever in doubt about how to apply the standards to a specific, real situation, ask your supervisor and/or Ethics Director for help.

7. *What is my responsibility if I become aware of someone who is violating the Standards?* If an employee believes that a fellow employee may be in violation of the Standards, it is his/her obligation to bring the situation to the attention of that employee for correction. If the employee suspected of a violation does not respond or take corrective action, it is then your responsibility to bring the matter to the attention of your supervisor or contact the Space Systems Division or corporate Ethics Program Director. Supervisors are required by company policy to bring all suspected violations of the Standards to the attention of the Space Systems Ethics Program Director.

8. *What happens if I violate the Standards?* In accordance with applicable company regulations and collective bargaining agreements, proven violations of the Standards will result in the imposition of one or more of the following mandatory sanctions: warning reprimand, probation, demotion, temporary suspension, discharge, reimbursement of losses or damages, referral for criminal prosecution or civil action.

9. *How does the Ethics Program apply to me?* The Ethics Program applies to all of us and is one of the five major initiatives taken as a result of the suspension agreement. We are all members of the Space Systems Division team, and we all contribute to the status of relationships. The Ethics Program's focus is on values at work in basic business relationships. The values include honesty, integrity, fairness, and loyalty. The relationships include those between company and customer, company and supplier, company and shareholder, company and community, company and employee, and employee with employee.

10. *What should I do if I am directed to do something that I believe is a violation of company standards?* If possible, first talk with your supervisor or the next person higher up in the chain of command. If that is not possible or desirable, call or talk with the Ethics Program Director. It is his responsibility to assist you in resolving the problem before it becomes a violation of General Dynamics' Standards.

Most control process involve at least three aspects:

1. Establishing standards;
2. Comparing performance with the standards;
3. Correcting deviations.

Chapters 3 and 4 dealt with the first aspect of the establishment of standards. The previous sections of this chapter have examined ways by which performance may be compared to the ethical standards. This section examines the issue of correcting deviations.

There are two requirements that must be met to control effectively unethical behavior. The control system must provide useful information, and it must mete out rewards and sanctions in a timely manner.

As Fayol indicated in his description of control processes, one of the purposes of the procedure is to identify mistakes and point out how they may be rectified and prevented from recurring. This requires the development of a system which can provide this type of information. This system will be organizational specific and must take into account the nature of the organization's structure. Sensing mechanisms like the ones discussed in the previous section must be established throughout the organization. In the event of an alleged instance of ethical misconduct, an investigation into the situation must ensue and the pertinent information collected. The situation can then be compared to what should have occurred and the problem areas identified.

Effective control systems are those systems which react quickly to a situation. This is particularly important when an instance of ethical misconduct has been uncovered.

Management's job is to ensure that this type of behavior does not continue. Merrill Lynch CEO and chairman, William A. Schreyer, in a speech given at the Federal Reserve Bank of Atlanta urged "vigorous enforcement and stiff penalties against unethical behavior are the best ways to promote 'universal adherence to the same set of values...which will assure a set and fair market.' " He went on to suggest "that strong deterrents are the only way to appeal to 'powerfully driven' young executives. 'Going to jail is something that even a 28-year-old, million-dollar hot shot can relate to.' "[10]

In a similar vein, Frank A. Olson, chairman of Hertz Corporation, is faced with a problem somewhat similar to that of Lee Iacoca's odometer problem. Hertz has admitted to overcharging motorists and insurers $13 million for repairs. This occurred even with the existence of a Hertz policy requiring employees to read an ethics code and sign a compliance code. Asked about how he would handle future problems like this, Olson responded, "If I catch one guy billing at something other than cost, I'll throw him out the window myself."[11]

In those instances where an individual or group of individuals has done the right thing even at the expense of increased profitability, this behavior should be recognized and rewarded quickly. Failure to either reward or punish quickly runs the risk that both good and bad behaviors will be ignored. This sends a strong signal throughout the organization that ethical behavior is not important. Further, for those instances in which an improper behavior has occurred, management may in actuality be institutionalizing the behavior. This can impact the organization's culture in an adverse manner and affect future behavior.

Ethics Audits

Many organizations are attempting to institute ethics audits in an effort to reduce instances of ethical misconduct. Typically these audits focus on such topics as equal opportunity employment, compliance, community involvement, safety, environmental protection, product and service quality, and conduct in multinational settings. The purpose of these audits is to "determine areas of ethical strain" and to measure an organization's progress.

10. Quote taken from *Economic Insight: A Newsletter from the Federal Bank of Atlanta*, 7, no. 6 (August 1987), 1, 3.
11. John A. Byrne, "Businesses are Signing up for Ethics 101," *Business Week*, February 15, 1988, p. 57.

Currently, ethics audits follow the same type of approach that social audits follow. Little consensus exists as to what types of indicators should be used. We would suggest the following framework for examining issues for their ethical content. The framework that we propose draws upon the two generally accepted moral philosophical strains of deontology and utlitarianism which were discussed in Chapter 3. It is not known to what extent individuals rely on any single moral philosophy or what combinatorial rules exist for their mutual application. It is our opinion that this is not that relevant. What is relevant is that this framework asks the necessary questions to help a decision maker think through the ethical consequences of a particular action. Aspects of each moral philosophy may be used and any particular weighting of the dimensions will be a function of a number of individual variables such as the decision maker's background, experience, beliefs, values, and education.

The framework begins with the recognition that there exists a situation with ethical consequences. This recognition motivates the subsequent inquiry. The self-interogatory begins with a series of questions extracted from a deontological perspective. Again, the actual starting point will depend on the nature of the problem and the individual's background.

The deontological perspective stresses the idea that there exist certain written/unwritten and spoken/unspoken obligations, commitments, and duties and moves to a consideration of whether the decision that is reached could become a company policy in regard to the particular situation under scrutiny. This line of questioning attempts to point out any explicit or implicit duties that the individual decision maker has. These duties might include truth telling, information disclosure, promise keeping, equal opportunity, and so on. These duties must be examined in light of the forseeable consequence that their abbrogation will have on certain impacted parties. The breaking of these duties and obligations with a concomitant harm to the identified parties suggests that the resulting decision is not ethical.

Utilitarian questioning, as Table 7-2 indicates, involves consideration of the costs and benefits which are attendant to a particular decision. Consequently, the decision maker begins with

Table 7-2
A Framework for Performing an Ethical Audit

Perceived ethical problem
Perceived alternatives

Deontological Evaluation

1. Who are the known impacted parties?
2. What explicit/implicit duties/obligations do I have to those parties?
   A. truth telling
   B. information disclosure
   C. delivery of a safe, tested product
   D. promise keeping
   E. equal opportunity
   F. environmental protection, etc.
3. Does my decision/action violate any of these written/spoken obligations/duties to these parties?
4. Does my decision/action violate any of these unwritten/unspoken obligations/duties to these parties?
5. What are the known negative consequences to these parties?
6. Is my decision/action such that I am comfortable with it becoming a basis for corporate policy?
7. Will this policy stand the test of time?

Utilitarian Evaluation

1. Who will be affected by my action/decision?
2. What kinds of costs/benefits will be generated by my decision/action?
3. What impacted parties, groups, individuals will be positively/negatively affected by my decision/action?
4. Will more people be better off or worse off because of my decision/action?
5. Does this balance change in the foreseeable future?
6. What is my intent in making this decision, or taking this action?
   a. to do the "right" thing?
   b. to better myself?
   c. to better my corporation?

listing all of the benefits that might accrue from taking a particular action. In addition, a list of all the potential harms that might result is also part of the analysis. Next, the decision maker needs to identify the impacted groups or parties in terms of the harms and benefits associated with a particular action. Once this is done, a naive cost/benefit analysis will point out the balance between harm and good that results from an action. If more forseeable harm than good results from the analysis, the action would be considered unethical. However, if more good results, the action would be justified as ethical on utilitarian grounds.

In most cases, when this analysis is performed by the same individual, the results are congruent. That is, deontological evaluations should lead to similar decisions as utilitarian deliberations. There will be exceptions, however. When exceptions do occur we suggest that they be reconciled with considerations about the responsibility of the action. Is the decision a socially responsible one? The decision maker can use the same core values that he or she has developed and used as guiding values in developing the corporate culture.

An example of this type of analysis may be helpful at this point. Consider the situation facing Stuart D. Watson, chairman of the board at Heublein, Inc.

HEUBLEIN, INC., A SOCIALLY QUESTIONABLE PRODUCT*

Stuart D. Watson, chairman of the board at Heublein, Inc., sat in his office to review a speech he was to give that evening. The occasion was the annual meeting of the Wine Institute, a trade association of wine producers and distributors. Watson had selected as his topic, "The Corporate Responsibilities at Heublein." He would focus in the speech on the importance of monitoring the social and political environment for contingency planning purposes.

*Abstracted from Roy Adler, Larry Robinson, and Jan Carlson, *Marketing and Society: Cases and Commentaries,* © 1981, pp. 30, 32, 34-39. Reprinted by permission of Prentice-Hall, Inc., Englewood Cliffs, N.J.

In particular, Watson intended to discuss the role at Heublein, Inc., of public affairs and the Corporate Responsibility Committee. Watson was proud of the research sponsored by Heublein on the causes and treatment of alcoholism. He was also pleased that the Corporate Responsibility Committee had provided strong guidance to senior executives on advertising, product, and distribution policies. As an example of the Committee's efforts, he intended to show some recent advertisements that were sensitive to the social consequences of alcohol consumption. The ads depicted people with and without cocktails, all having fun. The intention was not to glamorize drinking as the socially desirable thing to do. The text of the ads stressed moderation.

Just as Watson completed his review, he received a call from John J. Moran, vice president of public affairs. Moran began by saying, "Stuart, did you see the Today Show this morning? Well, I did. I could not believe my eyes. Betty Furness got some fifth graders drunk on Cows and then told America, 'This proves that Heublein is trying to appeal to kids.' Stuart, we cannot let this one lie like we did in November with the MacNeil-Lehrer Report." Watson agreed and asked Moran to prepare his recommendations for an appropriate response. He further requested Moran to add the issue to the agenda of the Corporate Responsibility Committee meeting scheduled for the following day.

Company Background

The Heublein product line featured over 200 well-known consumer product brand names, including Smirnoff Vodka, Black and White Scotch, A-1 Steak Sauce, Ortega Chiles and Sauces, Italian Swiss Colony, Lancers, Inglenook, Annie Green Springs, T.J. Swann, Jose Cuervo Tequilla, Black Velvet Canadian Whiskey, Irish Mist, Harvey's Bristol Cream, and Snap-E-Tom Cocktails. In addition, the company had acquired, in 1971, Kentucky Fried Chicken.

Heublein had been plagued by several serious problems in recent years which had the net effect of plummeting Heublein stock from 40 1/2 down to the 20s, even though sales and profits continued to be strong. The Christmas quarter of 1976, normally the strongest sales period, was disappointing, with sales down by 13 percent from the previous year. Preliminary estimates showed that company profits for the first half of the fiscal year 1977 would be up only 1 percent over the previous year.

Several reasons were cited by management for the declining performance of company products. First, in 1975, the Federal Trade Commission challenged Heublein's acquisition of United Vintners, a prestigious and profitable wine group, second only to the E&J Gallo Winery in market share. In negotiations with the FTC, Heublein offered to divest itself of the Petri, Italian Swiss Colony, and Lejon product lines while retaining the Inglenook, T.J. Swann, and Annie Green Springs brands. The FTC rejected this proposal, and the case was expected to go to court in late 1977.

Another problem area had been the declining performance of Kentucky Fried Chicken (KFC). As of June 1976, the KFC chain included 4,340 company-owned or franchised outlets, which spent over $30 million on advertising. KFC ranked second in fast-food-industry sales, behind McDonald's, and the company had planned to retain this position by relying on its superior marketing capabilities in spite of a trend of continuous and substantial price increases. Problems occurred when, as one industry analyst put it, "the oil shortage and the nation's economic problem resulted, the economics of a burger meal for the family began to look a lot more attractive than a $9 bucket of chicken...they priced themselves into a bind."[1] KFC planned to reduce prices and return to emphasizing a smaller sales package to recapture its declining market share.

The spirits groups also suffered problems during this period. The Black Velvet Whiskey campaign was given the "Keep Her in Her Place" Advertising Award in 1974 by the National Organization for Women for a campaign described as a demeaning "sex-sell." This was followed by an attack from the Oregon State Liquor Commission for "sexually suggestive" advertising.[2] Black and White Scotch, the leading brand of scotch in the 1950s, acquired by Heublein in 1974, experienced a decreasing market share. The company found itself unable to stop the decline. The trend, averaging a decrease of 110,000 cases per year since 1974, represented a drain on corporate profitability.

1. "Top 100 Advertisers," *Advertising Age*, August 18, 1976, pp. 145–46.
2. Ibid.

On the positive side, Heublein had Smirnoff Vodka, which was acquired in 1939 for a mere $14,000 and a small royalty by John G. Martin, grandson of Heublein's founder. Smirnoff was the largest selling vodka in the country, with sales of 5.5 million cases in 1976. Smirnoff accounted for nearly $15 million in profits in 1976. Smirnoff was the most heavily advertised distilled spirits product in the industry.

Beyond its more traditional liquor lines, Heublein was the industry leader in the prepared cocktail market, with a market share of over 75 percent. Although experts tended to see the company's expertise primarily in marketing, Heublein's research and development division was the largest and most active in the liquor industry. Researchers worked on developing and testing new products ranging from bottled martinis, manhattans, and canned whiskey sours through plum and peach wines to the "softer" coffee and chocolate liqueurs.

Over 1,000 ideas were generated by the marketing department and other sources throughout the year, and of that number, perhaps 100 were considered practical from a marketing or production viewpoint. The time span from conception to full distribution often took several years. A new product had to be salable and also retain quality and flavor over the months it might sit on a store shelf. Thirteen new drinks were introduced in 1974, the success of which contributed to the spirits division market increase from 9.9 percent to over 13 percent of the total market for distilled spirits.

Heublein noted a sharp trend toward lighter and sweeter drinks, with lower alcohol content. The prepared cocktail market was growing at over 20 percent per year. The forecast for 1976–1980 showed a continued trend for this category of distilled spirits. As a result, Heublein had its R & D division working on new prepared cocktail drinks. One result was the introduction in 1975 of Malcolm Hereford's Cows—a sweet 30-proof, milk-type drink—first conceived six years earlier.

Hereford's Cows was test marketed in Chicago in the spring of 1975.[3] The product was available in five flavors—banana, straw-

---

3. The details that follow were drawn from John J. O'Connor, "Heublein's Hereford's Cows Success Tips Marketers to Hot New Liquor Area," *Advertising Age*, December 1, 1976, pp. 1, 75.

berry, coconut, chocolate mint, and mocha. The successful results of the Chicago test market led to a decision to distribute nationally in March 1976. The product had originally been targeted for women in the age group 18 to 35. It was subsequently found to have strong appeal for other groups as well, including blacks, young males, and women over 35. Hereford's Cows was budgeted for over $3 million in advertising for 1976.

The product achieved market acceptance far in excess of forecasted levels. In fact, with first-year sales at over a million cases, it was the most successful distilled spirits new product introduction in the history of the industry. William V. Elliott, vice president, marketing, stated:

> There's a huge market here because Cows even appeal to non-drinkers....We could spend triple our promotional budget and it still won't be enough....The repeat business on this product has been phenomenal.[4]

Having seen the success of Cows' appearance on the market, Heublein introduced Kickers, a product almost identical to Cows except for packaging. Kickers was designed to increase demand for milk-type "fun" drinks by appealing to those individuals who considered themselves energetic, activity-minded and "young at heart."

The Controversy

Robert MacNeil, in the introduction to a November 5, 1976, airing of the MacNeil-Lehrer Report on the subject of teenage alcoholism, said:

> The appearance of Cows and similar drinks from other manufacturers has alarmed doctors and others concerned with alcoholism. In particular, they are worried that these pop drinks will exacerbate an already serious social problem, teenage drinking.[5]

4. Ibid.

5. "Teenage Alcoholism," The MacNeil-Lehrer Report, Library No. 290, Show No. 245, November 4, 1976.

The show, which focused on Heublein's 30-proof Hereford's Cows, represented a summation of the social objections which surfaced shortly after the product was successfully test marketed and introduced nationally.

Susan Papas, a spokesperson for Odyssey House, a New York center for rehabilitation of teenage alcoholics, said the sweet-tasting Cows "can cause the start or beginning of teenage problems." She explained:

> Kids that don't like Scotch or Vodka or other types of hard liquors might be more inclined to drink something that is like a milkshake. And milk is a very acceptable form of something to drink. And with a bottle like this, that's equal to two and a half cans of beer, I think they probably get a little surprised very quickly.[6]

Although Papas admitted that she had no statistics on Cows specifically, she said her experiences at Odyssey House taught her that teenage alcoholics begin by drinking sweet-tasting products. "It's the pop, the lightness; it's the way it's presented."[7]

In addition to objecting to the ready accessibility of these drinks to potential young alcoholics, Papas and others cited advertising that promoted alcohol as the answer to numerous adult situations, "which happen to be the very ones that teenagers find particularly frightening and painful."[8]

Referring to one of Heublein's ads for Kickers, a companion product to the Cows, Nicholas Pace, assistant professor of medicine at New York University-Bellevue Medical Center, president of the New York City Affiliate of the National Council on Alcoholism, and chairman of the New York State Advisory Commission on Alcoholism, told Robert MacNeil:

> It seems as if an awful lot of Madison Avenue…is sort of geared towards showing the use of the drug alcohol in a romantic way

6. Ibid.
7. Ibid.
8. Ibid.

that would allow people an escape or a method to dull their senses or to increase their sexual activity and so on.[9]

Other individuals active in fighting alcoholism objected to Heublein's attitude. Morris Chafetz, a medical psychiatrist who was a former head of the National Institute on Alcohol Abuse and Alcoholism, stated:

I must say that I am concerned about the Cow drinks. Not because I think they are designed to hook people to alcoholic problems, but because it reflects a lack of sensitivity on the part of the liquor industry.[10]

He further stated:

The liquor industry could be moving ahead faster...It's taking them a little longer to learn that there is no advantage to their product in people suffering from alcohol abuse and alcoholism.[11]

Pace, Chafetz, and Papas all agreed that they didn't believe government regulation of business practices and advertising was the answer to the types of problems they saw represented in Heublein's Cow. Chafetz, in summary, stated that he believed that the people in the liquor industry "are socially responsible and I would like them to downplay their product or remove it."[12]

Heublein did not respond publicly to the allegations and comments made on the MacNeil-Lehrer Report.

Heublein, the manufacturer of Hereford's Cows, declined to send a representative to join us tonight. A company spokesman objected that this program "was making a direct reference to certain products and had already made a decision that we (that's Heublein) were part and parcel of the problem." The Heublein man added, "It's like we're being placed on trial. Be-

9. Ibid.
10. Ibid.
11. Ibid.
12. Ibid.

sides we had late notice." In fact, our reporter first contacted Heublein a week ago. We should note that Heublein also refused to send a representative to a Senate hearing on this subject last March. The industry's main lobbying organization in Washington, the Distilled Spirits Council of the United States, also declined to join us. So did the advertising agency that handles the Cows account, and the American Association of Advertising Agencies. The U.S. Brewers Association and the Association of National Advertisers did not respond to our phone calls.[13]

In response to objections raised that advertisements for Kickers seemed to be primarily directed at teenagers, Heublein dropped its advertising campaign even though it disputed the complaint. A spokesman for the Institute of Alcohol Abuse later stated that "Heublein acted very responsibly in acknowledging our concern about the problem of teen drinking, which appears on the rise."[14]

The current crisis occurred against this background. Betty Furness, former Special Assistant for Consumer Affairs to President Johnson and currently consumer affairs reporter for NBC-TV, handed out Dixie cups filled with a beverage which later was found to be Strawberry Hereford's Cows to a classroom of 12- to 14-year olds.[15] The students were unaware that the cups contained an alcoholic beverage. This action was taped for a segment on NBC's Today show to back up earlier statements made by Furness in criticism of Heublein products.

In an effort to prove that kids were attracted by advertising for sweet milk-type drinks, and without disclosing her intentions to either school officials or the students' parents, Furness gave the teenagers a cup of the beverage. She then recorded their enthusiastic responses to her question of whether they preferred the sweet-cream Cows "rather than a shot of scotch." Furness closed the Today Show segment with the statement: "This is proof that Heublein is trying to appeal to young people." Furness did not question the stu-

13. Ibid.

14. The account of the incident was drawn from Mitchell C. Lynch, "The Day All the Kids Got Booze in Class from Betty Furness," the *Wall Street Journal*, February 12, 1978, pp. 1, 30.

15. Ibid.

dents about whether they had seen any of the advertisements being challenged or if they had heard of the product.

The Alternatives

Moran hung up the phone after his brief conversation with Watson. He began to consider the options available to Heublein in response to the latest incident involving the Hereford Cows.

Before laying out the alternatives, Moran reviewed the data provided by research and development and by marketing on the Hereford Cows. First, it was clear that most people could not drink more than two or three Cows at one sitting. The product was quite sweet and had a milk base. In fact, research in the R&D laboratory showed a high probability that a drinker would get physically sick before he or she would become drunk. Also, marketing research showed that the primary adopters of the product were 25- to 39-year-old women.[16] Further, an awareness study showed that only 8 percent of teenagers polled were aware of the product. Perhaps of most importance, the retail price of Cows, $4.50 to $6.00 per fifth, was well above the cost of the alcohol products typically consumed by teenage alcoholics. These data suggested to Moran that the charges were without factual basis.

He looked at his watch. It was nearly noon. The Corporate Responsibility Committee meeting was scheduled for 8:00 A.M. the following day. That left little time to prepare his recommendations for response to the latest incident which threatened the continued success of the Malcolm Hereford's Cows line of packaged cocktails.

Mr. Watson has recognized that an ethical problem exists. The question confronting him is what to do. We can assume that the original intent in the development and marketing of the Cow line was not to induce children to drink or to contribute to the problem of teenage alcoholism. Mr. Watson is dealing with unforseeable consequences of an initial action.

Turning to the deontological questions, Mr. Watson can clearly identify the impacted publics. They include not only children and teenagers but also their families.

16. "The Furness Fiasco," *Advertising Age*, February 6, 1978, p. 16.

What explicit or implicit duties and obligations does Mr. Watson have to these impacted publics? Mr. Watson must ask if he has an implicit or explicit duty to protect the children and the teenagers from themselves. He must ask if there exists some unwritten social contract between Heublein (or himself) and the people that he or the company attempts to serve that specifically seeks to protect those customers that cannot protect themselves. He must ask what his duties are in this situation. Even though there existed no intent to harm this group of people, harm is being done by the illegal misuse of his product.

In making this decision he can clearly identify what the known negative consequences are to not only the children and teenagers that are illegally using his product, but also to the parents and families of the users. Again, we would reiterate that Heublein and Mr. Watson are not to be faulted from an ethical standpoint for introducing the Cow product. The question of ethics, however, is clearly discernible now and Mr. Watson's response to this identifiable and actual problem is subject to criticism.

Mr. Watson must also ask whether he will be comfortable enough with his decision to allow it to become corporate policy so that if another situation like this arose, Heublein would have identifiable guidelines for responding to the problem.

Finally, Mr. Watson would want to ask whether or not his decision or action will stand the test of time. If for example, he decides to do nothing and shifts the burden of action to the legal system, how will he feel about his role in the decision two years from now? How will the public view his response to the problem?

If Mr. Watson has not reached a decision at this point in the analysis, he might approach his decision from a utilitarian perspective. In so doing he would be concerned about who would be affected by his decision. Again, children and teenagers are two clearly impacted publics, as are their families. In addition, Mr. Watson's decision may have ramifications for his employees and stockholders as well.

With these groups in mind, Mr. Watson must now ask who will benefit and who will be harmed by his decision. For example, to continue to market the product would certainly put children, teenagers, and their families at risk. That decision, at least in the short run, would economically benefit his employees and stockholders because of the profitability of the Cow product. At this point he should be able to answer the question "Will more people be better off or worse off by my decision?"

Will this balance change in the forseeable future? Here Mr. Watson might want to consider the potential concerns of product liability, litigation, and legislation against his company and the industry. We would suggest strongly that all calculations of cost/benefit be done so that a long-term perspective is incorporated within them. When these aspects of cost are factored into the calculation of cost/benefit, Mr. Watson may conclude that the balance does indeed change.

Finally, we suggest that Mr. Watson ask what his intent is in making this decision. This is a final check on the audit process.

Hopefully this example points out how these moral philosophies can be adapted to provide concrete guidelines for decision making. Clearly, different people may answer these questions differently. Individuals will bring to the problem a host of personal differences that bear on the response to the questions. Regardless of these differences, this suggested framework can help the decision maker think through the problem and formulate a response to it that has been made with regard to the attendant moral considerations.

Exercises for Chapter 7

Why Should My Conscience Bother Me?*

The B.F. Goodrich Co. is what business magazines like to speak of as "a major American corporation." It has operations in a dozen

*Excerpted from "Why Should My Conscience Bother Me?" by Kermit Vandivier from *In the Name of Profit*, edited by Robert Heilbroner et al. © 1972 New York: Doubleday, a division of Bantam, Doubleday. Dell Publishing Group, Inc. Reprinted by permission of the publisher.

"Why Should My Conscience Bother Me?" by Kermit Vandivier published in *In the Name of Profit* edited by Robert Heilbroner et al. © 1972 in *Business Ethics: Readings and Cases in Corporate Morality*, edited by W. Micheal Hoffman and Jennifer Mills Moore. New York: McGraw-Hill Book Company. Used with permission.

states and as many foreign countries, and of these far-flung facilities, the Goodrich plant at Troy, Ohio is not the most imposing. It is a small, one-story building, once used to manufacture airplanes. Set in the grassy flatlands of west-central Ohio, it employs only about 600 people. Nevertheless, it is one of the three largest manufacturers of aircraft wheels and brakes, a leader in a most profitable industry. Goodrich wheels and brakes support such well-known planes as the F111, the C5A, the Boeing 727, the XB70 and many others. Its customers include almost every aircraft manufacturer in the world.

Contracts for aircraft wheels and brakes often run into millions of dollars, and ordinarily a contract with a total value of less than $70,000, though welcome, would not create any special stir of joy in the hearts of Goodrich sales personnel. But purchase order P-23718, issued on June 18, 1967, by the LTV Aerospace Corporation, and ordering 202 brake assemblies for a new Air Force plane at a total price of $69,417, was received by Goodrich with considerable glee. And there was good reason. Some ten years previously, Goodrich had built a brake for LTV that was, to say the least, considerably less than a rousing success. The brake had not lived up to Goodrich's promises, and after experiencing considerable difficulty, LTV had written off Goodrich as a source of brakes. Since that time, Goodrich salesmen had been unable to sell so much as a shot of brake fluid to LTV. So in 1967, when LTV requested bids on wheels and brakes for the new A7D light attack aircraft it proposed to build for the Air Force, Goodrich submitted a bid that was absurdly low, so low that LTV could not, in all prudence, turn it down.

Goodrich had, in industry parlance, "bought into the business." Not only did the company not expect to make a profit on the deal; it was prepared, if necessary, to lose money. For aircraft brakes are not something that can be ordered off the shelf. They are designed for a particular aircraft, and once an aircraft manufacturer buys a brake, he is forced to purchase all replacement parts from the brake manufacturer. The $70,000 that Goodrich would get for making the brake would be a drop in the bucket when compared with the cost of the linings and other parts the Air Force would have to buy from Goodrich during the lifetime of the aircraft. Furthermore, the company which manufacturers brakes for one particular model of an aircraft quite naturally has the inside track to supply other brakes when the planes are updated and improved.

Thus, that first contract, regardless of the money involved, is very important, and Goodrich, when it learned that it had been awarded the A7D contract, was determined that while it may have slammed the door on its own foot ten years before, this time, the second time around, things would be different. The word was soon circulated throughout the plant: "We can't bungle it this time. We've got to give them a good brake, regardless of the cost."

There was another factor which had undoubtedly influenced LTV. All aircraft brakes made today are of the disk type, and the bid submitted by Goodrich called for a relatively small brake, one containing four disks and weighing only 106 pounds. The weight of any aircraft part is extremely important. The lighter a part is, the heavier the plane's payload can be. The four-rotor, 106-pound brake promised by Goodrich was about as light as could be expected, and this undoubtedly had helped move LTV to award the contract to Goodrich.

The brake was designed by one of Goodrich's most capable engineers, John Warren. A tall, lanky blond and a graduate of Purdue, Warren had come from the Chrysler Corporation seven years before and had become adept at aircraft brake design. The happy-go-lucky manner he usually maintained belied a temper which exploded whenever anyone ventured to offer any criticism of his work, no matter how small. On these occasions, Warren would turn red in the face, often throwing or slamming something and then stalking from the scene. As his coworkers learned the consequences of criticizing him, they did so less and less readily, and when he submitted his preliminary design for the A7D brake, it was accepted without question.

Warren was named project engineer for the A7D, and he, in turn, assigned the task of producing the final production design to a newcomer to the Goodrich engineering stable, Searle Lawson. Just turned 26, Lawson had been out of the Northrup Institute of Technology only one year when he came to Goodrich in January 1967. Like Warren, he had worked for a while in the automotive industry, but his engineering degree was in aeronautical and astronautical sciences, and when the opportunity came to enter his special field via Goodrich, he took it. At the Troy plant, Lawson had been assigned to various "paper projects" to break him in, and after several months spent reviewing statistics and old brake designs, he was beginning to fret at the lack of challenge. When told he was being assigned to his first "real" project, he was elated and immediately plunged into his work.

The major portion of the design had already been completed by Warren, and major assemblies for the brake had already been ordered from Goodrich suppliers. Naturally, however, before Goodrich could start making the brakes on a production basis, much testing would have to be done. Lawson would have to determine the best materials to use for the linings and discover what minor adjustments in the design would have to be made.

Then, after the preliminary testing and after the brake was judged ready for production, one whole brake assembly would undergo a series of grueling, simulated braking stops and other severe trials called qualification tests. These tests are required by the military, which gives very detailed specifications on how they are to be conducted, the criteria for failure, and so on. They are performed in the Goodrich plant's test laboratory, where huge machines called dynamometers can simulate the weight and speed of almost any aircraft. After the brakes pass the laboratory tests, they are approved for production, but before the brakes are accepted for use in military service, they must undergo further extensive flight tests.

Searle Lawson was well aware that much work had to be done before the A7D brake could go into production, and he knew that LTV had set the last two weeks in June 1968 as the starting dates for flight tests. So he decided to begin testing immediately. Goodrich's suppliers had not yet delivered the brake housing and other parts, but the brake disks had arrived, and using the housing from a brake similar in size and weight to the A7D brake, Lawson built a prototype. The prototype was installed in a test wheel and placed on one of the big dynamometers in the plant's test laboratory. The dynamometer was adjusted to simulate the weight of the A7D and Lawson began a series of tests, "landing" the wheel and brake at the A7D's landing speed, and braking it to a stop. The main purpose of these preliminary tests was to learn what temperatures would develop within the brake during the simulated stops and to evaluate the lining materials tentatively selected for use.

During a normal aircraft landing the temperatures inside the brake may reach 1,000 degrees, and occasionally a bit higher. During Lawson's first simulated landings, the temperature of his prototype brake reached 1,500 degrees. The brake glowed a bright cherry red and threw off incandescent particles of metal and lining materials as the temperature reached its peak. After a few such stops, the brake was dismantled and the linings were found to be almost completely disintegrated. Lawson chalked this first failure up to chance and, ordering new lining materials, tried again.

The second attempt was a repeat of the first. The brake became extremely hot, causing the lining materials to crumble into dust.

After the third such failure, Lawson, inexperienced though he was, knew that the fault lay not in defective parts or unsuitable lining material but in the basic design of the brake itself. Ignoring Warren's original computations, Lawson made his own, and it didn't take him long to discover where the trouble lay—the brake was too small. There simply was not enough surface area on the disks to stop the aircraft without generating the excessive heat that caused the linings to fail.

The answer to the problem was obvious but far from simple—the four-disk brake would have to be scrapped, and a new design, using five disks, would have to be developed. The implications were not lost on Lawson. Such a step would require the junking of all the four-disk-brake subassemblies, many of which had now begun to arrive from the various suppliers. It would also mean several weeks of preliminary design and testing and many more weeks of waiting while the suppliers made and delivered the new subassemblies.

Yet, several weeks had already gone by since LTV's order had arrived, and the date for delivery of the first production brakes for flight testing was only a few months away.

Although project engineer John Warren had more or less turned the A7D over to Lawson, he knew of the difficulties Lawson had been experiencing. He had assured the young engineer that the problem revolved around getting the right kind of lining material. Once that was found, he said, the difficulties would end.

Despite the evidence of the abortive tests and Lawson's careful computations, Warren rejected the suggestion that the four-disk brake was too light for the job. Warren knew that his superior had already told LTV, in rather glowing terms, that the preliminary tests on the A7D brake were very successful. Indeed, Warren's superiors weren't aware at this time of the troubles on the brake. It would have been difficult for Warren to admit not only that he had made a serious error in his calculations and original design but that his mistakes had been caught by a green kid, barely out of college.

Warren's reaction to a five-disk brake was not unexpected by Lawson, and, seeing that the four-disk brake was not to be abandoned so easily, he took his calculations and dismal test results one step up the corporate ladder.

At Goodrich, the man who supervises the engineers working on projects slated for production is called, predictably, the projects manager. The job was held by a short, chubby, bald man named Robert Sink. A man truly devoted to his work, Sink was as likely to be found at his desk at ten o'clock on Sunday night as ten o'clock on Monday morning. His outside interests consisted mainly of tinkering on a Model-A Ford and an occasional game of golf. Some 15 years before, Sink had begun working at Goodrich as a lowly draftsman. Slowly, he worked his way up. Despite his geniality, Sink was neither respected nor liked by the majority of the engineers, and his appointment as their supervisor did not improve their feelings about him. They thought he had only gone to high school. It quite naturally rankled those who had gone through years of college and acquired impressive specialties such as thermodynamics and astronautics to be commanded by a man whom they considered their intellectual inferior. But, though Sink had no college training, he had something even more useful: a fine working knowledge of company politics.

Puffing upon a Meerschaum pipe, Sink listened gravely as young Lawson confided his fears about the four-disk brake. Then he examined Lawson's calculations and the results of the abortive tests. Despite the fact that he was not a qualified engineer, in the strictest sense of the word, it must certainly have been obvious to Sink that Lawson's calculations were correct and that a four-disk brake would never have worked on the A7D.

But other things of equal importance were also obvious. First, to concede that Lawson's calculations were correct would also mean conceding that Warren's calculations were incorrect. As projects manager, he not only was responsible for Warren's activities, but, in admitting that Warren had erred, he would have to admit that he had erred in trusting Warren's judgment. It also meant that, as projects manager, it would be he who would have to explain the whole messy situation to the Goodrich hierarchy, not only at Troy but possibly on the corporate level at Goodrich's Akron offices. And, having taken Warren's judgment of the four-disk brake at face value (he was forced to do this since, not being an engineer, he was unable to exercise any engineering judgment of his own), he had assured LTV, not once but several times, that about all there was left to do on the brake was pack it in a crate and ship it out the back door.

There's really no problem at all, he told Lawson. After all, Warren was an experienced engineer, and if he said the brake would work, it would work. Just keep on testing and probably, maybe even on the very next try, it'll work out just fine.

Lawson was far from convinced, but without the support of his superiors there was little he could do except keep on testing. By now, housings for the four-disk brake had begun to arrive at the plant, and Lawson was able to build up a production model of the brake and begin the formal qualification tests demanded by the military.

The first qualification attempts went exactly as the tests on the prototype had. Terrific heat developed within the brakes and, after a few, short, simulated stops, the linings crumbled. A new type of lining material was ordered and once again an attempt to qualify the brake was made. Again, failure.

On April 11, the day the thirteenth test was completed, I became personally involved in the A7D situation.

I had worked in the Goodrich test laboratory for five years, starting first as an instrumentation engineer, then later becoming a data analyst and technical writer. As part of my duties, I analyzed the reams and reams of instrumentation data that came from the many testing machines in the laboratory, then transcribed it to a more usable form for the engineering department. And when a new-type brake had successfully completed the required qualification tests, I would issue a formal qualification report.

Qualification reports were an accumulation of all the data and test logs compiled by the test technicians during the qualification tests, and were documentary proof that a brake had met all the requirements established by the military specifications and was therefore presumed safe for flight testing. Before actual flight tests were conducted on a brake, qualification reports had to be delivered to the customer and to various government officials.

On April 11, I was looking over the data from the latest A7D test, and I noticed that many irregularities in testing methods had been noted on the test logs.

Technically, of course, there was nothing wrong with conducting tests in any manner desired, so long as the test was for research purposes only. But qualification test methods are clearly delineated by the military, and I knew that this test had been a formal qualification attempt. One particular notation on the test logs caught my eye. For some of the stops, the instrument which recorded the brake pressure had been deliberately miscalibrated so that, while the brake pressure used during the stops was recorded as 1,000 psi (the maximum pressure that would be available on the A7D aircraft), the pressure had actually been 1,100 psi!

I showed the test logs to the test lab supervisor, Ralph Gretzinger, who said he had learned from the technician who had miscalibrated the instrument that he had been asked to do so by Lawson. Lawson, said Gretzinger, readily admitted asking for the miscalibration, saying he had been told to do so by Sink.

I asked Gretzinger why anyone would want to miscalibrate the data-recording instruments.

"Why? I'll tell you why," he snorted. "That brake is a failure. It's way too small for the job, and they're not ever going to get it to work. They're getting desperate, and instead of scrapping the damned thing and starting over, they figure they can horse around down here in the lab and qualify it that way."

An expert engineer, Gretzinger had been responsible for several innovations in brake design. It was he who had invented the unique brake system used on the famous XB70. A graduate of Georgia Tech, he was a stickler for detail and he had some very firm ideas about honesty and ethics. "If you want to find out what's going on," said Gretzinger, "ask Lawson, he'll tell you."

Curious, I did ask Lawson the next time he came into the lab. He seemed eager to discuss the A7D and gave me the history of his months of frustrating efforts to get Warren and Sink to change the brake design. "I just can't believe this is really happening," said Lawson, shaking his head slowly. "This isn't engineering, at least not what I thought it would be. Back in school, I thought that when you were an engineer, you tried to do your best, no matter what it cost. But this is something else."

He sat across the desk from me, his chin propped in his hand. "Just wait," he warned. "You'll get a chance to see what I'm talking about. You're going to get in the act, too, because I've already had the word that we're going to make one more attempt to qualify the brake, and that's it. Win or lose, we're going to issue a qualification report!"

I reminded him that a qualification report could only be issued after a brake had successfully met all military requirements, and therefore, unless the next qualification attempt was a success, no report would be issued.

"You'll find out," retorted Lawson. "I was already told that regardless of what the brake does on test, it's going to be qualified." He said he had been told in those exact words at a conference with Sink and Russell Van Horn.

This was the first indication that Sink had brought his boss, Van Horn, into the mess. Although Van Horn, as manager of the design engineering section, was responsible for the entire department, he was not necessarily familiar with all phases of every project, and it was not uncommon for those under him to exercise the what-he-doesn't-know-won't-hurt-him philosophy. If he was unaware of the full extent of the A7D situation, it meant that matters had truly reached a desperate stage—that Sink had decided not only to call for help but was looking toward that moment when blame must be borne and, if possible, shared.

Also, if Van Horn had said, "regardless what the brake does on test, it's going to be qualified," then it could only mean that, if necessary, a false qualification report would be issued! I discussed this possibility with Gretzinger, and he assured me that under no circumstances would such a report ever be issued.

"If they want a qualification report, we'll write them one, but we'll tell it just like it is," he declared emphatically. "No false data or false reports are going to come out of this lab."

On May 2, 1968, the fourteenth and final attempt to qualify the brake was begun. Although the same improper methods used to nurse the brake through the previous tests were employed, it soon became obvious that this too would end in failure.

When the tests were about half completed, Lawson asked if I would start preparing the various engineering curves and graphic displays which were normally incorporated in a qualification report. "It looks as though you'll be writing a qualification report shortly," he said.

I flatly refused to have anything to do with the matter and immediately told Gretzinger what I had been asked to do. He was furious and repeated his previous declaration that under no circumstances would any false data or other matter be issued from the lab.

"I'm going to get this settled right now, once and for all," he declared. "I'm going to see Line (Russell Line, manager of the Goodrich Technical Services Section, of which the test lab was a part) and find out just how far this thing is going to go!" He stormed out of the room.

In about an hour, he returned and called me to his desk. He sat silently for a few moments, then muttered, half to himself, "I wonder what the hell they'd do if I just quit?" I didn't answer and I didn't ask him what he meant. I knew. He had been beaten down. He had reached the point when the decision had to be made. Defy them now while there was still time—or knuckle under, sell out.

"You know," he went on uncertainly, looking down at his desk, "I've been an engineer for a long time, and I've always believed that ethics and integrity were every bit as important as theorems and formulas, and never once has anything happened to change my beliefs. Now this....Hell, I've got two sons I've got to put through school and I just...." His voice trailed off.

He sat for a few more minutes, then, looking over the top of his glasses, said hoarsely, "Well, it looks like we're licked. The way it stands now, we're to go ahead and prepare the data and other things for the graphic presentation in the report, and when we're finished, someone upstairs will actually write the report.

"After all," he continued, "we're just drawing some curves, and what happens to them after they leave here, well, we're not responsible for that."

He was trying to persuade himself that as long as we were concerned with only one part of the puzzle and didn't see the completed picture, we really weren't doing anything wrong. He didn't believe what he was saying, and he knew I didn't believe it either. It was an embarrassing and shameful moment for both of us.

I wasn't at all satisfied with the situation and decided that I too would discuss the matter with Russell Line, the senior executive in our section.

Tall, powerfully built, his teeth flashing white, his face tanned to a coffee-brown by a daily stint with a sun lamp, Line looked and acted every inch the executive. He was a crossword-puzzle enthusiast and an ardent golfer, and though he had lived in Troy only a short time, he had been accepted into the Troy Country Club and made an official of the golf committee. He commanded great respect and had come to be well liked by those of us who worked under him.

He listened sympathetically while I explained how I felt about the A7D situation, and when I had finished, he asked me what I wanted him to do about it. I said that as employees of the Goodrich Company we had a responsibility to protect the company and its reputation if at all possible. I said I was certain that officers on the corporate level would never knowingly allow such tactics as had been employed on the A7D.

"I agree with you," he remarked, "but I still want to know what you want me to do about it."

I suggested that in all probability the chief engineer at the Troy plant, H. C. "Bud" Sunderman, was unaware of the A7D problem and that he, Line, should tell him what was going on.

Line laughed, good humoredly. "Sure, I could, but I'm not going to. Bud probably already knows about this thing anyway, and if he doesn't, I'm sure not going to be the one to tell him."

"But why?"

"Because it's none of my business, and it's none of yours. I learned a long time ago not to worry about things over which I had no control. I have no control over this."

I wasn't satisfied with this answer, and I asked him if his conscience wouldn't bother him if, say, during flight tests on the brake, something should happen resulting in death or injury to the test pilot.

"Look," he said, becoming somewhat exasperated, "I just told you I have no control over this thing. Why should my conscience bother me?"

His voice took on a quiet, soothing tone as he continued. "You're just getting all upset over this thing for nothing. I just do as I'm told, and I'd advise you to do the same."

He had made his decision, and now I had to make mine.

I made no attempt to rationalize what I had been asked to do. It made no difference who would falsify which part of the report or whether the actual falsification would be by misleading numbers or misleading words. Whether by acts of commission or omission, all of us who contributed to the fraud would be guilty. The only question left for me to decide was whether or not I would become a party to the fraud.

Before coming to Goodrich in 1963, I had held a variety of jobs, each a little more pleasant, a little more rewarding than the last. At 42, with seven children, I had decided that the Goodrich Company would probably be my "home" for the rest of my working life. The job paid well, it was pleasant and challenging, and the future looked reasonably bright. My wife and I had bought a home and we were ready to settle down into a comfortable, middle-age, middle-class rut. If I refused to take part in the A7D fraud, I would have to either resign or be fired. The report would be written by someone anyway, but I would have the satisfaction of knowing I had had no part in the matter. But bills aren't paid with personal satisfaction, nor house payments with ethical principles. I made my decision. The next morning, I telephoned Lawson and told him I was ready to begin on the qualification report.

In a few minutes, he was at my desk, ready to begin. Before we started, I asked him, "Do you realize what we are going to do?"

"Yeah," he replied bitterly, "we're going to screw LTV. And speaking of screwing," he continued, "I know now how a whore feels, because that's exactly what I've become, an engineering whore. I've sold myself. It's all I can do to look at myself in the mirror when I shave. I make me sick."

I was surprised at his vehemence. It was obvious that he too had done his share of soul searching and didn't like what he had found. Somehow, though, the air seemed clearer after his outburst, and we began working on the report.

I had written dozens of qualification reports, and I knew what a "good" one looked like. Resorting to the actual test data only on occasion, Lawson and I proceeded to prepare page after page of elaborate, detailed engineering curves, charts, and test logs, which purported to show what had happened during the formal qualification tests. Where temperatures were too high, we deliberately chopped them down a few hundred degrees, and where they were too low, we raised them to a value that would appear reasonable to the LTV and military engineers. Brake pressure, torque values, distances, times—everything of consequence was tailored to fit the occasion.

Occasionally, we would find that some test either hadn't been performed at all or had been conducted improperly. On those occasions, we "conducted" the test—successfully, of course—on paper.

For nearly a month we worked on the graphic presentation that would be a part of the report. Meanwhile, the fourteenth and final qualification attempt had been completed, and the brake, not unexpectedly, had failed again.

During that month, Lawson and I talked of little else except the enormity of what we were doing. The more involved we became in our work, the more apparent became our own culpability. We discussed such things as the Nuremberg trials and how they related to our guilt and complicity in the A7D situation. Lawson often expressed his opinion that the brake was downright dangerous and that, once on flight tests, "anything is liable to happen."

I saw his boss, John Warren, at least twice during that month and needled him about what we were doing. He didn't take the jibes too kindly but managed to laugh the situation off as "one of those things." One day I remarked that what we were doing amounted to fraud, and he pulled out an engineering handbook and turned to a section on laws as they related to the engineering profession.

He read the definition of fraud aloud, then said, "Well, technically I don't think what we're doing can be called fraud. I'll admit it's not right, but it's just one of those things. We're just kinda caught in the middle. About all I can tell you is, do like I'm doing. Make copies of everything and put them in your SYA file."

"What's an 'SYA' file?" I asked.

"That's a 'save your ass' file." He laughed.

On June 5, 1968, the report was officially published and copies were delivered in person to the Air Force and LTV. Within a week, flight tests were begun at Edwards Air Force Base in California. Searle Lawson was sent to California as Goodrich's representative. Within approximately two weeks, he returned because some rather unusual incidents during the tests had caused them to be canceled.

His face was grim as he related stories of several near crashes during landings—caused by brake troubles. He told me about one incident in which, upon landing, one brake was literally welded together by the intense heat developed during the test stop. The wheel locked, and the plane skidded for nearly 1,500 feet before coming to a halt. The plane was jacked up and the wheel removed. The fused parts within the brake had to be pried apart.

Lawson had returned to Troy from California that same day, and that evening, he and others of the Goodrich engineering department left for Dallas for a high-level conference with LTV.

That evening I left work early and went to see my attorney. After I told him the story, he advised that, while I was probably not actually guilty of fraud, I was certainly part of a conspiracy to defraud. He advised me to go to the Federal Bureau of Investigation and offered to arrange an appointment. The following week he took me to the Dayton office of the FBI, and after I had been warned that I would not be immune from prosecution, I disclosed the A7D matter to one of the agents. The agent told me to say nothing about the episode to anyone and to report any further incident to him. He said he would forward the story to his superiors in Washington.

A few days later, Lawson returned from the conference in Dallas and said that the Air Force, which had previously approved the qualification report, had suddenly rescinded that approval and was demanding to see some of the raw test data taken during the tests. I gathered that the FBI had passed the word.

Finally, early in October 1968, Lawson submitted his resignation, to take effect on October 25. On October 18, I submitted my own resignation, to take effect on November 1. In my resignation, addressed to Russell Line, I cited the A7D report and stated: "As you are aware, this report contained numerous deliberate and willful misrepresentations which, according to legal counsel, constitute fraud and expose both myself and others to criminal charges of conspiracy to defraud....The events of the past seven months have created an atmosphere of deceit and distrust in which it is impossible to work...."

On October 25, I received a sharp summons to the office of Bud Sunderman. As chief engineer at the Troy plant, Sunderman was responsible for the entire engineering division. Tall and graying, impeccably dressed at all times, he was capable of producing a dazzling smile or a hearty chuckle or immobilizing his face into marble hardness, as the occasion required.

I faced the marble hardness when I reached his office. He motioned me to a chair. "I have your resignation here," he snapped, "and I must say you have made some rather shocking, I might even say irresponsible, charges. This is very serious."

Before I could reply, he was demanding an explanation. "I want to know exactly what the fraud is in connection with the A7D and how you can dare accuse this company of such a thing!"

I started to tell him some of the things that had happened during the testing, but he cut me off saying, "There's nothing wrong with anything we've done here. You aren't aware of all the things that have been going on behind the scenes. If you had known the true situation, you would never have made these charges." He said that in view of my apparent "disloyalty" he had decided to accept my resignation "right now," and said it would be better for all concerned if I left the plant immediately. As I got up to leave he asked me if I intended to "carry this thing further."

I answered simply, "Yes," to which he replied, "Suit yourself." Within twenty minutes, I had cleaned out my desk and left. Forty-eight hours later, the B.F. Goodrich Company recalled the qualification report and the four-disk brake, announcing that it would replace the brake with a new, improved, five-disk brake at no cost to LTV.

Ten months later, on August 13, 1969, I was the chief government witness at a hearing conducted before Senator William Proxmire's Economy in Government Subcommittee of the Congress's Joint Economic Committee. I related the A7D story to the committee, and my testimony was supported by Searle Lawson, who followed me to the witness stand. Air Force officers also testified, as well as a four-man team from the General Accounting Office, which had conducted an investigation of the A7D brake at the request of Senator Proxmire. Both Air Force and GAO investigators declared that the brake was dangerous and had not been tested properly.

Testifying for Goodrich was R. G. Jeter, vice president and general counsel of the company, from the Akron headquarters. Representing the Troy plant was Robert Sink. These two denied any wrongdoing on the part of the Goodrich Company, despite expert testimony to the contrary by Air Force and GAO officials. Sink was quick to deny any connection with the writing of the report or of directing any falsifications, claiming to be on the West Coast at the time. John Warren was the man who supervised its writing, said Sink.

As for me, I was dismissed as a high-school graduate with no technical training, while Sink testified that Lawson was a young, inexperienced engineer. "We tried to give him guidance," Sink testified, "but he preferred to have his own convictions."

About changing the data and figures in the report, Sink said: "When you take data from several different sources, you have to rationalize among those data what is the true story. This is part of your engineering know-how." He admitted that changes had been made in the data, "but only to make them more consistent with the overall picture of the data that is available."

Jeter pooh-poohed the suggestion that anything improper occurred, saying: "We have thirty-odd engineers at this plant...and I say to you that it is incredible that these men would stand idly by and see reports changed or falsified....I mean you just do not have to do that working for anybody....Just nobody does that."

The four-hour hearing adjourned with no real conclusion reached by the committee. But the following day the Department of Defense made sweeping changes in its inspection, testing, and reporting procedures. A spokesman for the DOD said the changes were a result of the Goodrich episode.

The A7D is now in service, sporting a Goodrich-made five-disk brake, a brake that works very well, I'm told. Business at the Goodrich plant is good. Lawson is now an engineer for LTV and has been assigned to the A7D project. And I am now a newspaper reporter.

At this writing, those remaining at Goodrich are still secure in the same positions, all except Russell Line and Robert Sink. Line has been rewarded with a promotion to production superintendent, a large step upward on the corporate ladder. As for Sink, he moved up into Line's old job.

Questions

1. Perform a culture audit on B.F. Goodrich.
2. What control mechanisms would you institute to ensure that this type of situation did not occur again?

Chapter 8

Evaluating
The Parallel
Planning Approach

The purpose of this final chapter is to evaluate the potential effectiveness of the parallel planning approach. In order to accomplish this goal we begin with a discussion about *why* people in an organization act unethically. For this purpose the observations of three other authors will be used. After answering this question, the chapter continues by comparing the parallel planning system to each of the answers and evaluates its potential effectiveness in reducing unethical behavior.

WHY PEOPLE BEHAVE UNETHICALLY

In a *Harvard Business Review* article entitled "Why 'Good' Managers Make Bad Ethical Choices," Saul Gellerman identified "four commonly held rationalizations that can lead to misconduct:"[1]

A belief that the activity is within reasonable ethical and legal limits—that is, that it is not "really" illegal or immoral.

A belief that the activity is in the individual's or the corporation's best interests—that the individual would somehow be expected to undertake the activity.

A belief that the activity is "safe" because it will never be found out or publicized; the classic crime-and-punishment issue of discovery.

A belief that because the activity helps the company the company will condone it and even protect the person who engages in it.[2]

1. Saul Gellerman, "Why 'Good' Managers Make Bad Ethical Choices," *Harvard Business Review* (July–August 1986), pp. 85–90.
2. Ibid., p. 88.

About the first rationalization Gellerman says, "Put enough people in an ambiguous, ill-defined situation, and some will conclude that whatever hasn't been labeled specifically wrong must be OK—especially if they are rewarded for certain acts."[3] About the second rationalization he says, "...believing that unethical conduct is in a person's or corporation's best interests nearly always results from a parochial view of what those interests are....The sad truth is that many managers have been promoted on the basis of 'great' results obtained in just those (unethical) ways, leaving unfortunate successors to inherit the inevitable whirlwind."[4] About the third rationalization he says, "The most effective deterrent is not to increase the severity of punishment for those caught but to heighten the perceived probability of being caught in the first place."[5] And finally about the fourth rationalization he says, "How do we keep company loyalty from going berserk?...the practice of declaring codes of ethics and teaching them to managers is not enough to deter unethical conduct. Something stronger is needed."[6]

Another article by James Waters and Frederick Bird, published in the *Journal of Business Ethics*, focuses on "moral stress" as the important reason why managers make unethical choices.[7] These authors directly interviewed several managers in order to come to this conclusion. They argue that moral stress occurs "because of lack of clarity about practical, specific behaviors that are appropriate in various situations, and because of uncertain feelings of obligations to act in accord with moral standards."[8] They continue "...the interviewed managers frequently described the moral decision as one which had or would have been costly to them or their firms."[9] Then finally they state that "When the managers' implicit statements

3. Ibid., p. 88.
4. Ibid., p. 89.
5. Ibid., p. 89.
6. Ibid., p. 90.
7. James A. Waters and Frederick Bird, "The Moral Dimension of Organizational Culture," *Journal of Business Ethics*, (January, 1987), pp. 15–22.
8. Ibid., p. 15.
9. Ibid., p. 16.

about moral standards are viewed as a composite, the picture that emerges is one of ambiguity and competing principles."[10] Their argument that moral stress occurs in such circumstances seems undeniable.

The outlet for the moral stress experienced by managers is suggested as taking several different forms. Waters and Bird give several examples.

> they may...follow the fads and fashions of what others are in fact doing. They may also quite strictly and narrowly adhere to particular directives and rules, ignoring vaguer, more general principles. They may complain at length about the indiscretions of others, hoping by this strategy to expose the moral failings of others, and turn their own attention, as well as that of others, away from the uncertainties they may feel about their own actions. Finally, they may attempt to redefine moral issues into amoral matters of technique or taste, so that alternative courses of action are considered in relation to questions of available resources and personal inclination, rather than in relation to general normative standards.[11]

These two authors continue and suggest that "a key source of moral stress for individual managers is the general absence of institutionalized structures which accord a public character to moral questions..."[12] Thus, while ethical questions are very important to individual managers they are seldom discussed in the same way that managers discuss problems in the functional areas of the business (i.e., marketing, production, finance, and so on). The authors conclude that "morality needs to be...collectively recognized as an important dimension of an organization's culture and as an important aspect of everyday managerial life."[13]

The third and final explanation of why people in business make unethical decisions comes from a 1987 survey by *Personnel*

10. Ibid., p. 16.
11. Ibid., p. 17.
12. Ibid., p. 18.
13. Ibid., p. 18.

Journal.[14] The respondents were asked "to identify examples of unethical behavior" and their reasons or explanations for that behavior. The primary reasons given for unethical behavior in the workplace, with the percent of respondents citing it, are the desire for more power (74 percent), the desire for more money (73 percent), the desire for faster advancement (40 percent), and the desire for more recognition (38 percent).[15] Comments by the respondents provided more insight to the problem of unethical behavior.

> ...such specifics masked deeper reasons. One respondent expressed a popular viewpoint when observing that we live in a competitive society in which there is "pressure to do it faster, cheaper, better."
>
> Such pressures, in turn, put people in positions in which they feel unethical behavior is the only alternative they have to get ahead. As people move through careers, they "strive for a record of accomplishment and attainment of position," said one respondent. Another observed that, "Advancement is limited by the economy and demographics, and common sense frequently loses to expediency. People often feel that lapses in ethics don't hurt anyone."[16]

The article reporting this study goes on to suggest that many respondents felt that senior management must establish what is expected of employees. One respondent said "A corporation has a responsibility to make known its position with regard to ethical behavior and put into place written standards that will clearly spell out what it expects of its employees and what it will not tolerate."[17] Other suggestions included the firing of employees who act unethically, a videotape of the company chairman discussing the importance of ethical behavior for new employee orientation, "annual

14. Allen Halcrow, "Is There a Crisis in Business Ethics," *Personnel Journal* (November 1987), pp. 10–17.
15. Ibid., p. 14.
16. Ibid., p. 14.
17. Ibid., p. 14.

audits of compliance with ethical standards," the use of ethical standards in job descriptions, and the use of training programs.[18]

Each of the three explanations of why people behave unethically in organizations offers different insights. However, each explanation also has considerable similarity with the others. Table 8-1 summarizes and groups the explanations that were encountered in the preceding discussion. The authors believe that summary includes the essence of all of the ideas that have been presented. The section that follows compares the parallel planning approach to each of the explanations in Table 8-1 as a test of its potential ability to prevent unethical behavior.

Table 8-1
SUMMARY EXPLANATIONS OF WHY PEOPLE IN ORGANIZATIONS BEHAVE UNETHICALLY

I. There is a lack of clarity about what behaviors are appropriate or acceptable. Employees are likely to encounter ambiguous, ill-defined situations in which they do not know what the company expects. This situation creates ethical stress.

II. There is an individual understanding of what is right, as well as an understanding of what the company "says" they want me to do, but confusion concerning whether the company *really* means what it says. This situation also creates ethical stress.

III. There is a belief that the unethical activity is in the company's best interest. The belief focuses on the conflict that sometimes occurs between what is ethical and what is economically beneficial. This belief is perhaps accompanied by belief that the company will condone the unethical behavior and will reward the employee for undertaking it.

IV. There is a belief that the unethical activity is in the individual's best interest. The individual sees the activity as a route to power, money, advancement, and recognition. This belief may be accompanied by the belief that the activity will *not* be discovered—that the individual can "get away with it."

V Company owes me.

18. Ibid., p. 17.

EVALUATING PARALLEL PLANNING

The first explanation in Table 8-1 of why people behave unethically in organizations is concerned with a lack of clarity about acceptable behavior. The parallel planning system calls for a clear set of core values, integrated into the corporate culture. These values are specifically designed to confront the most difficult ethical problems that the organization is likely to encounter. Thus, in the worse scenarios, employees should have clear knowledge of what is expected from them. Further, the values are based on a carefully planned ethical profile which should also become part of the organization's culture. When the enculturation process has been achieved, employees at all levels of the organization should understand the acceptable boundaries of behavior. The keys to success in solving the problems of lack of clarity and ambiguity are (1) carefully and rationally selecting the core values and (2) diligent implementation of these values into the corporate culture.

The second explanation in Table 8-1 also deals with employee confusion. Here the company has a statement of policy, but the employee isn't sure that the company means what it says. Again, the parallel planning system produces a set of values that are reinforced in the lore of the organization. The implementation process builds stories about the rewards that come from following these values, and develops heroes who were successful against the odds. The openness of the ethical organization encourages people to talk about ethical and social responsibility problems. Thus, if the parallel planning process is followed by top management, there should be no confusion about what the company *really* expects of the employee.

The third explanation in Table 8-1 focuses on the conflict between attaining profits and behaving ethically. If an activity seems profitable, even though it is unethical, employees may believe that it is in the company's best interest. When this situation is accompanied by the belief that the company will condone and reward unethical behavior to attain profits, such behavior is likely to occur. And, of course, companies have rewarded unethical activities that produced profits—knowingly and unknowingly.

An analysis of the organization's impact on its environments, as part of the parallel planning process, helps to clearly define what is in the organization's short- and long-run best interest—something that top management in many of the examples used in this book failed to understand. "Best interest" includes both monetary and other concerns, and the parallel planning process forces a look at both. Top management can use that information to build a convincing case to employees about what is and what isn't acceptable behavior and *why*. When people know the reasons for requested behaviors they can act more intelligently in ambiguous situations and are often more willing to cooperate. The parallel planning approach calls for more openness in an organization's culture than is normally found, and this openness allows individual employees to use their own innate intelligence in a way that is most productive for the company.

The final explanation in Table 8-1 is concerned with the individual who is willing to act unethically in order to attain personal gain. It seems obvious that such an individual believes that he or she can "get away with it." The fact that in many organizations individuals do get away with unethical behavior, and are even rewarded for it, fosters a continuation of that behavior. It also encourages the spread of unethical behavior to others.

Core values can only be instilled in the organization with top management's understanding and support. That support includes strict enforcement. It should be clear to all employees that unethical behavior will be punished and that the core values are more than just words. On the other hand, when someone goes beyond what is expected to be ethical, they should be rewarded with power, money, advancement, and recognition. Stories of such incidents provide positive reinforcement to the culture and create the heroes that become part of "water fountain" conversation.

If enforcement and reinforcement of the core values is achieved, employees should understand that it is not in their personal best interest to behave unethically. Further, the belief that the activity is "safe" and will never be found out or publicized should be eliminated. If the organization is open with its employees, so that everyone knows "what's going on" surrounding their job, the issue of discovery is less likely to be a problem. In addition, if the company carries out an aggressive control function, unethical acts are more likely to be discovered. As suggested in the Gellerman article, increasing the probability of discovery is often a greater deterrent than increasing punishment.

A FINAL OBSERVATION: ETHICS PAYS

A publication of the Business Roundtable entitled *Corporate Ethics: A Prime Business Asset* reports on the ethical policy and practice of several large corporations. The following quotation comes from the conclusions in the summary section of the report.

> It may come as a surprise to some that, as details in this report indicate, corporate ethics programs are not mounted primarily to improve the reputation of business. Instead, many executives believe that a culture in which ethical concern permeates the whole organization is necessary to the self-interest of the company. This is required, they feel, if the company is to be able to maintain profitability and develop the necessary competitiveness for effective performance. In the view of the top executives represented in this study, there is no conflict between ethical practices and acceptable profits. Indeed, the first is a necessary precondition for the second. Sound values, purposes, and practices are the basis for long-range achievement.[19]

Thus, the conclusion of top executives from companies like Boeing, Champion International, Chemical Bank, General Mills, GTE, Hewlett-Packard, Johnson & Johnson, McDonnell Douglas, Norton, and Xerox is that, in the long run, "Ethics Pays."

19. *Corporate Ethics: A Prime Business Asset* (New York: The Business Roundtable, 1988), p. 9.

Exercises for Chapter 8

The Bay Area Rapid Transit (BART) Whistle-blowing Incident[1]
Lea P. Stewart*

Background

Whistle-blowing incidents do not occur in a vacuum, nor do they occur instantaneously. They develop over time, even though they may appear to occur suddenly and without warning.[2] The Bay Area Rapid Transit (BART) whistle-blowing incident is not atypical in this respect.

On November 6, 1962 voters in Alameda, Contra Costa, and San Francisco counties in California approved a $792-million bond issue and authorized construction of a 71.5-mile rapid transit system which included a Transbay tube under the bay between San Francisco and Oakland, subways under Oakland and Market Streets in San Francisco, and a tunnel through the Berkely Hills. The voters were promised an ultra-modern, computer-controlled, streamlined, and soundless transportation system. In 1962, the total cost of the system was estimated to be $996 million.

The board of directors of the Bay Area Rapid Transit District (BARTD) hired a consortium of three engineering firms (Parsons,

Original essay. Copyright © 1984 by Lea Stewart. Reprinted by permission of the author. *Department of Communications, Rutgers University.

1. For a complete discussion of the whistle-blowing incident and a history of the Bay Area Rapid Transit District see Lea P. Stewart, "The Ethnography of a Whistle Blowing Incident: Implications for Organizational Communication," Diss. Purdue University 1979, and R. M. Anderson, R. Perrucci, D. E. Schendel and L. E. Trachtman, *Divided Loyalties: Whistle-Blowing at BART* (West Lafayette, Indiana: Purdue University Press, 1980). Funding for these studies was provided by National Science Foundation Grant No. OSS76-14230, "An In-Depth Case Study of Ethical Problems of Professional Engineers: The BART (Bay Area Rapid Transit) Engineers."

2. Richard Austin Smith, *Corporations in Crisis* (Garden City, New York: Anchor Books, 1966), p. 3.

Brinckerhoff, Quade and Douglas; Tudor Engineering Company; and Bechtel Corporation) to engineer and manage the design and construction of the BART system. This consortium became known as PBTB, and received a contract that was described at the time as "probably...the largest contract ever let for engineering services."[3]

In the original contracts, full operation of the BART system was scheduled for late 1970.[4] At that time, however, construction of the system was not complete, and the transit cars were still being tested. Construction of the system was not completed until July 1971. Because BART was not an ordinary railroad, completion of construction did not mean the system was ready to operate. The BART system was designed to be controlled automatically, so the computer control system had to be tested thoroughly before the first passenger could ride the trains.

By 1972, BARTD management was under tremendous financial pressure. In 1969, the California state legislature had approved a 0.5 percent district sales tax to provide an additional $150 million to complete the system. Nevertheless, BART's costs continued to increase. The completion of the system was behind schedule and the money was running out.

BART also faced engineering problems. The BART system was to be run by a computer system which would regulate the speed of trains, stop them at the proper stations, and open and close train doors to let passengers in and out. Unfortunately, the development of this Automatic Train Control (ATC) system by Westinghouse did not proceed as smoothly as planned. The first successful test of the ATC software was not completed until October 1971, almost three years after the BART system was originally scheduled to open. As one local newspaper reported in January 1972: "Hailed many years ago when BART was just a dream as one of the innovative mass transit systems in the country, some fear the system will be outdated and plagued with problems within a year after it starts operation."[5]

3. Francis B. O'Gara, "Sharp Fight on Transit Engineers," *San Francisco Examiner*, Nov. 29, 1962, p. 17, col. 2.

4. Joseph H. Wujek, Jr., "Bart: Electronics Aids Rapid Transit," *Electronics World*, January 1969, p. 36.

5. "BART Depot Construction: The Beat Goes On," *Contra Costa Times*, Jan. 7, 1972, p. 2A, col. 3.

This was the state of the BARTD organization preceding the 1972 whistle-blowing incident.

The Engineers

In September 1966, Holger Hjortsvang saw a help-wanted advertisement for engineers for the BART system. He had been looking for work for several months, so he applied for a position and was hired as a train control engineer. He wanted to specialize in the central control of the BART system, so eleven months after he was hired he was sent to Pittsburgh for ten months to work with the system's designers at Westinghouse. When BARTD, PBTB, and Westinghouse began to coordinate the start-up of the system, Hjortsvang's "essential function" was to "specify and write maintenance procedures" and give "assistance to the technicians and maintenance foremen." He continued to monitor the development of the train control system as his "personal duty."[6] His direct supervisor was E. F. Wargin, superintendent of BARTD's Maintenance Engineering Division. (An abbreviated version of the BARTD organizational chart is included at the end of this case.)

In late 1969, Robert Bruder saw a want ad in the *San Francisco Chronicle*, applied for employment, and was hired by BARTD as an electrical and electronic engineer. His duties included coordinating the train control and communication contracts with the consultants in BARTD's operations group, PBTB and Westinghouse. He monitored the schedules to ensure that the contracts were being complied with. He reported directly to Frank Wagner, supervisor of Systemwide Contracts in BARTD's Construction Division.

In 1971, Max Blankenzee worked as a temporary programmer-analyst for Westinghouse Electric Corporation. Among other things, he worked on the computer programming to be used in the BART system's central control and, through this experience, became interested in working for BARTD. He met Holger Hjortsvang while working for Westinghouse and asked him if BARTD had any openings. Hjortsvang brought him an application form and took his

---

6. *Holger Hjortsvang v. San Francisco Bay Area Rapid Transit District*, Cal. Sup. Ct. 1973, No. 436443, Deposition of Holger Hjortsvang, p. 99.

resumé and completed application to E. F. Wargin. Wargin interviewed Blankenzee and hired him in May 1971 as a senior programmer and analyst. He worked on the "development, installation, operation and maintenance of the train control and central control system."[7] In the organizational hierarchy Blankenzee was considered subordinate to Hjortsvang.

Hjortsvang and Blankenzee shared an office in the basement of the Lake Merritt station in Oakland, California. They were physically separated from Wargin and BARTD upper management, whose offices were located in BARTD headquarters in San Francisco. Bruder contacted Hjortsvang and Blankenzee as a routine part of his work verifying the status of the train control contract. Hjortsvang and Blankenzee were involved primarily with the train and yard control computers and Bruder's job was to check the train control contract. In 1972, Hjortsvang was 60 years old, Bruder was 51, and Blankenzee was 30.

THE Whistle-blowing Incident

During early or middle 1971 Hjortsvang invited Bruder and Bruder's co-worker Jay Burns to lunch. Hjortsvang expressed concern that the BART project was not proceeding as it should. According to Bruder, Hjortsvang wanted the support of other professionals to "somehow get information up to upper management that things weren't being taken care of."[8] Bruder claimed Hjortsvang "was blocked in his own channels…and wanted to see if we could go up through our channels and get some solution to the general problem of the contractor not complying."[9] Hjortsvang suggested they go outside normal management channels of communication, possibly to a member of the BARTD board of directors, because "nobody in-

---

7. *Holger Hjortsvang v. San Francisco Bay Area Rapid Transit District*, Cal. Sup. Ct. 1974, No. 436443, Answer of Plaintiff Max Blankenzee to Interrogatories of Defendant, p. 9.

8. Telephone interview with Robert Bruder conducted by Robert Perrucci, June 15, 1977.

9. *Robert Bruder v. San Francisco Bay Area Rapid Transit District*, Cal. Sup. Ct. 1973, No. 436444, Deposition of Robert Bruder, p. 25.

side is listening."[10] Burns and Bruder discouraged him. Burns told him it would be better to work within normal lines of command and communication. Bruder refused to get involved.

During the middle of 1971 Hjortsvang spoke to Gilbert Ortiz, a BARTD employee who was also a union organizer. Ortiz said he could arrange a meeting for Hjortsvang with any of the labor-supported members of BARTD's board of directors. Hjortsvang reported: "After thinking about that...for a while, I decided that I did not want to...start anything, anything that could be dangerous for me personally."[11]

Several months later, on September 8–10, 1971, Hjortsvang and Blankenzee attended a seminar given by the Advanced Institute of Technology on standards in program development. During September, October, November, and December, Blankenzee sent his supervisor, Ed Wargin, a series of memoranda criticizing various aspects of the ATC system and offering to give BARTD management a half-day presentation on what was wrong with the system and how to correct the problems. He was never given permission to make the presentation.

Hjortsvang also wrote a series of memoranda between April 1969 and December 1971 which pointed out problems in the train control system and called for the creation of a Systems and Programming Division of the Department of Operations to coordinate operating procedures, train control, and computer programming. As with Blankenzee's memoranda, BARTD management did not act upon the suggestions in Hjortsvang's memoranda. Nonetheless, an unsigned memorandum titled "BART System Engineering" and dated "Nov. 18, 1971" played a key role in the whistle-blowing incident. Although the memorandum was unsigned, Hjortsvang acknowledged that he was the author.

According to E. F. Wargin, Hjortsvang's supervisor, the November 18, 1971, memorandum was "circulated to a large number of employees on the BART technical staff, including most, if not

10. Telephone interview with Robert Bruder conducted by Robert Perrucci, June 15, 1977.
11. Hjortsvang Deposition, p. 124.

all, of the engineers under my supervision."[12] Wargin's supervisor, General Superintendent of Power and Way C. O. Kramer, sent a copy to his supervisor, Director of Operations E. J. Ray, and one to Assistant General Manager D. G. Hammond. Kramer claimed he discussed the memorandum with Hammond, and they disagreed with its proposal to restructure the BARTD organization to include a systems engineering group. Kramer claimed he did not make an effort to find out who wrote it. Because of the writing style, Wargin believed it was written by Hjortsvang.

According to Bruder's supervisor, Frank Wagner, in late 1971 Bruder spoke to him and several other BARTD managers about forming a systems engineering group to provide a better method of coordinating operations. Wagner and the other BARTD managers with whom Bruder talked did not recommend the formation of such a group.

Thus, during 1971, the three engineers became increasingly concerned about the BART system. Each engineer communicated his concerns to his supervisor, but did not receive an answer he felt answered his questions satisfactorily.

Each of the three engineers was concerned about somewhat different problems affecting the BART system. Hjortsvang was concerned, first, about the ability of the ATC system to control the trains in the way the specifications required because, in his opinion, the train control components were inadequate and were not being tested properly, the Westinghouse design deviated from good engineering practice, and the friction he perceived within the Westinghouse organization could cause trouble getting the system coordinated properly. In addition, he believed BARTD's internal management structure was not adequate to monitor the progress of the ATC system to ensure the development of a "satisfactory system."[13]

Blankenzee also had two main concerns about the development of the BART system. First, he believed the system was not being tested adequately. Second, he felt that BARTD engineers

12. *Holger Hjortsvang v. San Francisco Bay Area Rapid Transit District,* Cal. Sup. Ct. 1974, No. 436443, Declaration of E. Wargin, p. 2.

13. Hjortsvang Deposition, p. 77.

would be unable to maintain the system because they lacked documentation which would allow them to understand the "internal workings of the system."[14] Bruder believed that BARTD management, made up mostly of nonengineers, did not have the technical expertise to supervise development of the train control system adequately and that it was publicly announcing unrealistic opening dates.

By late 1971, Hjortsvang and Blankenzee were both concerned about the development of the BART system and frustrated in their attempts to receive answers from their supervisors. Hjortsvang spoke to Ortiz again, and Ortiz reported he could put Hjortsvang and Blankenzee in contact with members of the board of directors to open up a line of communication with BARTD's top management.

Several days later Ortiz told Hjortsvang and Blankenzee that he had tried to set up a meeting for them with BARTD directors William C. Blake and Nello J. Bianco, but was unsuccessful. He suggested Blankenzee phone Blake personally. Blankenzee phoned Blake and told him several engineers were concerned about problems in the development of the BART system and would like to present their concerns to him so he could talk to BARTD's upper management about the problems. According to Blankenzee, Blake told him to set up a meeting which Blake would attend. In addition, Blankenzee claimed he told Blake the engineers did not have anyone to back up their story, but that Blake could hire a consultant to confirm their concerns. According to Blankenzee: "We wanted him to get the independent consultant, but since he did not have the time we said we would get it."[15] Blankenzee attempted to set up a meeting but was unable to reach Blake again.

While he was attempting to set up this meeting, Blankenzee searched for an independent consultant to verify his and Hjortsvang's concerns. He contacted an acquaintance who recommended Edward Burfine. Blankenzee contacted Burfine and asked him "on behalf of the directors" to visit the BART system and "pass

14. Telephone interview with Max Blankenzee conducted by Robert Perrucci, Feb. 21, 1977.

15. *Max Blankenzee v. San Francisco Bay Area Rapid Transit District*, Cal. Sup. Ct. 1973, No. 436445, Deposition of Max Leopold Blankenzee, p. 88.

judgment on our statement of BART."[16] According to Burfine, Blankenzee told him he wanted a short study of the ATC system to be given to the board of directors, and that a group of directors was seeking the report.[17] Burfine spent one day in November 1971 at the Lake Merritt station talking to Blankenzee, Hjortsvang, and Bruder and looking at specifications for the system, computer hardware, and various documentations.

Shortly after his visit to the BART system, Burfine sent a draft of a report to Hjortsvang and Blankenzee. They corrected some errors in the report, and Burfine wrote a corrected version with a cover letter addressed to the BARTD board of directors. Blankenzee, Hjortsvang, and Bruder all received a copy of the final "Burfine Report." Since Blankenzee and Hjortsvang had been unable to meet with directors Blake and Bianco, Ortiz told them Director Daniel Helix, who had just become a board member in October 1971, was interested in talking with them. According to Helix: "I asked both directors Bianco and Blake about this prior to my meeting with the engineers. They confirmed that they were aware of the problem and encouraged me to meet with the engineers and with Gil Ortiz."[18] (Later, both Blake and Bianco adamantly denied ordering the Burfine Report.)

According to Hjortsvang, the contact with Helix was a "last-ditch attempt" to attract BARTD management's attention to a situation which they felt was threatening the successful completion of the system.[19] Blankenzee, Hjortsvang, Ortiz, and Helix met in early January 1972 in the local union office in Oakland. The engineers told Helix the BART system would not be ready to open as scheduled; Helix became concerned about the safety of the system after listening to them. He asked them why they came to him instead of going to Assistant General Manager Hammond or General Manager Stokes, and they told him they tried to go through their supervisors but could get no response.

16. Blankenzee Deposition, p. 89.

17. *Holger Hjortsvang v. San Francisco Bay Area Rapid Transit District*, Cal. Sup. Ct. 1974, No. 436443, Declaration of Jerome C. Dougherty, Exhibit F, p. 5.

18. Letter received by R. M. Anderson from Daniel Helix, Aug. 14, 1978.

19. Gordon G. Friedlander, "The Case of the Three Engineers vs. BART," *IEEE Spectrum*, October 1974, p. 70.

Hjortsvang gave Helix a copy of the November 18, 1971, memorandum. According to Blankenzee, he and Hjortsvang told Helix that they had retained Burfine to provide independent verification of their concerns.

On January 9, 1972 Hjortsvang's November 18, 1971, memorandum appeared in an article in the *Contra Costa Times,* a local newspaper. The article described Helix's concerns about the safety of the BART system and labeled the anonymous memorandum a "memo to the board of directors."[20] Later on, Hjortsvang claimed he gave copies of the memorandum to Helix "to hand to the members of the board, but it was certainly not intended for further distribution, or publication."[21]

According to Blankenzee, the second meeting with Helix was held in Concord, California, and was attended by Blankenzee, Bruder, Hjortsvang, Helix, and a computer specialist brought by Helix. Helix read the Burfine Report and asked questions. Following this meeting, Helix gave a copy of the Burfine Report to General Manager Stokes without disclosing the names of the three engineers.

While waiting for a response from Stokes, Helix, who was the vice mayor of Concord, California, talked about the BART system after a Concord city council meeting and mentioned the Burfine Report. Justin Roberts, an investigative reporter for the *Contra Costa Times,* overheard Helix's remark and questioned him about the report. Helix said the report was about the BART system and that he had given a copy of the report to the BARTD general manager. Roberts asked for a copy; Helix gave it to him after Roberts promised not to release it until Helix received a response from General Manager Stokes.

Stokes arranged a meeting for Helix and representatives of PBTB which Helix later felt was "a royal snow job." According to Helix, the PBTB representatives said "not to worry about anything, that there were no problems that they were not aware of or couldn't handle, that things were going along just fine and that the system

---

20. Rick Vogt, "Local BART Director Checking Into Reasons for System Delays," *Contra Costa Times,* Jan. 9, 1972, Sec. A, p. 7, col. 1.

21. Letter received by R. M. Anderson from H. Hjortsvang, July 28, 1978.

was going to open in March or April 1972 on schedule."[22] After the meeting, Helix told Roberts he could release the Burfine Report because the situation was "shaping up to be a massive cover-up."[23]

The Burfine Report appeared in the *Contra Costa Times* on January 20, 1972, and the story was picked up by other local papers. According to Bruder, the Burfine Report had already been given to all BARTD board members and top management, but nothing was done about it until it appeared in the press.

Once the Burfine Report appeared in the press, BARTD management attempted to find out who was responsible for it. According to Blankenzee, Wargin called him into his office and asked Blankenzee if he knew who the "ring-leader" of the group of engineers speaking to Helix was. Wargin asked if Hjortsvang was the leader and explained that he wanted to know "because BART couldn't tolerate that type of person in its organization."[24] Blankenzee denied knowing the ringleader. On February 7, 1972, Director of Operations Ray met with Hjortsvang and asked him if he had been talking to Helix. Hjortsvang said he had not.

The BARTD board of directors met on February 24, 1972. Board of Directors' President George Silliman began the meeting by suggesting that the engineers who had been speaking to Helix speak with General Manager Stokes. Silliman said he had been assured that Stokes' "office was open to any complaints by staff members and that if there are any 'corrective measures' to be taken, Stokes would see they are taken."[25] During the meeting Stokes said "his door was always open" to employees who wanted to discuss problems concerning the BART system.[26] The issue was closed, and a vote of confidence was given to Stokes.

22. *Holger Hjortsvang v. San Francisco Bay Area Rapid Transit District*, Cal. Sup. Ct. 1974, No. 436443, Declaration of Daniel Helix, p. 4.

23. Personal interview with Daniel Helix conducted by Dan E. Schendel, July 26, 1977.

24. *Holger Hjortsvang v. San Francisco Bay Area Rapid Transit District*, Cal. Sup. Ct. 1974, No. 436443, Supplemental Answers of Plaintiff Max Blankenzee, p. 3.

25. Rick Vogt, "Helix Loses as BART Supports Staff," *Contra Costa Times*, Feb. 25, 1972, Sec. A, p. 1, col. 3.

26. Justin Roberts, "3 BART Engineers Fired for Aiding Burfine Inquiries," *Contra Costa Times*, Mar. 7, 1972, Sec. A, p. 1.

In reference to the engineers who had been speaking to Helix, one of the other directors declared: "I have very little sympathy for the people involved at this point. If I was running the organization, I think I'd fire them."[27] Another director noted: "The unnamed employees went behind the back of their supervisors. Put yourself in that position and you suffer the consequences."[28] After the meeting, L. A. Kimball, assistant general manager for administration, said there were no plans to fire the engineers who asked Burfine to study the computer system.

Up to this point, BARTD management did not know the names of the engineers who had supplied information to Helix. Apparently the engineers' identity was discovered almost accidentally. In late February 1972 Bruder visited his supervisor, F. H. Wagner, in his home and told Wagner he had participated in a conference call with Helix, Hjortsvang, and Blankenzee, in which they discussed appearing before the board of directors. After Bruder left, Wagner phoned his own supervisor, J. B. Fendel, and reported the conversation. The next day he reported the conversation to Fendel's supervisor, E. A. Tillman.

During the week of February 28, General Manager Stokes, Assistant General Manager Hammond, Director of Operations Ray, and General Superintendent of Power and Way Kramer met and decided that problems with the ATC system had been misrepresented to persons outside the BARTD organization. According to a memorandum written after the meeting by Ray, they agreed to discharge the participating employees because the employees supplied information to external parties directly contrary to BARTD policy and because of the severity of the action.

On March 2, 1972, at 9:30 A.M., Ray and Kramer called Hjortsvang into Ray's office, and Ray told Hjortsvang that for the good of the district his employment was being terminated. He was given the option of resignation or termination. Hjortsvang again claimed he had not participated in the dealings with Burfine and had met with Helix only once. Hjortsvang was escorted to his office

27. Harre W. Demoro, "BART Train Control Issue Ends," *Oakland Tribune*, Feb. 25, 1972, p. 13.

28. Demoro, p. 13.

by a person from BARTD's Security Division, picked up his personal belongings, and left the building before noon.

Blankenzee saw Hjortsvang before he left, and Hjortsvang told him he was fired. Ten to twenty minutes later, Blankenzee was called into Ray's office. Ray told Blankenzee he would have to resign or he would be terminated by order of the general manager. Blankenzee asked to talk to the general manager, and Ray said he was not in. Blankenzee was then taken to his office by a security guard. He claimed that as he went through his files an assistant to Kramer and the head of security told him what he could take with him.

The next morning, March 3, 1972, Tillman told Kimball he was satisfied that Bruder had lied about his participation in the Burfine-Helix incident. At 11:40 A.M., Tillman met with Bruder and Fendel in Tillman's office. Tillman asked Bruder if he was involved with Helix; Bruder denied involvement. Tillman said he had evidence that Bruder was involved, but Bruder continued to deny it. Tillman offered Bruder the opportunity to resign. Bruder refused and was fired.

All three engineers suffered personally after their dismissal from BARTD. Bruder went on welfare and received food stamps. He sold his house and could not find professional employment for eight months. Blankenzee was separated from his wife for forty-five days, lost his house, and was unable to find employment for four and a half months. Hjortsvang became "agitated and tense" and required sleeping pills.[29] He could not find full-time employment for fourteen months.

On May 21, 1973, the three engineers filed a lawsuit which charged BARTD management with breach of contract, interference with prospective business relations, and deprivation of First and Fourteenth Amendment rights guaranteed by the United States Constitution and asked for $875,000 in damages. The lawsuit was scheduled for jury trial on February 3, 1975; however, on January 29, 1975, the engineers and BARTD settled out of court for $75,000 minus 40 percent for lawyers' fees. The engineers were advised by their attorney that they could not win the lawsuit in court because they had denied hiring an outside consultant when questioned by BARTD management.

29. *Holger Hjortsvang v. San Francisco Bay Area Rapid Transit District*, Cal. Sup. Ct. 1974, No. 436443, Points and Authorities, p. 29.

Case Study—When E. F. Hutton Speaks...
Joanne B. Ciulla*

On May 2, 1985, E. F. Hutton pleaded guilty to mail and wire fraud. The brokerage house had been charged with fradulently obtaining the use of more than $1 billion in interest-free funds by systematically overdrawing checking accounts at some 400 banks. Hutton's attorneys bargained with the Justice Department and agreed on a $2 million fine plus $750,000 to cover the cost of the investigation. Since the fine for mail fraud was $1000 per case, Hutton's attorneys pleaded guilty to 2000 counts of fraud. (Ironically, around the time of Hutton's settlement the fine for mail fraud was raised to $500,000 per count.)

Robert Fomon, CEO of E. F. Hutton, hoped that the guilty plea would minimize public scrutiny and put an end to the scandal—but it didn't. Investigations of the firm continued and were closely monitored by the press. E. F. Hutton, one of the most respected brokerage houses on Wall Street, became "the company that pleaded guilty to 2000 counts of fraud."

Company Background

E. F. Hutton was founded by Edward F. Hutton and George Ellis, Jr., in 1904. The Hutton partnership aimed at maintaining a strong financial base and providing complete service to elite investors. It was the first New York Stock Exchange firm to open an office on the West Coast. Since Western Union had no wires over the Rockies, Hutton advanced it $50,000 to complete its first coast-to-coast wire. The system was completed in 1905, establishing Hutton as a firm dedicated to speedy service.

Because of the importance of the wire to their business, brokerage firms were called "wire houses." This ability to move funds and to buy and sell quickly benefitted Hutton's West Coast clients. For example, during the 1906 San Francisco earthquake Hutton office managers retrieved their records from the destroyed of-

*Joanne B. Ciulla, "E. F. Hutton." Reprinted by permission of the author.

fice, and knowing that clients would need cash but could not be reached, liquidated their positions before news of the quake hit the East Coast.

While sharing in the prosperity of the 1920s, Hutton pursued a conservative course in keeping within margin requirements. So when the market crashed in 1929, it lost less than $50,000 on its unsecured accounts. Even during the depression, Hutton continued to expand and improve its communications networks. By 1962 the firm had grown so much that it dissolved the partnership and became a corporation.[1]

Robert Fomon and the Hutton Organization

After graduating from the University of Southern California with a degree in English, Fomon was hired by Hutton as a sales trainee in 1951. He told one interviewer that his first impression of the securities industry was an unrealistic one which came from reading F. Scott Fitzgerald novels.[2] Nonetheless, Fomon learned the business and worked his way up to the head of the company's West Coast corporate finance, syndicate, and institutional sales. He then became CEO in 1970. The choice of Fomon was controversial. Some people in the firm had wanted John Shad, who was then head of corporate finance, to be CEO (Shad later left Hutton in 1981 to become chairman of the SEC).

When Fomon became CEO, Hutton was losing money because the market was depressed and the firm's staff had grown too large—commissions accounted for almost 68 percent of Hutton's revenues (by 1979 commissions would shrink to 38 percent). Fomon began his term of office by firing 600 employees and trimming losses that had reached $1 million a month. This aggressive move, combined with the healthy market of 1972, got Hutton out of the red.

In 1972 Hutton became a publicly owned company, but Fomon continued to run the firm in the loose style of a partnership. The

1. "The Story of E. F. Hutton's Founding and Growth," published by E. F. Hutton.

2. "The Undoing of Robert Fomon," by James Steingold, the *New York Times*, Sept. 29, 1985, sec. 3, p. 10.

managing partners all sat on the board of directors. There were no outsiders on the board until 1974 when Harvard Business School Professor Warren Law became a member. Ten years later Edward F. Hutton's daughter, actress Dina Merrill, and California attorney Edward Cazier, Jr., joined the board. Baseball commissioner Peter Ueberroth became a member in 1984.

Disliking tight organizational systems, Fomon believed that "charts and boxes do not solve your problems." He said, "It's much more important to select the right people and I think that I'm pretty good at that."[3] But Fomon, who was described as moody and aloof, took little interest in the details of management. He did, however, pay close attention to business deals and was known to veto certain projects for ethical reasons or because of his personal tastes. For example, he refused to let Hutton underwrite a casino project and once vetoed a deal because it included a fast food business.[4] Under Foman's leadership, Hutton went from 95 branch offices and 1250 account executives in 1972 to 400 offices worldwide and 6600 account executives in 1985.

Hutton's strength was its retail sales force and distribution system. Hutton's rewards system plus its decentralized management system engendered a strong independent entrepreneurial spirit among employees in its branch offices. While the large and bureaucratic Merrill Lynch was symbolized by the herd, Hutton was best symbolized by the lone cowboy. At Hutton it was said that the client belonged to the account executive, whereas at other places like Merrill Lynch, the client belonged to the company.

Interest Income in the Securities Industry

Interest income is very important to a brokerage firm. Basically, said one industry specialist, "Wire houses are giant factories designed to collect money from customers and lend it out." In order to do business with a brokerage house, both retail and institutional customers must either have money on hand to buy shares, or they

3. Ibid., p. 11.
4. "Bob Fomon: Is Being Tough Still Enough?" by Gregory Miller, *Institutional Investor*, April 1985, p. 62.

can buy shares on credit (or margin). To buy on margin, they must borrow from the broker and deposit the shares as collateral. If clients want to sell short (sell stocks that they do not own so as to profit from a falling market), they must deposit the cash value of those shares in their brokerage account. This system boosts profits whenever interests rates rise—especially since customers often hold their profits in their brokerage account until another investment opportunity comes along.

Brokerage firms are allowed by the SEC to use the credit balances left by customers to lend out to other clients. For example, in 1981 the Bache Group described its policy this way:

> A portion of the funds loaned to customers by the company is derived from sources which are largely interest free to the company. [As a result of this] the company earns income in some cases equal to the entire interest rate charged to its customers. A primary source of such funds are the excess funds left with the company by its customers.[5]

With interest rates at 17 percent in 1981, Shearson Loeb Rhoades was able to cover all of its overhead with "Saturday and

	(1) Pre-tax Earnings $m	(2) Net Interest Revenues $m	(2) As % of (1)
Merrill Lynch	366.1	251.8	69
E. F. Hutton	155.8	95.8	61
Shearson Loeb Rhoades	105.0	71.5	68
Dean Witter Reynolds	62.3	61.2	98
Bache	47.5	52.6	110
Donaldson Lufkin & Jenrette	15.9	21.8	137
Paine Webber	−16.2	20.3	—

Source: *The Economist,* June 20, 1981, p. 9.

5. Ibid., p. 60.

Sunday money," which is interest income derived from waiting until Monday to move customers' money into their private accounts.

Motivation in the brokerage business was mostly based on monetary rewards. The main source of account executives' income was the 1/2 to 2 percent commission they made on each trade—the more they traded, the higher the commission. High producers were treated like prima donnas. Firms regularly tried to steal good sales people from each other by offering them bonuses—which were sometimes as much as $300,000—to defect. The top producers at Hutton tended to gravitate to managerial positions. Branch managers received 10 percent of the net profit of their office; however, some successful sales people preferred to stay in sales, where they could earn more money.

George Ball

In 1977 Fomon named 38-year-old George Ball as President and head of retail operations. Ball was an aggressive salesman who had quickly worked his way up through the branch system. He began as an account executive trainee in 1962, became the Newark branch manager in 1967, and then regional sales manager in 1969. A charismatic public person, Ball was always out talking to employees—making sure that new sales ideas were in the pipeline. As one ex-Hutton employee said: "It wasn't a surprise to see him [Ball] anywhere. But when Fomon went anyplace other than the twelfth floor [the site of the executive offices], people would say, 'what the hell is he up to?' "[6] Ball's managerial abilities complemented those of the moody and sometimes reclusive Fomon, who was described as a "backroom deal maker" and talented investment banker.

All of the regional offices reported to Ball. The chain of command was short and loose—account executives reported to branch managers, who reported to their regional VPs, who reported to Ball. Ball and the executive VPs reported directly to Fomon. But in actual

6. "The Productivity Game at E. F. Hutton," by Nigel Adam, *Euromoney*, Dec. 1981, p. 79.

practice Ball was the dominant figure in the company and other senior officers reported to him ex-officio (see Exhibit 1). Hutton was described as a "comfortable" organization without a fixed hierarchy. The benefit of this arrangement, according to Ball, was that without a formal organizational chart, management could make fast decisions.[7]

Cash Management at Hutton

In 1980, with interest rates hovering around 18 percent, Hutton began to explore ways to maximize its interest earnings. Hutton managers recognized that if they could receive one-day credit on checks deposited with local banks, while checks written by Hutton required two days to clear, they could capture some of the "float" inherent in the banking system. By drawing checks on Monday, e.g., based on anticipated deposits on Tuesday, sufficient funds would be available in the bank to cover Hutton's checks when presented for payment on Wednesday. This required an estimate of the next day's deposits. A formula was derived which used past experience to produce a reasonable estimate. Since checks were written when funds were not on deposit, Hutton was technically overdrafting its account. If next day deposits were overestimated, the account would be overdrawn and in reality have a negative balance. This could cause the bank either to demand immediate reimbursement by wire transfer of funds or refuse payment of Hutton's checks—although sometimes, for various reasons, the banks did nothing.

William Sullivan, designated as Hutton's "money mobilizer," had designed Hutton's cash management system in the late seventies. The system moved money from branch office accounts to regional office bank accounts and then to national concentration accounts where the funds could be used by the company. Often delays in the processing of Hutton's checks between banks denied the company same-day availability of funds. To remedy this delay, funds were transferred as soon as possible. The objective of this system

7. Appendix to "The Hutton Report," by Griffin B. Bell, Sept. 4, 1985, Exhibit 45.

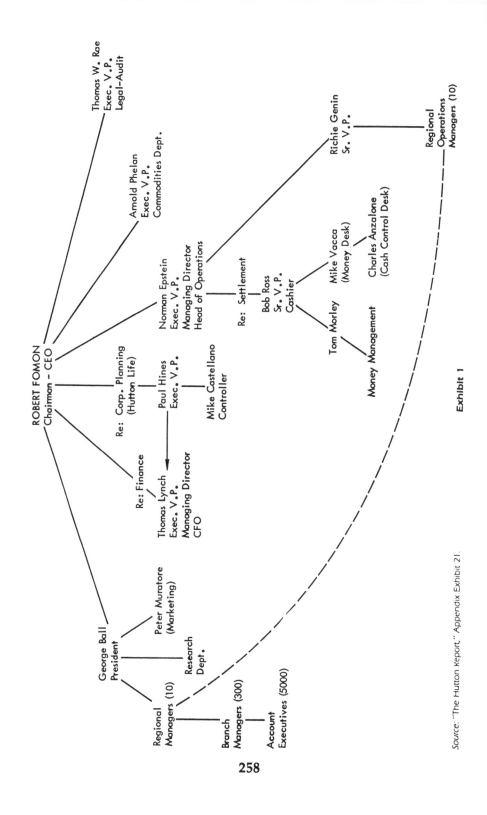

ROBERT FOMON
Chairman – CEO

Thomas W. Rae
Exec. V.P.
Legal–Audit

Arnold Phelan
Exec. V.P.
Commodities Dept.

Richie Genin
Sr. V.P.

Regional
Operations
Managers (10)

Norman Epstein
Exec. V.P.
Managing Director
Head of Operations

Re: Settlement

Bob Ross
Sr. V.P.
Cashier

Mike Vacca
(Money Desk)

Charles Anzalone
(Cash Control Desk)

Tom Morley

Money Management

Re: Corp. Planning
(Hutton Life)

Paul Hines
Exec. V.P.

Mike Castellano
Controller

Re: Finance

Thomas Lynch
Exec. V.P.
Managing Director
CFO

George Ball
President

Peter Muratore
(Marketing)

Research
Dept.

Regional
Managers (10)

Branch
Managers (300)

Account
Executives (5000)

258

Source: "The Hutton Report," Appendix Exhibit 21.

Exhibit 1

was to leave enough money in the bank account to compensate the bank for its services and withdraw the rest. From Hutton's point of view, it was compensating itself by overdrafting for the day in which the bank was holding its money.

When these alterations had been made in the cash management system, Sullivan and other Hutton officials met with its auditors, Arthur Anderson & Co. (AA&Co), to discuss the legality of the new procedures. A memorandum dated March 7, 1980, described that meeting:

> After the discussion of the procedure employed and its legality, Joel Miller, AA&Co engagement partner, requested that Tom Rae (Hutton's general council and former SEC lawyer) render a written legal opinion stating that Hutton's activities in this area don't present any legal problems. Mr. Rae declined to render such an opinion, stating that the banks are fully cognizant of Hutton's procedures, that this is an accepted banking practice, and that there is no question as to the propriety of such a transaction, again making reference to the "means of payment" principles. [The legal concept of check writing requires that you have the intent and the ability to cover the check on time.] After Tom Rae declined to issue an opinion on this matter, Bill Sullivan offered to call one of the banks that Hutton uses, Morgan Guaranty, and ask them what the banks would do if a company were to issue checks with no book balances. Joel Miller then stated that he would discuss the matter with other partners at AA&Co, whose clients include major money center banks, to ascertain what the banks' "point of view" is regarding these transactions.[8]

The Banks

Banks are compensated for their services to corporate customers by either requiring a minimum balance in the account or by charging set fees, or a combination of both. Most of the banks Hutton used required the firm to leave an average amount of money in the account so that the bank could produce a yield that would com-

8. "The Hutton Report," by Griffin Bell, Sept. 4, 1985, p. 21.

pensate it for its services. The bank and the customer agreed on the sum of the average balance and the time period over which the adequacy of compensation would be measured. If this arrangement did not yield enough compensation for a particular bank, it would inform the customer. Bank of America charged Hutton set fees for its services and only required Hutton to have sufficient funds in its account to cover a check when it was presented for payment—the rest of the time the account could have a zero balance.

Commercial banks, however, normally required corporate customers to maintain average account balances at negotiated target levels, and did not expect corporate customers to overdraft their accounts without prior consent. Nevertheless, bank managers expected occasional overdrafts to occur because of errors or inadvertence, such as the failure of an incoming wire to arrive on time. Most bank managers tolerated overdrafting by creditworthy customers as long as the amounts of money were relatively small and the overdrafts were infrequent.

The time that it takes for a check to clear, called "collection float," is based on the inefficiency of the payments system in this country. A check that is not cashed in person must be physically taken from the bank to a clearing house before its funds can become available. Electronic banking systems would eliminate this time lag by moving funds instantly. However, according to one Federal Reserve Board representative, an electronic payments system is not likely to displace checks during the remainder of this century.[9]

The Campaign for Interest Profits Begins

On October 21, 1980, a memo written by Tom Morley (who had replaced William Sullivan as the money mobilizer) was sent to all branch managers. The memo emphasized the importance of interest income and suggested ways to increase interest profits. The memo pointed out that "net interest income accounted for approximately 50 percent of the average branch's profits. And by paying insufficient attention to net interest profits, a branch may be

9. Appendix to "The Hutton Report," Exhibit 35.

ignoring potential revenue." Four major areas generated interest profits: margin accounts, short positions, free credit balances, and interest on general ledger balances. Morley pointed out that the last category had the greatest potential for profit. The memo said:

> The branch earns interest on all credit balances in its general ledger and is charged for all debit balances, both at the call rate. The lion's share of the interest profit generated in this category is due to the float earned on Bank of America checks and over-drafting the branch's account.[10]

At the time, interest from overdrafting was reported as part of a single line item on profit and loss statements. This item included interest generated by the overdrafting of branch bank accounts as well as interest generated by other bank transactions. Morley's memo broke down the components of interest in the Southeast Region. He noted that the first three categories accounted for approximately 55 percent of the interest earned, while the general ledger interest accounted for 45 percent of the net interest profits.

In November 1980 Morley gave a speech to the regional operations managers and noted that it was a good idea for branch managers to inform local banks of Hutton's cash management system. However, one of Morley's staff members later sent a memo in June 1981 to Regional Operations managers, advising: "If an office is overdrafting its ledger balance consistently, it is probably best not to request an account analysis."[11]

Explaining the Cash Management Policy

Tom Morley told branch managers how to use Hutton's money management system in a memo dated March 10, 1981:

> In collecting our branch receipts, we usually assign one-day availability to our local deposit. In doing this we anticipate our drawdown check clearing the bank the next business day, which will be when our local deposit becomes available. If the

10. Ibid., Exhibit 6.
11. Ibid., Exhibit 31.

drawdown check fails to clear the bank the next business day, we attempt to capture the excess balances by increasing subsequent drawdowns. In handling our collections in this manner, we give the same clearing value to our drawdown check as we expect to receive on our branch deposit. This system is the standard cash management collection process used in the industry. What the system fails to address and cultivate is the situation where we can receive one day availability on our drawdown check, but it actually takes two days for the check to clear our bank.[12]

With the emphasis on interest income, the branch office cashier's job became more important because the cashier was the one who moved the money in and out of a branch office's account. In a memo to Tom Morley dated May 12, 1981, Tom Lillis, the vice president of accounting services, emphasized the importance of a good branch cashier, giving the following example:

One branch had earned a consistent $30,000 per month in interest "just from overdrafting of the bank account." When the branch manager changed cashiers, the office only earned $10,000 from overdrafting.[13]

The overdrafting principle was implemented through a formula that incorporated a multiplier, which took weekends into account. Many cashiers found the formula difficult to understand and use. In July 1980 and May 1981 Morley's assistant, Kevin Mahoney, suggested automating the procedure at the branch office level. Using a computer software program, offices could only overdraft as much as would allow Hutton to maintain a zero balance.[14] Hutton did not, at either time, purchase this software.

The Mountain Region offices received instructions on how to use the formula in a memorandum. The Pacific region was given instructions by telephone. Some branch offices did not get any instructions on how to use the formula. Traditionally, branch office

12. Ibid., Exhibit 13.
13. Ibid., Exhibits 26, 27, & 28.
14. Ibid., Exhibit 20.

practices were determined by the instructions that the branch manager gave to the office cashier.

Branch operations personnel in the Atlantic Region learned how to use the formula in a seminar. A memo from that seminar titled "Reminders from Seminar," dated June 2, 1981, contains this tip: "Drawdown as discussed. You may drawdown more than formula but not less! This will depend on individual branch/bank circumstances."[15]

Interest profits became a frequent topic of conversation at meetings of branch and regional personnel. Branch managers were concerned with interest profits because their compensation and job evaluation was based on their office's net profit. However, because of the sharp division in the Hutton organization between sales and operations, branch managers were mainly responsible for sales and reported to the regional vice president of sales, while their cashiers were answerable to the regional operations managers. Under this arrangement it was possible for a branch manager to assume that if the drawdown worksheets were being used incorrectly, he or she would be notified by operations.

George Ball's Encouragement

Throughout 1981 Ball wrote memos encouraging greater interest profits. A memo dated April 27, 1981, named New England as "The Region of the Month." In it, Ball recommended that managers get in touch with Tom Morley to find out how to maximize interest income and said, "Interest is an excellent way to legitimately optimize a branch's or region's results."[16] On June 25, 1981, Tom Lillis wrote in a memo

> I noticed that George Ball suggested to a number of RVPs [regional vice presidents] that they get in touch with Tom Morley to see if they can improve their interest profits. Tom Morley is only concerned with overdrafting at the branch level and I

15. Ibid., Exhibit 40.
16. Ibid., Exhibit 39.

believe that there is far more to be done to improve interest profits.

Lillis went on to say

I would like to spearhead a retail system campaign to make branch managers aware of interest profit opportunities, but without a means of monitoring branch performance the program would be at best hit or miss. I need a priority for the proposed interest program so that we can improve the profitability of this $100,000,000 product.[17]

Ball continued to encourage interest earnings. In his memo dated August 5, 1981, he wrote: "High fences make good neighbors and high interest profits create good margins."[18] His December 18, 1981, memo states, "We have certainly had the luxury of high interest profits, profits which may be importantly lower in the year ahead. Our corporate goal is to earn in excess of $100,000,000 [in interest]. Together we can do it, but it will take a mighty push."[19]

The Branches Push

Branch managers became very conscious of their interest income stacked up against other branch offices. Baltimore branch manager, Anthony Read, worried about his branch's poor interest earnings. His cashier informed him that the way in which managers increased interest was to arbitrarily increase drawdowns. Read began to do so periodically, adding $500,000 to $3 million to his account. The bank complained to Morley and Hutton deposited a large sum of money and left it there for several days. Read was charged with the interest on that money and stopped overdrafting his account.

Alexandria branch manager, Perry Bacon, was known as a bright young manager. After someone in the Alexandria branch inadvertently added an extra zero to an overdraft, making the figure

17. Ibid., Exhibit 13.
18. Ibid., Exhibit 13.
19. Ibid., Exhibit 19.

9 million instead of 900 thousand, Bacon noticed that the bank did nothing. So he began to aggressively overdraft his account. Letters from Bacon's local bank indicated that he maintained excellent relations with it.

In November 1981 Bacon's office was ranked as the number one profit center in the central region. George Ball sent a memo to the Central Regional vice president asking why the Alexandria office's interest earnings were so high. Ball queried, "Were these accounting adjustments?" The response was, "No, but the office does a superb job of money management."[20] Ball, Morley, and others later suggested that branch managers get advice from Bacon on how to increase their interest income.

Earnest Dipple, a VP for the Central Region, told Louisville branch manager, William Wilcox, to contact Bacon about how to improve his branch's interest earnings. Wilcox increased the multiplier used in connection with the drawdown formula and arbitrarily increased the amount of the branch drawdown. However, unlike Bacon and Read, Wilcox had negotiated a minimum service fee with his bank, The First National Bank of Louisville, in the fall of 1981. In order to assess the fees owed to it, the bank closely analyzed Wilcox's account and was fully aware of its status from day to day.

The Big Overdraft

In December 1981 the Genesee County Bank in Batavia, New York, was presented with a large check that had been deposited in a New York bank. Genesee had received Hutton checks drawn on the United Penn bank in Wilkes-Barre, Pennsylvania. The Genesee branch manager called United Penn to see if Hutton had $8 million available in its account. United Penn said Hutton only had uncollected money in the form of checks that were deposited the day before. Genesee and United Penn then refused to honor Hutton checks and closed the firm's account. Hutton immediately wired $18.8 million to United Penn and $20 million to Genesee.

---

20. "Hutton Auditor Defends Role," by Nathaniel Nash, the *New York Times*, October 4, 1985, sec. D, p. 3.

This movement of money between the Genesee Bank and United Penn was called "chaining" (see Exhibit 2). The system had been developed by the Atlantic Region's operations manager, Arthur Jensen, and similar systems were used in other regions. These chains served the purpose of generating clearing delays in order to ease the region's task of concentrating funds from branches within the region. Clearing delays increased interest profits by giving Hutton one-day availability of checks written to Hutton and two-day clearance of checks written by Hutton. It was generally considered convenient and it improved the availability of funds. Unlike overdrafting, which was used to compensate Hutton for the float that was built into the banking system, chaining created additional float.

Hutton's Auditors Ask Questions

Hutton's AA&Co auditors called a meeting in early 1982 with CFO Tom Lynch, General Council Tom Rae and his assistants, and an attorney from Hutton's outside law firm, Cahill, Gordon & Reindel. They discussed Hutton's overdraft policy, the $8 million overdraft at the Genesee County Bank, and inquiries by banking regulators into excessive overdrafting of accounts at Manufacturers' Hanover Bank and Chemical Bank. A memo describing the meeting said the Federal Reserve Board had expressed concern that Hutton might be "creating float" as opposed to taking advantage of the float inherent in the banking system. The

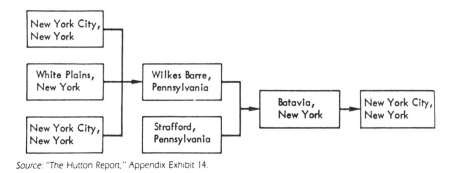

Source: "The Hutton Report," Appendix Exhibit 14.

Exhibit 2: The Genesee Chain as Identified by the Department of Justice.

266

memo reported that "We were assured of the fact that no action has been brought against Hutton and that Hutton officials believed that banking regulators had no jurisdiction over their firm." The memo further stated that "the major concern of management was the potential negative publicity if the media were informed."[21]

Many other questions began to surface at Hutton. George Ball, in a March 19, 1982, memo again questioned the interest profits of the Alexandria office. Commenting on the contents of a memorandum on interest earnings, Ball said: "Note—commentary seems very aggressive. Who is calling the shots, and were the shots well called?"[22]

Four months later, in July 1982, to the surprise of some and the disappointment of many, Ball left Hutton to become the president and chief executive of Prudential-Bache Securities. His departure was based on the desire for professional advancement and did not, according to Ball, have anything to do with problems at Hutton.[23] Ball's departure left a huge managerial gap in the Hutton organization. Fomon was without his public "hands on manager."

Hutton Attracts Attention

The Genesee incident attracted the attention of a young Assistant U.S. Attorney from the Middle District of Pennsylvania named Albert Murray. Murray doggedly traced the movement of Hutton's checks between banks and initiated a Justice Department investigation of Hutton's activities. On May 10, 1982, the Justice Department subpoenaed CEO Robert Fomon and Controller Michael Castellano, asking for virtually every document in E. F. Hutton's files.

At that time Attorney General Edwin Meese III had just taken office. Meese's appointment had been opposed by congressmen and senators who questioned the propriety of some low interest loans that Meese obtained while working in the White House. The

21. Appendix Exhibit 40.
22. "E. F. Hutton Appears Headed for a Long Siege," by Scott McMurray, the *Wall Street Journal*, May 4, 1985, p. 1.
23. "What Did Hutton's Managers Know—And When Did They Know It?" by Anthony Bianco, David Wallace, and Daniel Moskowitz, *Business Week*, May 20, 1985, p. 110.

Democrats in particular not only questioned Meese's moral character, but worried that he would be soft on white collar crime.

The Justice Department's investigation covered the firm's overdrafting from mid-1980 to February 1982. Hutton was charged with overdrafting its accounts and intentionally delaying check collection. Altogether, the Justice Department estimated that by shuffling $10 billion in uncollected funds from one account to another, Hutton obtained the interest free use of $1 billion in uncollected funds from July 1980 through February 1982 (which was when the short-term interest rates were 18 percent to 20 percent).[24]

Hutton's Response

The investigation dragged on from February 1982 until May 1985. When it was completed in the spring of 1985, the audit committee of the board of directors met. The committee, which consisted of the outside members of the board of directors, did not think that the case against Hutton was very strong (a representative of the Justice Department later testified that, in the department's opinion, chances of convicting Hutton were fifty-fifty).[25] However, a guilty plea would avoid a long jury trial with the attendant publicity, and the risk that Hutton employees would be found guilty of fraud (in which case they could be barred from the securities industry). It was tentatively agreed to enter a guilty plea, if a satisfactory settlement could be worked out with the Justice Department.

One factor contributing to this decision was a memo that surfaced in February 1985. It was written on April 23, 1982, by Perry Bacon in response to a memo by Washington branch manager, Steve Bralove. Bralove had complained to Bacon about causing problems with the bank by overdrafting excessively. Bacon replied in reference to overdrafting:

24. "Why the E. F. Hutton Scandal May Be Far from Over," by Chris Wells, *Business Week*, Feb. 24, 1986, p. 98.

25. "The Undoing of Robert Fomon," sec. 3, p. 1.

```
TO:      Steve Bralove                              EFHutton
FROM:    Perry H. Bacon      INTER-OFFICE MEMORANDUM
DATE:    April 23, 1982
SUBJECT: Your Memo—Banking Activities
```

Our banking activities during the last six months have been no
different than our banking activities off and on for the last
five years. Additionally, I believe those activities are encouraged by the firm and are in fact identical to what the
firm practices on a national basis. Specifically, we will from
time to time draw down not only deposits plus anticipated
deposits, but also bogus deposits. One day prior to that in-
cremental drawdown arriving at our bank, we may need to cover
with a New York (Chemical, U.S. Trust) check. As long as the
local bank honors that check with same day availability, the
firm profits at both the branch and the national level. We
profit at the branch level by creating a surplus in general
ledger revenues which are credited at the broker call rate. We
profit at the national level for two reasons: (1) Because New
York is doing the same thing with the U.S. Trust check by
reacting to our bank wire and floating checks based on those
deposits which deposits may not really exist. (2) Because
those bogus deposits create a reduction in our net capital
ratio requirement which allows the firm to deploy capital elsewhere. Furthermore, we (as a firm) learned to use the float because it is exactly what the banks do to us (see enclosed
article). I know of at least a dozen managers at E. F. Hutton—
managers who along with Bill Sullivan and Tom Morley taught me
the system—who do precisely the same thing. Presumably, any
manager who was willing to take the time to learn the system
would want to use the system.

The obvious drawback to the system is that it can cost the
bank money. If the bank honors a New York deposit check with
same day availability and subsequently have those funds
withdrawn by a New York drawdown check before they get FED
usage of the funds, they have a net debit. On the other hand,
the bank is not quite the defenseless amoeba that your memo
suggests. FIRST, the system only exists because, peculiarly,
our mammoth federal banking system is more hand processed than
automated—NB—a system which the banks well know how to use as
the enclosed article discusses. SECOND, the system we use does
not happen the day we open an account. We spend months working
up to larger drawdowns leaving the bank surplus deposits, and
I do not recall any bank offering to send us their earnings on
those deposits.

NB—There is not much difference between what we do and when a
bank tells you not to write checks on your out of state
deposit for 10 days, clears that check through the FED in 2
days, and enjoys the float for 8 days. Essentially, the bank
has created a net debit against you in the form of 8 day non-
usable funds. By the way, Tom Morley believes that within 2-3
years the entire system will be automated and all domestic
checks will clear in one day. Therefore, as Tom stated in our
New York BOM meeting, the time to take advantage of the system
is now. (See second enclosed article.)

THIRD, all banks either know or eventually figure out our system. When they do, they simply cease giving same day availability, and often will not count regular checks as collected funds. In fact, contrary to your implication that all banks are now holding your checks, NBW (a bank with whom we have never dealt) had been doing that to you months before this issue arose. FOURTH, if a bank is slow to move on #3 above, documents a net loss and asks us for same, we will probably give it to them. Our objective is not to steal money from the banks. Whatever the bank may have lost, we have enjoyed a greater profit due to the spread float.* I am aware of four branches that have had to write checks within the last six months for just the reasons listed above. On the other hand, many banks accept their losses as a cost of doing business and never ask for the money.

This last point leads to some of the specific remarks in your memo. FIRST, when you called a few months ago and asked if I was aware that due to our overdrafts, 1st American was giving you trouble with your secondary account there, you will recall that I replied that I was not aware, and I replied that I would not do any more overdrafting at that bank. If I sounded unconcerned, it was because your terse interrogatory was limited to your secondary bank account. The first time I heard about an institutional problem was from Ernie some weeks ago. Your conclusion that my attitude to Hutton's reputation in the city is "indifferent" is ridiculous. I confess to an emotion somewhere between indifference and astonishment at your suggestion that the solution to your secondary account problem was to call and offer money to a bank that had not, and to this date has not called me to complain, ask for money or request to discuss the issue—in fact has never called me at all. SECOND, your remark that since 1st American has contacted all of the area banks and now all banks are holding checks is not only contradicted by your knowledge that NBW had already been doing that, but would further suggest violation of any number of federal and banking statutes regarding collusion and antitrust. THIRD, and what really troubles me, is that your constant use of terminology such as "excessive," "blatant disregard," "casually damaged" and "indifferent" is way out of line—and I think you know it. I plead guilty to simply never having considered that an institutional relationship could be jeopardized. Importantly, if our zeal with the bank has in any way impaired your ability to do business with that bank, I am genuinely sorry and would like to apologize to you and anyone else adversely effected. However, your sweeping implication that such an isolated incident immeasurably damages our reputation and ability to transact…

*Ex.—The average balance that we earned on during the months to which you refer was significantly greater than the 2 million figure that the bank stated.

Source: "The Hutton Report," Appendix Exhibit 17.

I believe those activities are encouraged by the firm and are in fact identical to what the firm practices on a national basis. Specifically we will from time to time draw down not only deposits plus anticipated deposits, but also bogus deposits. (See Exhibit 3.)

Some Hutton insiders said that this memo was "the nail in the coffin" that forced Hutton to plead guilty.[26] But the most compelling reason why Fomon chose to plead guilty was the hope that it would end the affair quickly.[27]

Hutton's board of directors later approved the settlement and the firm pleaded guilty to the agreed-upon 2000 counts of fraud. Attorney General Meese said that the government had foregone prosecution of Hutton employees in order to avoid lengthy litigation. Meese believed that the overdrafting was a "corporate scheme" and "no one personally benefited from defrauding the banks."[28] The Justice Department had also agreed to send a letter to the SEC saying, "the interests of the U.S. government have been served."

But many constituencies were not satisfied with the Justice Department's investigation. The Chairman of the House Judiciary Crime subcommittee, N. J. Democrat William J. Hughes, believed that individuals in the corporate hierarchy should be charged. Stephen Trott, Justice Department Criminal Division chief, was unhappy with the way that Hutton delivered subpoenaed documents and thought the case should be reopened. And the SEC wanted its own investigation. On top of all this, some banks considered filing a class action suit under the Racketeer Influenced & Corrupt Organizations Act.

So it did not look like the guilty plea was going to put the scandal to rest. The press was keeping a watchful eye on Hutton and its publicity-shy CEO. After two years of investigations, even Fomon was not sure what had gone wrong. One thing that the 34-year Hutton veteran did know was that he would have to do something to keep his prized employees from defecting, and regain Hutton's credibility as a financial institution.

---

26. "What Did Hutton's Managers Know—And When Did They Know It?" p. 111.
27. "Why the Hutton Scandal May Be Far from Over," p. 101.
28. Special thanks to Professor E. Raymond Corey for his helpful advice on this case.

Index